Building a Language-Focused
Curriculum for the Preschool Classroom

Volume II:
A Planning Guide

Building a Language-Focused
Curriculum for the Preschool Classroom

Volume II:
A Planning Guide

by

Betty H. Bunce, Ph.D., CCC-SLP
Director
Language Acquisition Preschool
Adjunct Assistant Professor
Department of Speech-Language-Hearing
University of Kansas, Lawrence

·P A U L·H·
BROOKES
PUBLISHING C?

Baltimore • London • Toronto • Sydney

Paul H. Brookes Publishing Co.
Post Office Box 10624
Baltimore, Maryland 21285-0624

Typeset by Brushwood Graphics, Inc., Baltimore, Maryland.
Manufactured in the United States of America by
BookCrafters, Chelsea, Michigan.

Building a Language-Focused Curriculum for the Preschool Classroom is a two-volume set:
   Volume I: *A Foundation for Lifelong Communication*
   Volume II: *A Planning Guide*
To order Volume I, contact Paul H. Brookes Publishing Co., Post Office Box 10624, Baltimore,
Maryland 21285-0624 (1-800-638-3775).

This book is printed on recycled paper.

Library of Congress Cataloging-in-Publication Data
Building a language-focused curriculum for the preschool classroom.
   Includes bibliographical references and index.
   Contents: v. 1. A foundation for lifelong communication   /   edited by Mabel L. Rice and
Kim A. Wilcox—v. 2. A planning guide   /   by Betty H. Bunce.
   1. Language arts (Preschool)   2. Language experience approach in education.   3. Educa-
tion, Preschool—Curricula.   I. Rice, Mabel.   II. Wilcox, Kim A.   III. Bunce, Betty H.
LB1140.5.L3B85 1995   372.6   94-49085
   ISBN 1-55766-177-4 (v. 1)
   ISBN 1-55766-192-8 (v. 2)

British Library Cataloguing-in-Publication data are available from the British Library.

Contents

About the Author

Betty H. Bunce, Ph.D., CCC-SLP, Director, Language Acquisition Preschool; Adjunct Assistant Professor, Department of Speech-Language-Hearing, University of Kansas, 3031 Robert Dole Human Development Center, Lawrence, Kansas 66045

Dr. Bunce was born and raised in a bilingual, bicultural community in southern Colorado. She earned a bachelor of science degree in education from the University of Colorado, a master of arts degree in speech from Temple University, and a doctoral degree in child language from the University of Kansas. She received her certificate of clinical competence in speech-language pathology in 1977. Dr. Bunce has taught kindergarten and preschool-age children and has worked as a school speech-language pathologist. She has also taught coursework at the university level in reading and language arts, early childhood education, and speech-language pathology.

Dr. Bunce has written several chapters and articles on preschool education, bilingual and bicultural children, referential communication, and intervention techniques for both preschool- and elementary-age children. She has presented workshops to practitioners in the fields of early childhood education and speech-language pathology and has presented papers at several national and state association conventions. She is the director of the Language Acquisition Preschool at the University of Kansas, where an important part of her job is to train speech-language pathology graduate students in conducting naturalistic language intervention in classroom settings. Dr. Bunce's fields of scientific interest include child language, language intervention therapy and research, preschool education, English as a second language, and relationships between oral language abilities and literacy skills. Her most recent research has focused on naturalistic intervention techniques and their effectiveness.

Preface

This book was developed as a companion volume to *Building a Language-Focused Curriculum for the Preschool Classroom, Volume I: A Foundation for Lifelong Communication*, edited by Mabel L. Rice and Kim A. Wilcox. Both books describe components of a language-focused curriculum (LFC) but differ in their organization and focus. The first volume addresses the operating guidelines for the development of an LFC and describes its different features. This second volume provides specific details about how to implement a language-focused curriculum and includes sample planning guides and activity plans.

This book arose from my interactions with both speech-language pathologists and early childhood educators. While presenting workshops about utilizing a language-focused curriculum and a concentrated normative model of intervention, many participants asked questions concerning the actual activities used in the Language Acquisition Preschool at the University of Kansas. The major concern of speech-language pathologists was how to embed the intervention activities in classroom settings. The early childhood educators were concerned about how to support language intervention while providing appropriate activities for the children's development of cognitive, motor, and social skills. This book attempts to answer these questions.

This volume outlines important assumptions underlying the LFC and then provides sample lessons illustrating these assumptions and the guidelines discussed in Volume I. Specifically addressed are techniques for embedding language intervention in preschool activities. The activities described include those that are routine and those that change, as well as both child-centered and adult-directed activities. In addition, a 4-month sample curriculum guide is provided as a springboard for staff undertaking the development of LFCs for their programs.

The use of weekly thematic units provides an overall structure for preschool programming, yet it allows flexibility in the development of activities appropriate for children with varying competencies. The daily dramatic play activities are the core of the LFC. For many people, "dramatic play activities" means playing house or acting out community helper roles (e.g., doctor, firefighter). The activities listed in this volume include these dramatic plays but also many more. In addition to the dramatic play activities, approximately 50 art and group lesson plans are also provided. Within all of the activities, there is a language emphasis as well as a focus on developing appropriate social, cognitive, and motor skills.

This book is intended for speech-language pathologists and early childhood educators who work with preschool-age children. This is not a cookbook of activities designed to replace or eliminate teacher and speech-language pathology planning for particular settings. Rather, I hope this book will serve as a model to follow in the development of appropriate language-focused activities for all children—those with and without language impairments. The planning guides and activity plans provided in this volume may be used as a base from which to build a curriculum appropriate to a particular setting. The activities have been field tested in the Language Acquisition Preschool with approximately 120 children and have been implemented by many professionals. The activities have also been used in both public school and university training programs in several states. For these endeavors, I acknowledge the contributions of my colleagues, graduate students, and, of course, the children who participated. In particular, I thank Mabel L. Rice, Kim A. Wilcox, Ruth V. Watkins, Pamela A. Hadley, Sean Redmond, and Julie F. Sergeant for their comments and input regarding this book. The children have taught all of us much about how to implement a language-focused curriculum. We pass this knowledge on to you.

To the memory of my husband,
John W. Bunce,
and
in honor of my two children,
Steven and Kathie

In acknowledgment
of the many LAPPERS
(children and staff members)
who have made this book possible

In particular,
thanks to
Mabel L. Rice, Kim A. Wilcox,
Ruth V. Watkins, Pamela A. Hadley, and Julie F. Sergeant
for their helpful comments and support

Building a Language-Focused
Curriculum for the Preschool Classroom

Volume II:
A Planning Guide

`1`

CURRICULUM DEVELOPMENT

~1~

The General Philosophy of the Language-Focused Curriculum

The philosophy underlying the language-focused curriculum (LFC), which was developed in the Language Acquisition Preschool (LAP), is described in detail in this book's companion volume, *Building a Language-Focused Curriculum for the Preschool Classroom, Volume I: A Foundation for Lifelong Communication* (Rice & Wilcox, 1995). In general, the LFC focuses on development of language skills as a key to learning. The curriculum also is designed to be appropriate for 3- to 5-year-old children and to follow developmentally appropriate practices with regard to development of cognitive, social, and motor skills. The children are viewed as active learners who construct their own knowledge. Teachers, speech-language pathologists, and other staff teach or assist learning by providing opportunities. To do this, the environment is structured so children experiment with materials and procedures. Errors and atypical responses are not viewed in a right-or-wrong dichotomy; rather, they are analyzed to provide information for further experimentation and refinement of skills. Teachers also teach by modeling, providing feedback, and interacting with children both verbally and nonverbally. The role of staff in the LFC is to facilitate learning and to encourage children also to learn from their peers through interaction and observation.

The LFC developed at the Language Acquisition Preschool of the University of Kansas was designed for 4 half days per week. The curricular examples provided in this volume involve plans for a 4-day week; however, the curriculum could be easily adapted to 3 or 5 days per week. In LAP, there are two sessions each day, with the children enrolled in either the morning or afternoon session. The classroom includes children with speech and language impairments, children developing language typically, and children learning English as a second language. Eighteen to 20 children attend each session, with each group of children approximately equally represented.

Language intervention is provided in a least restrictive environment during natural interactions in the classroom setting. The LFC was developed based on the belief that the most effective language teaching occurs throughout the entire curriculum. All children are viewed as candidates for language enhancement, and language teaching is most effective when it focuses on the interests of individual children. The challenge to the adults is to embed targeted linguistic forms in naturally occurring interactions so that language input is also functional for the child. Adults must convey the targeted linguistic forms without being obtrusive or violating communicative intent. On a more specific level, targeted therapy structures for children with speech and language impairments are implemented and negotiated with the child during daily classroom activities.

LAP's classroom staff members include a teacher who is also a speech-language pathologist, an assistant teacher who is a certified early childhood teacher, and speech-language clinicians in training. Although the clinicians add to the adult–child ratio, the curriculum is designed for implementation by two qualified personnel. It would be possible to have other professionals, such as occupational therapists, provide therapy in the classroom. In LAP, there is also a family services coordinator whose duties include facilitating communication between families and the preschool staff. This LFC model has been adapted to other settings including those involving children with multiple disabilities (see Bunce, Watkins, Eyer, Torres, Ray, & Ellsworth, 1995, for descriptions of different adaptations).

ASSUMPTIONS ABOUT CHILDREN AND LANGUAGE LEARNING

Rice (1995) has described a model of specific language learning principles that guide the language-focused curriculum. This model is called the concentrated normative model (CNM). The *normative* aspect of the model emphasizes the "commonalities across children and the strong potential of young children's developmental momentum" (p. 28). The *concentrated* aspect relates to the specific emphasis placed on language and the "need to highlight specific language skills in order for children to notice the differences between linguistic forms, as well as the functional uses and outcomes of communication" (p. 29). The operational guidelines for the model are as follows:

1. *Language intervention is best provided in a meaningful social context.* This environment is most likely to generate meaningful language that a child can use in other settings, thereby ensuring generalizations. This guideline suggests that language teaching should take place in a classroom with a number of children interacting with each other as well as with adults.

2. *Language facilitation occurs throughout the entire preschool curriculum.* There is no need to isolate language teaching into a special activity time. Instead, children's communication should be encouraged in different activities, and different activities should be constructed to elicit different kinds of competencies.

3. *The language curriculum is rooted in content themes.* A general theme allows for consistency in the topic of conversation and a coherence of cognitive constructs. For example, if the theme for the week is "construction," then individual activities can focus on various ways of building things, the people who build, what to build with, and so forth. This topic can be addressed, for example, in play materials, art activities, and storybooks for consistency and planned redundancy across a day's activities.

4. *Language begins with the child. It is most effective when it is child centered and child initiated.* This guideline is an extension of the belief that children are *not taught* language, but instead they *construct* it from their daily experiences (see below for elaboration upon this principle).

5. *Verbal interaction is encouraged.* Children have many opportunities to practice their language skills in real interactions with other children and adults. The curriculum is designed so that there are opportunities for talking and much to talk about.

6. *Passive language learning and overt responses are encouraged.* Children do not need to practice out loud while they are working out new linguistic rules. In fact, much of initial comprehension may occur with few external signs of new knowledge. Therefore, it is not necessary for children always to respond to a teacher's input.

7. *Children's utterances are accorded functional value.* It is believed that if children's utterances are treated as meaningful attempts to communicate, they are more likely to achieve that status.

8. *Valuable learning occasions can arise in child-to-child interactions.* Therefore, children are provided with ample opportunities to interact with each other in a spontaneous fashion. For example, times when young children are negotiating for a favorite toy are meaningful occasions for learning how to ask politely or how to justify their needs. In some situations, for example, it makes a big difference whether the child says, "Gimme that" or, "If you let me have that, I'll let you play with my new truck." The authenticity of this kind of learning situation is nearly impossible to simulate in adult–child interactions.

9. *Parents are valuable partners in language programming.* Parents are the most important people in young children's lives, and they are the most powerful sources of communication development. Therefore, parents should be part of the teaching team. This does not mean that parents are to be language trainers in the conventional sense. If we do not teach that way in the classroom, we should not expect parents to practice drill material at home. Instead, teachers and therapists will want to learn from the parents about their child's interests and the family activities that may be incorporated into classroom activities.

10. *Routine parent evaluations are an integral part of the program.* A parent evaluation form is used to provide a structured way to collect parental input. In addition, parent notebooks are available to facilitate communication with staff members in writing. Parents are also encouraged to meet with staff members if they have concerns or questions. Two formal parent group meetings are scheduled each year to address parental concerns. Individual conferences are also scheduled each year, which provide opportunities for parents to evaluate the program as well as their child's progress.

These principles affect how speech and language intervention is provided for children with speech and language impairments. For example, in LAP, intervention is provided in the classroom. A variety of intervention techniques based on the CNM are described by Bunce and Watkins (1995) and are elaborated upon in Chapter 3 of this volume. The techniques capitalize on following the children's interests and providing models and focused contrasts of targeted structures. In addition, the adults expand or recast the children's utterances in a naturalistic manner to provide additional models of the target forms and content. More than one child may be involved in the interactions. For example, two children may be playing with a ball. The adult can model the *is verbing* structure many times as the play proceeds (e.g., Jane *is rolling* the ball. Look, Sara *is bouncing* the ball. She *is bouncing* it high.). The children hear the structure describing their own actions. Many models can be provided within a typically occurring activity without disrupting the activity. Opportunities to respond are available, but verbal responses are not required. The target may be a sound, a specific grammatical structure, vocabulary, or development of appropriate conversational skills with peers. This child-centered intervention utilizes the naturally occurring interactions to provide the focus and content of the intervention.

This style of interaction is in contrast to the traditional therapy session involving one adult and one child, with the adult providing the content and focus of the therapy. Typically, the adult models the structure for the child, expects the child to respond, and then judges the correctness of the child's response. For example, the focus of the therapy may be to improve production of the *is verbing* structure (e.g., *is walking*). The adult might present action pictures and ask the child to describe the picture either with or without the adult model. The child responds and the adult then acknowledges whether the responses are correct or incorrect. Some children have difficulty staying on task; others may have learned to respond to the pictures but not to use the structure in their conversational speech.

Although it is possible to provide child-centered therapy in one-to-one settings, it is more difficult to do so because of the type of setting and number of participants. For example, a therapist in a one-to-one therapy session may follow the child's topic of conversation but is restricted in the activities available. There are fewer opportunities for a child to choose alternative activities than occurs in a classroom setting. Also, there are usually only two interactants, the adult and the child, so that additional input from a peer is not available. To a great degree, the traditional therapy model assumes that language acquisition is adult directed. Instead, we believe that language development is child directed, and it is the job of the teacher and/or speech-language pathologists to maximize the opportunities for a child to figure out how language works.

ADDITIONAL GUIDELINES UNDERLYING THE LFC

There are several other guidelines that underlie or expand the CNM principles. Although described as independent concepts, these guidelines are interrelated and are part of a philosophy that views the child's role as constructing knowledge and the teacher's role as facilitating that constructive process.

The Development of Language and Communication Is Supported by the Curriculum

In order for a curriculum to support the development of language and communication skills, opportunities for both child–child and child–adult communication must exist. The activities within the curriculum must allow for a variety of conversational interactions with a number of participants on various topics. A highly directive environment in which children are expected to listen and not talk for extended periods of time is not conducive to facilitating a full range of language and communication skills. When children are allowed to choose their activities and partners, such as during center times, a number of appropriate communication opportunities arise. Other preschool activities, such as snacktime, outdoor play, and sharing time, also can be effective in stimulating communicative interactions.

Developmentally Appropriate Activities Are Used

Providing opportunities to interact is just the first step in developing a program to facilitate language and learning. Developmentally appropriate activities are needed to provide a framework for these interactions and to enhance language, cognitive, motor, and personal/social skills. Developmentally appropriate activities for 3- to 5-year-old children encourage the children to learn through active exploration of materials and settings. This exploration may involve both verbal and physical manipulations. Children learn best by doing or by being actively involved in an activity while the teacher scaffolds (i.e., provides the framework and support for the activities). Scaffolding may take a variety of forms that vary in the amount of support provided. Providing examples, materials, situations, comments, and demonstrations are all effective methods of scaffolding. Hands-on, experiential manipulation of materials, rather than paper-and-pencil tasks, are important for this age group. Dramatic play, manipulation of blocks and puzzles, experimentation with art and other materials, and interactive story reading are appropriate activities to foster cognitive, language, social, and motor skills.

Individual Differences Are Respected

Individual differences among children are viewed as positive. Each child has a unique contribution to make to the classroom, an ideal that is fostered by providing a supportive environment that allows children to express their own personalities and interests. All children have their own learning style and rate of learning, and not all are expected to do every activity or achieve in the same manner. Each child is provided opportunities to learn in the way most helpful to him or her. Therefore, not all children choose to or are required to participate in all activities. Likewise, family and cultural differences are respected. Family contributions to the curriculum are encouraged and vary widely according to individual preferences.

Children's Self-Esteem Is Fostered

Children's self-esteem is valued; its growth is fostered in the classroom by allowing the children to have as much control over participation in the activities as possible. During center time and outdoor playtime, children can choose in which activities they want to participate. They also decide to what degree they will engage in these activities. This includes the right to be passive participants. The children's participation in a new activity is encouraged and supported by the teachers. Activities can be modified to help the children achieve success because each successful activity builds children's confidence in their abilities and fosters a willingness to try other new activities. Other encouragement toward competence is provided throughout the day by allowing children to get a drink of water when they are thirsty, pour more juice for themselves at snacktime, and attend to personal toileting needs without teacher direction or permission. However, teacher support is readily available when needed. During transitions between activities, children are expected to entertain themselves independently. For example, some children finish their snacks more quickly than others. If they are finished, they may read books or work puzzles in the quiet area while they wait for others to finish. This gives the children opportunities to make choices and exercise self-control. All of these procedures work together to help children become self-confident and competent people who can take care of their own needs.

Child-Centered Activities Are Emphasized

It is important that child-centered activities be a primary focus of the curriculum in order for the children to be able to construct their own knowledge. In LAP, approximately two thirds of the school day is devoted to child-centered activities. These activities take place during arrival, center time, and outdoor playtime. In child-centered activities, the child plays an active role in choosing in what activity to engage and how the activity will proceed. The teacher follows the child's lead and in some cases the teacher "steps out" of the interaction when facilitation is not needed. Often the teacher may be following the lead of several chil-

dren as they play together, drawing different children into an interaction when appropriate. For example, if several children are building a house, the teacher can hand a block to a child who is standing nearby and is avidly watching the others play; that child is assisted in joining the group. In this manner, interactions among children are encouraged. There are usually many child–child, as well as teacher–child, interactions during child-centered activities.

Learning Is Also Facilitated Through Teacher-Directed Group Activities

Teacher-directed activities are also important in facilitating language and learning. During these activities, the teacher engages the attention of a group of children at various times throughout the day for approximately 10 minutes at a time. In LAP, these activities occur during circle time, storytime, sharing time, large and small group time, and music time (see Chapter 2 for a sample schedule and description of activities). Some of the activities involve daily events (e.g., roll call during circle time) whereas others involve the presentation of new information (e.g., classifying according to shape during large group time). In these group activities, the teacher gives formal instruction on when to talk and when to listen. Even though the teacher is more directive in these group activities, the children still participate in the interactions through their verbal and nonverbal initiations (e.g., questions, body movements) and responses.

The Process of Learning Is Advocated

Activities are designed to be process, rather than product, oriented. This means that the child's learning is more important than the evidence of that learning. For example, the fact that a child tries to make an art project outweighs the importance of how the project turns out. However, as children "practice," the form of the production (i.e., art or language) usually improves. "Errors" are not viewed as requiring immediate correction, but rather as stages in the learning process. Most activities and materials are open ended and offer a variety of uses and ways to proceed rather than one correct way. Close-ended materials such as worksheets are not well suited to a process-oriented program. Again, the teacher's role is not to transmit knowledge that must be portrayed in a "correct" way; rather the role is to facilitate the children's construction of their own knowledge.

Naturalistic Development of Language and Literacy Is Fostered

Relationships between language and literacy skills are fostered through naturalistic activities. Rather than requiring the children to memorize the alphabet, practice writing their names on a worksheet, or learn phonics, the curriculum is planned to provide the children with opportunities to learn these skills as they relate to everyday activities. Naturalistic learning is evidenced as the children learn to recognize their names during roll call or from labels on their coat cubbies. They learn the letters of the alphabet by singing a song and later pair the letters in the song to the alphabet letters displayed in the room. Still later, the children begin to recognize the individual letters of their names as well as the names of their classmates. During dramatic play activities, children may note words on pretend canned goods, make shopping lists by copying words, "read" to their babies, take telephone messages, and practice many other literacy events. After repeated readings of a story, the children often are able to retell it accurately and begin to recognize individual words. The children have access to writing materials and may "write" words, letters, and stories. Invented spelling is acceptable. After special activities are completed, a group story is often written describing the activity. In these ways, language and literacy relationships are formed naturally with the child's interest being the primary driving force.

Naturalistic Development of Inquiry and Math Concepts Is Encouraged

Inquiry and mathematical skills are facilitated in much the same manner as language and literacy relationships. Opportunities for observing, manipulating, and experimenting with objects and events occur during daily activities and routines. The teacher's role is to facilitate the children's ability to note, question, manipulate, and experiment. For example, testing the ability of objects to roll might occur during outdoor playtime with balls and tricycles and during center time with arts and crafts materials such as cardboard tubes, beads, and round macaroni wheels or with round and tubular wooden blocks. Counting and number relationships can be fostered during calendar time, when each day's date is discussed, or during child-centered activities, when objects can be counted. Snacktime is a particularly good time to foster one-to-one matching and number concepts as the crackers and juice are distributed. Addition concepts can be taught as children have seconds on the crackers. They can take two or three more crackers adding to the ones they already have. Subtraction concepts can be taught as the children eat their crackers (e.g., first they have five crackers, then they eat one, and now they have four). Other concepts such as size and shape or quantity judgments (e.g., more or less) can be incorporated naturalistically throughout the curricular activities.

Parents Are Viewed as Central to the Program

Close communication with the child's family is important for a variety of reasons. First, the families are the primary social agents for the child. As such they are the most knowledgeable about the child's communicative interests and needs. Parents or other primary caregivers and teachers provide each other with important information about the child's needs and progress. Second, the transfer of skills learned in the classroom to other settings can be fostered by knowledgeable parents and other family members. This means that parents and family members should be aware of the child's activities and helped to foster the skills in the home environment. Close communication between school and family can be achieved in a variety of ways. One way is through daily contact when a child is dropped off or picked up at the preschool. Another way is through conferences, both in person and over the telephone. A third way to communicate is through a newsletter specifying what the curricular activities will be for each week (see Appendix A at the end of this book for a sample newsletter, *LAPlines*). In this way parents are aware of what is *going to happen* (rather than what has already occurred). This means that they can ask their children specific questions about their day rather than a general "What did you do today?" (the usual answer being "nothing!"). Through awareness of the day's activities, the parents have the knowledge needed to facilitate their children's talk about preschool activities. They can ask such questions as, "How did you make the pudding?" and "What does a vet do?" Finally, student clinicians and parents of the children with speech and language impairments can exchange information through personal contact, telephone calls, notes describing weekly progress at school or at home, individualized education program (IEP) meetings, and progress reports written by the clinician at the end of each semester.

GUIDELINES FOR CLASSROOM MANAGEMENT

The Schedule of Activities Is Important in Management

The schedule of activities lends structure to the curriculum and adds structure for the children. It is this structure that helps the children know what to expect and how to behave. By alternating between teacher-directed activities and child-centered activities, the children do not have to sit still for long periods of time. In this way, their attention spans are not overextended, and their interest in learning is maintained. Interested, motivated children who are active in their own learning are less likely to misbehave than those who are bored or disinterested. It is also important in developing a schedule to consider such factors as when children need to have a snack, when they need variation, and when they need to move around. For example, placing snacktime just after outdoor play provides the children with food and drink after being active, a time to calm down after strenuous outdoor play, and important maintenance of energy. Scheduling music at the end of the day provides an opportunity for the children to express themselves through songs and motions. It is an activity in which all children can participate, ending the day on a positive note.

A Variety of Activities Is Needed

It is important to have a variety of activities available in order to accommodate different children's interests and abilities. Children who are interested and willing to try an activity will learn from their participation. Children who can succeed at an activity will want to continue that activity and talk about it. Children who have difficulty with an activity become bored and frustrated. By having alternative activities available, these children are able to find something that interests them. This variety also facilitates classroom management. Children who are actively involved in learning are not likely to misbehave.

Established Routines Are Helpful

Routines for classroom management are helpful for both children and teachers. Routines help children predict what will happen next. After children have learned a routine, they know what to do without much teacher direction. The teacher can then pay attention to individual children without constant direction to all.

The ability to follow a routine also encourages children's development of self-discipline and competence. Picking up toys is taught during clean-up time by helping a child to perform the activity until the help is no longer necessary. These self-help tasks are particularly important for children with speech and language impairments and those who are learning English as a second language because they can be accomplished without any talking. The children can demonstrate nonverbal competence even if they cannot demonstrate verbal competence. The competence displayed by children in attending to their own needs also helps in classroom management.

Wait Time Should Be Minimized

Minimizing wait time is also important in preschool classroom management. Having alternative activities available for those who are waiting can be helpful. For example, instead of having all children wait at the snack table until everyone has finished, staff should let the children clean up their own place and then get a book to read. Or, while waiting in line, the teacher can initiate fingerplays or songs.

OVERVIEW OF THIS VOLUME

All of the underlying guidelines discussed in this chapter, regarding language learning, curriculum development, and classroom management, influence how a classroom using a language-focused curriculum is conducted. The preschool child is an active learner, and classroom routine and structure must support this constructive process. Specific details on the structure of the LFC used in LAP are outlined in Chapter 2. Also addressed in Chapter 2 are the reasons for having both teacher-directed and child-centered activities and for having activities that are routine and those that vary daily. In addition, the focus and use of dramatic play activities is explained. The chapter includes a detailed schedule that outlines the purpose of the different types of daily activities.

Chapter 3 then describes effective classroom-based intervention techniques within the classroom setting. Examples from children enrolled in LAP are used to illustrate the way therapy can be embedded in daily classroom activities. The use of therapy is demonstrated as well. With Chapter 3, the first part of this book concludes, having addressed the general philosophy of LAP and the LFC, general procedures and structure for implementation, and intervention techniques.

Part II then provides examples of both general curriculum planning guides and specific lesson plans that describe how to implement the LFC. Chapter 4 focuses on how to plan a language-focused curriculum and provides guidelines for selecting activities. Activities can be selected from the lesson plans provided in Part III. These plans feature dramatic play, art, and group activities and suggestions for how they can be used to implement a variety of weekly themes. Suggestions for how to incorporate music and story activities are also given. Finally, suggestions are made on generating new dramatic play, art, and group activities.

Chapter 5 provides sample monthly calendar plans for 4 months to demonstrate how activities could be developed for a semester. Sample curriculum plans for 2 weeks follow to illustrate how lesson plans can be developed around a thematic unit. General curriculum guides provide an overview of the activities planned for a specific week. Daily lesson or activity plans describe individual lessons (e.g., classifying objects according to whether they sink or float).

Part III then begins with a listing of possible weekly thematic units. Possible dramatic play activities that relate to the themes are also listed. Following this listing, daily lesson or activity plans involving dramatic play, art, and group activities are organized in the following manner:

- Lesson plans for dramatic play activities are organized alphabetically with an index indicating page numbers.
- Art activities are organized according to the following categories: cutting, drawing, painting, pasting, and miscellaneous.

- Group activity plans are categorized according to whether they focus on classification, labeling and matching, or sequencing skills. Pre-academic skills involving letters and numbers and daily living concepts involving health and safety issues are also included in the group activity plans.

Two reference lists follow Part III. First is the references cited. Second is a bibliography of children's stories used as examples in a sample semester's (20 weeks) overall curriculum plan. Then Appendix A features an example of the Language Acquisition Preschool parent newsletter, *LAPlines*. Appendix B contains blank forms for curriculum planning. The forms include a monthly calendar guide, a weekly planning guide, a daily planning guide, and activity plans for dramatic play, art, and group activities.

~2~

The Curriculum Structure for Naturalistic Learning

Once staff understand the basic principles of the LFC, the classroom structure can be shaped by them. This chapter outlines the general types of activities included in the LFC structure. General lesson formats for child-centered and teacher-directed activities are also described. (Specific details about lesson plans and ways to develop an LFC are addressed in Chapter 4.) A major focus of the curriculum structure is the center time activities, particularly the dramatic plays. The rationale for including dramatic play activities is discussed in detail in this chapter, and other center time activities are also described. Finally, a sample schedule and a description of activities typically used in LAP illustrate the overall structure of the LFC.

GENERAL CATEGORIES OF ACTIVITIES

Activities in the LFC can be categorized as those that change daily (or frequently) and those that are routine. In addition, each of the activities can be categorized as primarily either child centered or teacher directed. For example, a dramatic play activity typically changes daily and is primarily child centered. The group activity also may change daily but is teacher directed. For example, classifying objects that are large or small is a group activity that is directed by the teacher. Sharing time is a routine activity that is teacher directed, whereas snacktime is a routine activity that is child centered. Sharing is a show-and-tell activity that follows a prescribed format wherein the teacher assists one child to ask another child questions about an object (see below). Routine phrases such as "More crackers, please" typically occur at snacktime but are not teacher directed. Figure 1 illustrates the sample of possible cross-categorization of the different activities.

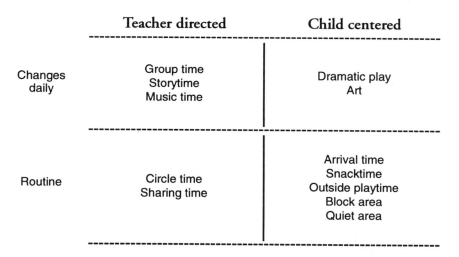

Figure 1.   The activities of the LFC can be categorized as shown in this matrix. (From Bunce, B.H., & Watkins, R.W. [1995]. Language intervention in a preschool classroom: Implementing a language-focused curriculum. In M.L. Rice & K.A. Wilcox [Eds.], *Building a language-focused curriculum for the preschool classroom: Vol. I. A foundation for lifelong communication* [p. 67]. Baltimore: Paul H. Brookes Publishing Co.; reprinted by permission.)

Changing Versus Routine Activities

It is important to have both activities that change and activities that are routine. The activities that change daily allow for new concepts, vocabulary, and language structure to be taught. They also are interesting to the child because of their novelty. They provide a challenge to the children, stretching their intellect, language, social, and motor skills. These activities provide new information to the children. The routine activities provide known structure and, to some degree, a level of comfort for the children. The children know what to expect from the routine activities and can predict what they are to do or say. These activities allow for the practicing of skills within a known format. Many of the children with speech and language impairments and those who are learning English as a second language will first begin to participate verbally when involved in routine activities such as sharing time or snacktime when functional language forms are similar from day to day. A balance of both kinds of activities is needed to provide an appropriate learning environment for all of the children.

Child-Centered Versus Teacher-Directed Activities

It is also necessary to have a balance between activities that are child centered and those that are teacher directed. The child-centered activities allow children to focus on what is of interest to them. Adults then can describe or comment on what each child or several children are doing. The children hear language describing their own activities and are more likely to talk about the activities. Children are also more likely to be understood if the topic is known. This is particularly important for the child who is hard to understand as a result of speech and/or language problems. Teachers (or other children) will know what the child is saying when the talk is focused on the child's own activity. Also, the child who is interested will be more likely to stay on task and continue to try even if difficulties arise.

However, it is also essential to teach the children new information. With teacher-directed activities, the teacher can present new information. Although the teacher controls the pace during teacher-directed activities, the children are encouraged to participate. Also, teacher-directed activities help children learn to listen and follow directions. Often concepts introduced in a teacher-directed activity are later incorporated into the child-centered activities.

GENERAL LESSON FORMATS

Child-Centered Activities

During child-centered activities, the children are free to choose the activities in which they want to participate. They also are free to choose their level of participation, which may range from active interactions to observing the play of others. As a facilitator, the teacher must be aware of the child's level of competence and provide appropriate structure and materials, but be ready to change the structure, materials, or activities based on the child's interest and needs. This means the teacher must be aware of each child's needs and be flexible enough to meet changing needs. The teacher follows the child's interest and provides support, which may take the form of finding needed extra materials and/or helping to problem-solve.

During dramatic play activities, this facilitation may take the form of providing verbal scripts (i.e., modeling), responding to the children's productions, finding additional props, problem solving how to construct an important prop, and in general surrounding the children with appropriate language necessary to achieve their needs and wants. During play in the block area, the facilitation of language and learning may be achieved by commenting on the children's and the adult's actions, responding to an individual child's requests and comments, and providing additional blocks, noting arrangements, and adding appropriate toys (e.g., small cars, animals, people). Facilitation in the arts-and-crafts area may include modeling the procedures to be used, providing models for the child to observe, or providing "technical" help in cutting, glueing, and painting. Language facilitation may be achieved by describing the procedures, responding to the child's initiations, expanding or recasting the child's utterances, and in general carrying on a conversation with the child. Language and learning facilitation in the quiet area may involve helping the child do a puzzle or learning center activity such as matching letters or numbers or helping one or more children play classification games or board games. Story reading is also a popular quiet area activity. The adult may read a story to one or more children or the children may look at the books by themselves.

Facilitating language and learning also takes place during outdoor time. The children and adults interact through group games or in one-to-one play. Again, language facilitation occurs through expansion and re-

casting of the child's utterances and by commenting on actions of the
child or adult. Cognitive skills are fostered through observation of the
properties of natural objects. For example, sand can be poured, plants
have leaves and seeds, some also have thorns, pine cones are prickly, and
so forth. The properties of manipulative toys can also be noted (e.g., tricycles have pedals and can roll). Learning to play group games (e.g.,
"Duck, Duck, Goose") fosters learning to follow rules. Motor skills are
facilitated through use of the outdoor play equipment (e.g., pouring sand,
batting balls, throwing and catching balls, riding tricycles, climbing). Social skills are fostered through sharing of and negotiating for play equipment and through playing group games.

Teacher-Directed Activities

During teacher-directed activities, the children listen to the teacher as a
group. The children learn how to interact nonverbally by pointing or
raising their hand and/or verbally as directed by the teacher. As a facilitator of children's learning, the teacher must be able to vary the demands
of each task to meet the different children's needs and skill levels. Instead of rotely asking each child to perform the same task, the teacher
has them perform alternative tasks that achieve a similar goal. There
may also be group participation, such as answering a question in unison
or counting to find out the day's date. A general format usually guides
the teacher-directed activities so that the children know what is expected. For example, circle time typically begins with a standard roll call
and ends with a description of upcoming center activities. The children's
participation at storytime can vary with the type of stories read or told
(e.g., from a book, on a flannel board, with a puppet). For example, the
children soon learn that if a line is repeated several times, they are to
join in.

For teacher-directed group activities, the following general format is
employed. To begin, there is an introductory task (e.g., a demonstration,
a problem posed). Then an interaction between the children and teacher
(or between two children) further develops the concept through child
manipulation and exploration of the task. Finally, when appropriate, a
brief summary task or project is completed. For the introductory task,
the teacher may demonstrate the particular concept through videotapes
or object manipulations. The teacher may also pose a problem verbally
(e.g., does a nail float?) or by demonstration (e.g., showing that an object
will not fit into another if turned a particular way). The children respond
by suggesting solutions or answers, which are then tried by the teacher
or other children. The children are encouraged to make predictions, try
new ideas, and demonstrate their knowledge both verbally and nonverbally. Although there is a general format used, the type of group activities varies greatly (e.g., acting out a story, doing science experiments,
reciting the alphabet). (See Part III for specific group lessons plans.)

For sharing time, the procedure is to have two children come up to
the front of the group, each standing on one side of the teacher. The
teacher prompts one child to ask the other child three questions about
the object the second child has for sharing time. The three questions are,

"What do you have?", "What do you do with it?", and "Where did you get it?" The second child responds to each question in turn. The questions can be simplified to, "What have?" or "Have?", "What do?" or "Do?", and "Where get?" or "Get?" In this way, most of the children are able to ask the questions verbally. When necessary, the teacher provides models of the questions or answers for the children. Other questions can also be asked, such as "What color is it?", "What's its name?", and so forth. After the questions are answered and the item shown to the other children, the child who responded to the questions sits down. The child asking the questions becomes the child who answers the questions, and a new child is chosen as the questioner. At the end, the child who first answered the questions becomes the last questioner. It is helpful if the large group is broken into smaller groups so that plenty of time can be used to demonstrate or show the item. All of the children can take part in the sharing activity. If an item is not brought from home, a favorite item from the classroom can be shared. If they desire, children may also tell about an event rather than showing something. As the year proceeds, the children learn to ask and answer questions with less and less teacher support. Sharing time teaches children to ask and answer questions within a real context. The ability to ask questions provides a way for children to obtain information both in and outside of the classroom. A child asking a question such as "What do you have?" almost always gets a response from an adult or another child. This response provides new vocabulary knowledge about items in which the child is interested.

USE OF DRAMATIC PLAY ACTIVITIES

Fostering of Linguistic Skills

The dramatic play activities form a basis for the LFC because they facilitate language, social, and cognitive development. Several scholars (French, Lucariello, Seidman, & Nelson, 1985; Pelligrini, 1984) have noted that dramatic play activities can facilitate preschool children's language abilities, particularly in the production of imaginative language, the use of pronouns, and the use of displaced references (i.e., talking about objects or actions not present in the environment—"then and there" topics). French et al. also noted that in *nonscripted play settings* (e.g., playing with blocks), the language usually focused on object talk and discussions about objects and actions taking place in the "here and now." Lucariello, Kyratzis, and Engel (1986) suggested that children can learn new syntactic and semantic forms to perform the same function when acting out a script. This may be a result of the language being embedded in a familiar routine. For example, in a fast-food restaurant schema, many children have watched parents place an order and pay. Likewise, if a grocery store scenario is used, children are familiar with pushing a cart, choosing items, and paying for them. The new language knowledge in turn may also facilitate the development of new script knowledge. Although most of these studies have observed typically developing children, there is evidence suggesting that the use of scripts and/or routines may facilitate development of language abilities in children with language impairments as well (Constable, 1986).

Encouragement of Social Interaction

A second reason for using dramatic play activities is that they encourage social interaction. Many opportunities for talking occur in the dramatic play area as children establish the schema and enact their roles. Dramatic play activities allow for the children to play many different roles and to interact with many different partners. More talking, particularly among peers, occurs in this area than occurs in the block, art, or quiet areas (Pelligrini, 1984). The dramatic play schema facilitates these conversations among the children. Although controversial, there is some indication that if children share a schema or script, the interaction will be sustained longer than in nonscripted interactions (Nelson, 1981; Nelson & Seidman, 1984). Nelson suggested that one reason for this is that children may use their understanding of a particular script to guide their social interactions. Also, the interactions are based in "real-world" scenarios, which may allow for generalization to and from school and home environments of both linguistic and social interaction skills.

Expansion of Knowledge and Organizational Skills

A final reason for using dramatic play activities is that children may also extend their knowledge by first observing a script and then having the opportunity to enact it themselves (e.g., observing a guest speaker such as a veterinarian and then playing at being a vet). Children may acquire a basic structure of a particular script after an initial experience with it. The scripts then become elaborated each time they are repeated (Fivush & Slackman, 1986). Thus, script frameworks may be one way knowledge is organized and extended.

Different Types of Dramatic Play Activities

Not all dramatic play activities have the same strengths for developing language, social, cognitive, and motor skills. Some are interactive with defined roles (e.g., fast-food restaurant). These dramatic play activities have excellent verbal exchanges and lend themselves to promoting discourse. Other dramatic play activities may be strong in vocabulary development or classification activities as well as in interaction. For example, a grocery store script lends itself to classification activities (e.g., identifying fruits, meat, cereals) as well as providing a known schema for interaction. Some dramatic play activities emphasize sequential development of the action. For example, going on a picnic could involve preparing the lunch basket, getting to the park, eating the lunch, and going home. Other dramatic play activities may be action oriented and provide many opportunities to model verb, adverb, and adjective structures. Firefighter and matchbox car racing activities are examples of action-oriented dramatic plays. Still other dramatic play activities lend themselves to promoting problem solving. Mechanic or construction activities are good examples of dramatic play activities where problem solving can be demonstrated. The adult or child can present a problem to be solved (e.g., how to fix windows, shingle a roof, or put together a car) and then all can help find a solution. Finally, some dramatic play activities promote the development of both gross and fine motor skills. Hammering with a plastic hammer to make sure a shingle is glued or turning a plastic screw when building a car are examples of the use of a variety of muscle movements.

It is important to note that within each type of dramatic play some verbal and/or social interaction can take place. Children learn to share desired items and to get their needs met in socially accepted ways. The shy child is supported in interactions with others; often pretending itself allows the child to experiment with roles and dialogues. The dramatic play activities can entice a child to take a risk to learn by getting involved. In developing dramatic play activities, then, it is important to take advantage of particular strengths of each dramatic play in facilitating language, social, cognitive, and motor skills.

COMPONENTS OF DRAMATIC PLAY

A dramatic play activity has four major components: the schema, the roles, the props, and the verbal exchanges.

Schema

It is important that the children have a sense of the overall schema involved in a dramatic play theme. If the child has no idea what is involved in a particular dramatic play activity, then he or she will usually choose not to participate. This does not mean that only activities thoroughly familiar to a child can be used. It does mean that for unfamiliar schema, more involved introductions may be necessary during circle time before the children will take part. This introduction may involve a demonstration by a guest speaker, the viewing of a brief video clip (e.g., activities on a farm or at a rodeo), the reading of a story (e.g., one describing an airplane trip), and/or a demonstration of the overall schema by having adults and, when possible, children act out various roles.

As the children become more familiar with a particular dramatic play, they enjoy playing a variety of roles. The children know what to expect and can perform the role. However, it is possible that children may become so familiar with a particular dramatic play that they become bored with it. Therefore, some novelty added to familiar dramatic plays often increases interest in participation. This novelty can often be achieved through the addition of new or different props or a new focus (e.g., instead of just fishing, go ice fishing or go on a picnic where fishing is just one of the activities).

Roles

Another component in a dramatic play activity is the number of different roles that can be assumed. In most dramatic plays, there are a variety of roles available. For example, when playing "house," there can be parents, children, neighbors, and pets. When playing "doctor," there can be doctors, nurses, parents, sick children, receptionists, and so forth. Having a variety of roles in a particular dramatic play is important because it allows several children to play together and promotes the use of a variety of linguistic structures. It also allows children to change roles and switch identities. Children can elaborate on a particular role and even extend the dramatic play. For example, playing house may extend to going shopping so there is food to cook for supper. Additional roles of cashier and other grocery store personnel can then be added.

Props

The available props are an aspect of successful dramatic plays. Props are important because they provide contextual support for the dramatic play. They help the child identify the particular role to be played. To some extent they define the dramatic play. Props that can be manipulated in some way appear to be the most popular. It is not necessary to have actual objects or even miniature representations of the actual objects; however, it is necessary to have objects that can be used to perform the function of the needed props. It is also important that the props have the distinctive features of the particular object. For example, a chair with a man's tie can become a car with a seatbelt, particularly if a round Frisbee (or plastic lid) is used as a steering wheel. The features of a seat, a seatbelt, and a steering wheel form some of the key features of a car. If, however, the car is part of the "mechanic" dramatic play, then key features might also include having a hood that can be raised with some kind of "engine" inside. A box (or actual toy vehicle) with a liftable lid can be used to represent the car. For a "fishing" dramatic play, a fishing pole can be made with a stick and a string with a magnet on the end. The magnet is used to catch paper fish, each of which has a metal paper clip attached. Having the fish in a container or on a blue area (e.g., a blanket) to define a lake or pond adds to the reality of dramatic play activity.

The use of objects to represent other objects in the dramatic play often adds to the fun. One child might use a toilet paper tube as a flashlight. It becomes a flashlight because it is so designated and because the child uses it as a flashlight. The use of props in this way fosters imaginative play. Props also provide motivation and interest. Sometimes a child will be drawn into play interactions because of the props. For example, the opportunity to experiment with a typewriter may entice a child to be part of an "office" dramatic play.

Props also stimulate the need for negotiation. A favorite prop will often need to be shared. The modeling by teachers and/or peers of specific ways to get access to a favorite object is one way children can expand their ability to get their needs met. Over the course of the semester or year, the children can repeatedly practice their verbal negotiation skills in getting a turn using various props.

Verbal Exchanges

The verbal exchanges involved in dramatic play activities are varied. The same role in a dramatic play might elicit long, complex sentences or just one word. For example, in playing fast-food restaurant, one child cashier might say, "That will be $10 for your hamburger, French fries, and drink"; another child in the same role might just say "Money." Therefore, it is not the case that children must be able to use multiword sentences in order to participate in a dramatic play activity. In addition, one child may do a lot of nonverbal acting whereas another child may use verbal means to achieve a role. Usually, the children will combine both nonverbal and verbal means while participating in the dramatic play activity. For example, when playing "mechanic," a child may pretend to fix a car through actions, but will verbally "explain" to another child why the car will not run. (A common explanation is that it needs a new battery!) Child-produced "sound effects" are common in some dramatic play activities. Much language facilitation can take place through verbal interactions developed during dramatic play times. It is through the verbal exchanges that an adult (or another child) may provide models not only for content and form of language but also for its use. The adult or peer may model the role by using the props and acting the part. For example, an adult may report to the child "mechanic" that something is wrong with his or her car by saying, "My car needs to be fixed. I think it needs a new battery." The child can then respond nonverbally by "changing the battery" or verbally by saying, "Let me look at the car," "Let me get a new battery," "It will take 5 hours," or "I need some tools," and so forth. The adult can then switch roles with the child in order to provide models for additional types and forms of responses.

In summary, successful dramatic play activities need to be about familiar settings or schemas, or there needs to be appropriate modeling of the schema. Different dramatic play activities have different strengths: Some foster social interaction and discourse between children; others may emphasize vocabulary, classification, or problem-solving skills; and still others may be more action oriented. It is important that each dramatic play have a variety of potential roles or provide several different activities in order to involve several children at once. Manipulative props help maintain interest, provide learning opportunities, and provide support for verbal exchanges. The dramatic play activities, therefore, promote language use and the elaboration of language form and content, social interactions, and cognitive skills.

IMPLEMENTATION OF DRAMATIC PLAY ACTIVITIES

There are several steps involved in implementing the dramatic play activities. First, the activity must be introduced to the children. For this introduction, the teacher may model or act out portions of a dramatic play, often including children in the action. Videotapes or books may give the children a visual image of an unfamiliar schema, such as a rodeo. Guest speakers (e.g., a parent) may demonstrate activities by using props and actions rather than just telling the children about a topic. An example would be a beautician who uses a doll to show how she washes and styles (or cuts!) hair. Questions from the teachers and children often facilitate the demonstrations. Props to be used in the dramatic play activity need to be part of the demonstration whenever a new schema is presented.

Second, props are arranged in the dramatic play area to set the context or scene of the action. These props can be arranged by an assistant teacher while the children are in circle time, or the props can be arranged earlier. It is usually best not to arrange the easily portable props until center time. We have found it best to have the dramatic play props and area available only during center time. (Other areas, such as the art, block, and quiet centers, can be open during transition times.) A major reason for having the dramatic play activity available only during center time is that the activity typically requires an introduction or demonstration. The main transition time, during which the children play in the other three areas, occurs during arrival time—before the children would have been introduced to the dramatic play activity. Also, because the novelty of the activity helps keep the children's interest, it is important that they do not always have access to all of the props all of the time. (For similar reasons, the center time art project is different from the art activities available during arrival time.)

Third, the children are allowed to develop the schema in a manner meaningful to them. While playing "pizza parlor," a child may pretend to pick up a telephone and order a pizza to be delivered, adding an unplanned dimension to the dramatic play.

Fourth, the role of adults in a dramatic play activity is to provide modeling of roles while following the children's lead. In the above example, an adult may grab a chair and a paper plate steering wheel to create a delivery car and model the role of a driver delivering a pizza to a customer.

Fifth, if a dramatic play activity is overwhelming to some children, they must have the option to "escape" to another play center, such as the less threatening book and puzzle area. Conversely, a child should also have the option of observing the dramatic play setting from another area before deciding to become involved in it. Again, passive learning is fostered. Overt responses are not a requirement. Having the option to leave or to watch an activity places control over the amount of participation with the children. By giving the children this control, they will stay motivated to learn and be active learners.

In summary, dramatic play activities are first introduced to the children through demonstration and/or enactment using a variety of props appropriate to the activity. The children then develop the scenarios with the support of the adults who role play, problem-solve, and provide models or additional props as needed. The children are allowed to choose the level of their participation in the activity, including just observing. There is no requirement for participation in the dramatic play activity; rather, during center time, the children are free to participate in any of four different center activities, only one of which is dramatic play.

OTHER CENTER-TIME ACTIVITIES

The three other activities typically available to the children during center time are located in the art, block, and quiet areas. As mentioned previously, the art activities change daily whereas activities in the block and quiet areas remain relatively stable. The children, therefore, have a choice of two areas with new activities and two areas with familiar activities. One of the beliefs on which LAP is based is that language, social, cognitive, and motor skills can be facilitated in each of the areas although from day to day there may be differences in each area in the types of language used or the types of social, cognitive, and motor demands made. It is our experience that most children enjoy playing in all of the areas and by the time their first semester is completed, they are usually participating in all areas at some time during the day or across a week's time.

The Art/Science Area

The art activity changes each day so it is introduced at the end of circle time following the introduction of the dramatic play activity. The introduction usually consists of demonstrating the use of the art materials and tools. Art activities often reflect the daily theme. One way this is accomplished is to have the children make a prop that can be used in the dramatic play. For example, children can make binoculars to be used in an African safari dramatic play or a camping and hiking dramatic play. Another way to incorporate the theme is to make a picture out of items associated with a particular dramatic play. An example would be to make a "doctor kit" by glueing Q-tips, cotton balls, and tongue depressors onto paper. During the weekly theme of "Discovering things we do with our hands," one child was observed spending time detailing the hands on a simple figure, laboriously counting each finger as she painted. At times, the children's endproduct may relate to the dramatic play, such as car or vehicle rubbings for car racing day or an animal puppet for circus day. Often, the art activities do not have an endproduct. For example, during Play-Doh activities children use cookie cutters, Popsicle sticks, and their hands to manipulate the Play-Doh. At the end of center time, the Play-Doh is rolled into a big ball and stored for future use.

Different science concepts are also facilitated at the art table. For example, children experiment with colors when painting to learn that different color mixes make new colors (e.g., red and yellow make orange). Some projects may involve change of state, such as cornstarch and water constructions. Children can form objects with the mixture, but when they are finished the object "melts." Other science concepts involve learning about shapes, sizes, and textures, particularly when making collages. Art projects might also involve representing different life-stage sequences, such as making or drawing caterpillars, then cocoons, and then butterflies.

Language and social interaction at the art table varies with the children and with the type of activity. Children at the art table often work individually on a particular project (although group murals are also done). They may choose not to talk to others while they are painting, pasting, cutting, or developing their own project, or they may talk only to request needed supplies. Other children may do a lot of conversing and readily discuss their art projects with other children or with adults.

Various types of art activities demand different fine motor abilities. Cutting with scissors uses different muscles and coordination than painting or pasting activities. It is important to offer a range of art activities that allow for different motor skill levels so that all children can benefit from participating in art.

It is also important to allow the children opportunities to be creative. They learn much about their world when given opportunities to experiment. For example, when painting they find out what happens when two colors are blended together. They learn about shapes, forms, textures, and colors when making designs. Art activities provide children with opportunities to use and improve language, social, fine motor, and cognitive skills.

The Block or Manipulative Area

A block or manipulative area often includes many different types of blocks and other manipulative toys such as miniature furniture, toy cars and trucks, animals, and dolls. The area also might also include a dollhouse, garage, and barn. Occasionally, items can be added or taken away from the area, but in general, several kinds of blocks and miniature toys should be available consistently every day. Additional items relating to specific dramatic play activities may be added to the block area. For example, a miniature space ship and station might be added to the block area during a "Discovering Space" theme.

In the block area, children can play alone, beside other children, or with other children. Activities range from stacking blocks to creating a miniature town or farm. The amount and kind of language used in the block area varies depending on what the children are doing and on the children's level of language competence. The motor control needed to play with the items also varies with the type of toys used. Play with Lego blocks tends to be an individual or side-by-side activity requiring fine motor skills; large cardboard bricks generally encourage children to cooperate in building a cave or house to crawl into or out of. A variety of cognitive skills are facilitated in the block area. Experimenting with different sizes and shapes of blocks helps a child learn about relationships among large, medium, and small objects or relationships between different shapes (e.g., put two right-angle triangles together to make a square). Problem solving is promoted as children determine how to build the fourth wall of a house out of small blocks because all of the large blocks are already in use. Again, the block area activities can help foster the children's development of language, social, motor, and cognitive skills.

The Quiet Area

Activities in a quiet area could involve reading and looking at storybooks, working puzzles, playing board games, or writing on the chalkboard. A children's size book rack can display books so that children can see them. Books can be rotated occasionally, with some of the books corresponding with the weekly theme. Books read during storytime can later be put in the book rack so the children can look at them again or have an adult reread them. It is important that the books contain both male and female characters from different ethnic groups in a variety of roles. The children will often insist that a few of their favorite stories are kept available. The book rack could contain books in a variety of formats, including books that label, rhyme, repeat, or tell complex stories. Books containing artwork in the form of photographs, collages, pencil drawings, watercolors, block prints, or chalk drawings will broaden the horizons of the children reading them. A large, wooden crate turned on its side and filled with pillows provides a comfortable and quiet place to look at books or share secrets with a friend or a stuffed animal. A large beanbag chair could also be used as a quiet place to sit with friends and look at books together. The children may look at books together, by themselves, or with an adult. Adults may read a story to a child or small group of children but will often follow the child's lead and encourage the child to tell the story, labeling pictures when necessary.

Puzzles should vary in difficulty and be changed periodically. The children may work puzzles by themselves or with others, discussing where a specific piece fits. One "puzzle" in this area could be a Lego wall board. (A Lego wall board is similar to a Lego table but is mounted on the wall. At the bottom of the board is a container that stores the Legos, which are of different colors and designs and can be used to make a variety of patterns.) The children tend to work independently or side by side at such a board and frequently match colors or shapes as they work. Work on puzzles facilitates eye–hand coordination, fine motor skills, problem solving, and figure–ground skills. A variety of board games, such as card games, memory games, and matching games, can be available for individual or joint play. The children can choose a game and play it on the floor or at a small table. Turn taking is often an important skill learned when playing board games.

A chalkboard located in the quiet area provides opportunities for the children to draw or write. Children enjoy drawing and/or writing their name or alphabet letters with colored chalk. Younger children simply cover the board with color, learning to control arm and hand movements, which will enable them to write letters later. Children often work at the chalkboard in pairs, which requires negotiations for space or turn taking. If a chalkboard is not available, setting up a writing center may be feasible with paper, pencils, or markers. Activities in the quiet area facilitate language, preacademic, motor, social, and cognitive skills.

TYPICAL DAY IN LAP

A sample schedule from LAP (Figure 2) illustrates how all of the components of the LFC can be incorporated. A brief description of each activity taken from the LAP curriculum manual (Bunce & Liebhaber, 1989) is presented below.

Arrival

Upon arrival, each child receives a brief health check (e.g., throat examined, stomach and limbs checked for rashes), which is a child care licensing requirement. If the child appears ill, the child is sent home. The health check is also a good language-learning opportunity as the teacher can briefly label body parts during the health check. It is also a time when a child can tell about a home happening with a parent present to explain or elaborate so the teacher can understand (e.g., "It was Uncle Joe who came, not Uncle 'Soe' "). After the children are checked in, they have a 15-minute play period. The play period gives them an opportunity

DAILY SCHEDULE

Time/class

A.M.	P.M.	Activity
8:30–8:45	1:00–1:15	**ARRIVAL** Health checks and free play.
8:45–9:00	1:15–1:30	**CIRCLE TIME** Children and teachers greet each other; discuss helper of the day, today's date, and topic for the day; and choose where they will play.
9:00–9:50	1:30–2:20	**CENTER TIME** Children can play at one of four centers (art/science, blocks, quiet area, dramatic play).
9:50–10:05	2:20–2:35	**CLEAN UP/STORYTIME** Children clean up the toys. Then, they listen to a story.
10:05–10:15	2:35–2:45	**SHARING TIME** Children gather back in circle area to share information or toys. They take turns being the questioner or respondent.
10:15–10:45	2:45–3:15	**OUTSIDE TIME** Children play individual games, as well as organized group games (e.g., "Duck, Duck, Goose").
10:45–11:00	3:15–3:30	**SNACKTIME** Children assist in preparing snack. This is a good time to encourage conversation and table manners.
11:00–11:15	3:30–3:45	**SMALL/LARGE GROUP TIME** Each day different activities will be planned. Sometimes the children will be split into small groups during this time; on other days, the whole class will participate in a group project.
11:15–11:30	3:45–4:00	**MUSIC TIME** Children sing songs, play instruments, and/or dance.
		DISMISSAL Children sing a good-bye song and are dismissed.

Figure 2.   LAP's daily schedule. (From Bunce, B.H., & Watkins, R.W. [1995]. Language intervention in a preschool classroom: Implementing a language-focused curriculum. In M.L. Rice & K.A. Wilcox [Eds.], *Building a language-focused curriculum for the preschool classroom: Vol. I. A foundation for lifelong communication* [p. 58]. Baltimore: Paul H. Brookes Publishing Co.; reprinted by permission.)

to greet their friends and acclimate themselves to the classroom for the day. They may play in the block and/or quiet area or draw pictures at the art table.

Circle Time

During the 10- to 15-minute circle time, the teacher welcomes the children and then takes roll. Roll-call involves the teacher holding up 3″ × 5″ index cards on which the children's names are written. Initially, the teacher will say the name as each card is displayed, but later the card is presented alone. Upon seeing his or her name on the card, the child raises his or her hand. After each child has responded, the helper of the day places his or her card on a special chart. The helper of the day is determined by the namecard on top of the pile. (At the end of the day that child's card is placed on the bottom of the pile.) The helper's duties include flipping the lights to indicate "clean-up" times, being the line leader, and helping the teacher to put up the date on the calendar. All of the children count to make sure that the correct date is posted. The "days of the week" song is sung with the helper's assistance. Discussion of the weather and other events or announcements are made at this time. The alphabet song may be sung, or the first letter in the helper's name may be discussed. The teacher then introduces the theme and the activities of the day. Finally, the children choose the center area in which they will participate first. During circle time, the children are encouraged to do the following:

- Participate
- Take turns talking
- Listen to others
- Ask questions
- Make decisions about what activity to join

Center Time

Center time lasts for approximately 50 minutes. During this time, the children can choose to play in any of four centers: art/science, blocks or manipulatives, quiet area, or dramatic play. The children are free to pursue their interests in any of these areas. Some children manage to play in all four areas during center time. The focus of center time is to stimulate verbal interactions between the children, to model speech and language skills, for the children, and to encourage the use of context-appropriate verbal skills, as well as to foster learning, motor, and social skills. During center time, the children are encouraged to do the following:

- Choose their own activities
- Explore everyday scripts
- Explore new scripts
- Learn new concepts
- Develop verbal interactive skills, vocabulary, grammar, and discourse competencies appropriate for enacting the script
- Play with other children

- Take turns with toys
- Ask for what they want
- Be creative
- Practice fine and gross motor skills

Clean Up/Storytime

To signal the end of center time, the helper of the day flashes the classroom lights. The children then help clean up by putting away the props, toys, and blocks, cleaning up the art table, and putting away the books and puzzles. The children then gather for storytime.

Storytime lasts approximately 10 minutes each day. Stories or poems are read or told to the children using children's literature books, puppets, and/or flannel board stories. Throughout the story, the children are asked to predict what will happen, provide some of the dialogue, and in general, interact with the story. Sometimes favorite nursery rhymes or stories are acted out. Occasionally, children will make up a story that the teacher writes down. Sometimes a story will be read in another language and then retold in English. Short videotaped stories or segments of "Sesame Street" also are sometimes incorporated into storytime. During storytime, the children are encouraged to do the following:

- Help with clean up
- Listen to the story
- Learn to comprehend verbal information
- Respond appropriately to the story
- Note repetitive lines
- Enjoy the story

Sharing Time

After storytime, the children gather together for a 10- to 15-minute sharing time. One child asks another child about the item brought to share. Typical questions include "What do you have?" and "Where did you get it?" Each child has the opportunity to be both the questioner and the respondent (i.e., the one who shares). During sharing time, the children are encouraged to do the following:

- Ask questions
- Speak to the group
- Listen to others
- Answer questions

Outside Time

Outside time lasts for approximately 30 minutes. The children line up with the helper of the day in the lead and walk single file down to the play yard. The playground equipment includes slides, a merry-go-round, a climbing platform, rope ladders, a sliding pole, and a sand area. There are also several different styles of tricycles available. While on the playground, the children share the facilities with other preschool classes. Therefore, the children learn to negotiate for turns and play with children other than those who attend LAP. The equipment fosters development of gross motor skills involved in climbing ropes and stairs, sliding down poles and slides, riding, running, jumping, digging, throwing, catching, and so forth. These different actions encourage the use of different verb structures as well as adverbs and adjectives.

Sometimes the teacher will lead group games, such as "Duck, Duck, Goose." For this game, the children sit in a circle while one child taps the other children on the shoulder one at a time saying, "Duck, duck, duck, . . . (and eventually) goose." When the child says "goose," the child who is tapped gets up and chases the first child around the circle. The first child runs until he or she reaches the open space where the second child had been sitting. Then, the first child sits down. The second child repeats the game by saying, "Duck, duck, duck, . . . goose" and then running when he or she designates the "goose." The game is played until all children have had a turn being the one who says, "Duck, duck, duck, . . . goose." Other group games include "Red Light/Green Light," "Simon Says," and "Mother (Father), May I?"

During outside time, the children are encouraged to do the following:

- Experiment with sand and sand toys
- Climb on climbing toys

- Ride tricycles and scooters
- Negotiate for turns
- Run and generally have fun
- Play cooperatively (e.g., throw and catch balls)
- Observe changes in nature

Snacktime

When the children come in from outside, they wash their hands to get ready for snacktime. One adult monitors the bathroom and helps children with the routine of toileting and hand washing. During snacktime, the children sit at tables and enjoy a snack (e.g., crackers and juice). There is at least one adult at each table. During snacktime, children practice politeness skills by waiting until all are seated and by asking other children for more crackers or juice as needed. The routine phrase "More crackers, please" is often one of the first phrases learned by children with speech and language impairments and children who are learning English as a second language. The phrase can be expanded to "May I have more, please?"

Snacktime is also a good time to use counting skills and perform simple addition and subtraction. One child might have five crackers but after eating one will note that only four crackers remain. Or another child will count to three as three more crackers are taken from the tray. Other children will comment that when three crackers are added to the one on their napkin, they have four crackers. The children often comment on the shape of the crackers, noting that some are round like circles, some are square or rectangular, and occasionally some are triangular. During snacktime, the children are encouraged to do the following:

- Wait until everyone is seated at the table before starting to eat
- Engage in appropriate conversation with tablemates
- Use good table manners
- Ask for more juice or crackers using appropriate words, including "please" and "thank you"
- Pour their own juice
- Take turns washing hands after snacktime
- Clean up after themselves

Small/Large Group Time

Group time lasts for approximately 10–15 minutes and consists of activities that vary from day to day. The children are split into small groups during small group time, and the whole class participates together in large group activities. Activities may involve experiments (e.g., mixing colors and seeing what happens, deciding what sinks or floats, cooking pudding), sorting and matching activities, and/or sequencing activities involving repeated patterns. A summary chart of what happened during the experiments may be composed by the children with the teacher writing the information on a big chart. Class thank-you notes to visitors are composed during group time. Often the children will each draw a picture or add their name to the letters. Short alphabet and phonic lessons, as well as mathematical and inquiry activities, are presented during group time (see Part III for specific group lesson plans). During group time, the children are encouraged to do the following:

- Pay attention
- Learn to comprehend verbal information
- Participate
- Learn key vocabulary and concepts
- Ask questions
- Generate ideas and sentences
- Learn alphabet letters and letter–sound correspondence
- Learn number concepts
- Follow directions

Music Time

Music time occurs during the last 10–15 minutes of the day. It is a time when the children can relax and have fun singing. Many of the songs have actions or fingerplays to accompany them. Rhythm instruments are sometimes used. Favorite songs are learned and sung over and over. Music activities are particularly good to end the day because all of the children can participate. For some children with limited language competency, it is during music time that they first begin to participate actively in an activity. Doing actions, fingerplays, or singing in a group may be less threatening than talking. Also, singing in a group is a fun way to learn to follow directions, learn words to a song, and learn about music. During music time, the children are encouraged to do the following:

- Participate
- Enjoy different melodies
- Enjoy different rhythms and patterns
- Learn and enjoy rhymes
- Follow directions

After music time, the children sing the good-bye song:

> Good-bye everyone,
> Good-bye everyone,
> Good-bye everyone,
> We'll see you again tomorrow

When the song is completed, the children are released to their parents.

SUMMARY

The language-focused curriculum used in LAP and described in this chapter is designed to foster language and learning for 3- to 5-year-old children with varying levels of linguistic competence. Language intervention and enhancement are provided in a least restrictive environment during natural interactions. It is within these communicative interactions that the children learn new language content, forms, and uses. A thematic approach is used in designing the curricular activities. In particular, the dramatic play, art, storytime, group, and music activities are designed to develop the day's theme. Although language development is viewed as central to the learning process, developmentally appropriate activities are also utilized to facilitate cognitive, motor, and personal/ social skills.

~3~

Language Intervention in the Language-Focused Curriculum

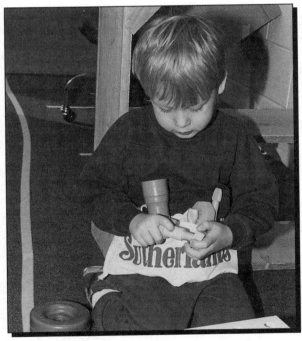

Children with speech and language impairments may need more intense language stimulation than is provided by the general language facilitation guidelines outlined in Chapter 2. Several scholars have suggested that children with specific language impairment (SLI) learn in a manner similar to children whose language development is typical; however, the children with language impairments need many more presentations of the target vocabulary or structures to reach the same level of competency (Rice, Buhr, & Nemeth, 1990; Watkins, Rice, & Moltz, 1993). For example, Rice, Buhr, et al. (1990), using a story presented through videotape, found that children with typical language development needed four presentations of a new word before they could identify it correctly. Children with SLI also learned the new words through the video format, but they needed more presentations.

Although children with SLI may need more information, it is often the case that they receive less (Rice, 1993; Silliman & Wilkinson, 1991). Part of the reason for this reduction is that they are often not active participants in verbal exchanges and may not initiate interactions or respond when addressed. This lack of initiation or response limits some potential stimulation. For example, a child who asks, "What's this?" will receive a lot of information about objects in the environment. A child who is not able to ask questions or fails to ask them will not receive the same amount of information. Similarly, a child who responds when spoken to encourages the speaker to continue the interaction. If the child makes no response, then the interaction usually ends, thus limiting the opportunities to learn more about communication and language. Therefore, in a language-focused curriculum, the children with speech and language impairments receive much stimulation or input even when they fail to respond. The stimulation is provided by both adults and other children. The children with speech and language impairments are not required to produce verbal language, although they are provided with many opportunities to do so. The focus of this chapter is on describing specific language intervention for children with speech and language impairments using a LFC based on a concentrated normative model. This model, as described in detail by Rice (1995), proposes that intervention be provided in a naturalistic setting to capitalize on the children's developmental momentum while providing a concentrated focus or highlighting specific language skills (see also Bunce & Watkins, 1995).

SPECIFIC LANGUAGE INTERVENTION STRATEGIES

Providing language opportunities in a rich and stimulating environment and allowing language use are central to all other strategies for linguistic enhancement. However, provision of a stimulating environment is not enough. Other strategies are needed in order to focus children's attention on linguistic forms and uses. These strategies or techniques include focused contrasts, modeling, event casts, open questions, expansions, recasts, redirects and prompted initiations, and scripted play.

Focused Contrasts

A focused contrast is a production by an adult that highlights contrastive differences in speech sounds, lexical items, and/or syntactic structures. This technique works on two levels. The first level is one of corrective feedback in which negative evidence is provided to the child. Focused contrasts make explicit the error versus the correct form in a manner that allows the child to recognize the differences. The procedure can be a brief focusing of attention on the crucial features in an interaction or it can involve several exchanges. For example, the adult might say to the child, "You said 'Otay,' but I say 'Okay' " to focus the child's attention on the differences between the production of /t/ versus /k/. The exchange might continue with the teacher writing a "t" and then a "k" on the chalkboard to further emphasize the contrast.

The second level involves modeled contrasts in adult talk. These verbal productions or contrasts are embedded in the ongoing descriptions. For example, if the plural marker /s/ is the target, both the singular form and the plural form would be used. To illustrate with a child who is playing with cars, the clinician could request one car and then ask for two other cars. Gestures to indicate what was desired would accompany the verbal requests. During play, the adult would continue to contrast the forms. The focused contrasts highlight for the child features that are relevant or crucial to the distinction to be made. To some extent, other strategies (e.g., modeling, event casts, expansions, recasts, scripted play) provide focused contrasts to help the child attend to the crucial features of the targeted linguistic form. These two levels, corrective feedback and modeled contrasts, may be especially well suited to advancing the language skills of children with speech and language impairments and children learning English as their second language.

Modeling

One frequently used language facilitation strategy is modeling, or giving the child a model of a target sound, word, or form. Models such as these often contain structures that the child does not yet produce. The child is offered the opportunity to repeat or respond to the model but is not required to do so. Models are most often incorporated in naturally occurring interactions, although extra emphasis or stress may be placed on particular features to highlight them. Models usually take the form of a statement or comment. For example, if the structure "*is* verb*ing*" is the target, then the adult would use this form in describing what the child or other children are doing. To illustrate, the adult might say, "Sara *is* jump*ing*" or "Now, she *is* runn*ing*."

Event Casts

Event casts provide an ongoing description of an activity and are similar to the voice-over description of athletic events provided by sports broadcasters. Teachers and other adults frequently use event casts (cf. Heath, 1986) as a means of language enrichment. Event casts can be used by adults during relatively teacher-directed times of the day; for example, in a group pudding-making activity, the teacher might narrate the event with, "I'm opening the package, and now I'm pouring the mix into the bowl. Now, it's time for the milk. I'll put the milk in. What should I do now? Okay, stir it. I'll get out all the lumps." Furthermore, a classroom adult can use event casts during play with children who are quiet, hesitant, or shy in the classroom setting. Describing a child's play actions or one's own activities can promote language production by the child.

Event casts serve two facilitative functions. First, event casts provide a sort of language "bath," insofar as they can accompany and describe ongoing activities. This language bath allows children to hear language pertinent to ongoing events. Second, event casts can be used to encourage children to use oral problem-solving strategies by modeling their use. As the classroom teacher solves a bridge-building problem, she can narrate her activities, "I wonder if this block will fit. No, it's too big. Oh, maybe if I turn it around. Yes, now it fits." This oral problem-solving model can assist children in learning to use such a strategy in working through their own daily challenges.

A cautionary note should be added here regarding the use of event casts. Although event casts are useful in describing ongoing activities, constant or highly frequent use of this intervention strategy would result in an adult-dominated classroom language environment. Thus, event casts are best used sparingly, during moments in the classroom day when descriptions of events or activities are desired. The descriptions can provide a means for children to connect events and language and may be particularly helpful in modeling problem-solving strategies.

Open Questions

Open questions are questions that have a variety of possible answers. Examples of open questions include, "What do you think will happen next?", "Why do think that happened?", and "What do you think we should do next?" Open questions contrast with "test," or closed, questions. Test questions usually demand a specific answer often consisting of one- or two-word utterances. Examples of test questions include, "What color is this?" and "What is this?" There is pressure to respond and to respond "correctly." Test questions are appropriate for testing the child's knowledge but are not necessarily a good way to facilitate language acquisition. Because open questions are real questions to which the adult does not necessarily know the answer, there is less pressure to provide a specific response. If a child draws a picture and then shows it to the adult, more language may be generated by the child if the adult says, "Can you tell me about your picture?" than if the adult says, "What's that?"

Expansions

Expansions occur when the adult repeats a child's utterance, filling in the missing features. For example, if a child omitted a verb ending, as in the phrase "he ride bus," the adult could respond by saying, "Yes, he rides the bus." Expansions serve two purposes. First, they affirm that the child has communicated effectively; and second, they provide a model for achieving more adult-like forms.

Recasts

A recast is a conversational adjustment through which basic semantic information is retained while syntactic structure is altered (Baker & Nelson, 1984). Children's utterances can be recast by maintaining meaning but changing the grammatical form. For example, the utterance, "He walks home now" could be recast as, "You're right. He is walking home." Thus, a recast 1) is temporally adjacent to the child's original utterance, 2) maintains the basic meaning of the child's utterance, and 3) changes one or more elements of the original utterance. Recasts are believed to promote linguistic development because they maintain the child's original ideas or meaning and present them in grammatically altered sentences. Thus, the child's attention may be drawn to the new forms or words expressed. The use of recasts shows alternative ways to form sentences without disrupting communication. Recasting is a natural response that does not appear artificial or contrived and does not disrupt conversational interactions with young children. Furthermore, recasting can be both tailored to a specific child's goals or provided in a more general manner to promote linguistic abilities.

Another way recasts can be incorporated into the language of the classroom is for teachers and classroom personnel to recast their own utterances. This technique is particularly useful in teacher-directed moments of the classroom day. The teacher simply provides pairs of original and recast sentences in his or her language (e.g., "Today is Tuesday. It's

Tuesday." or "Mike's drinking his juice. He's drinking apple juice"). These sentence pairs can aid children in recognizing relations between varied syntactic forms expressing the same meanings and highlight new words and their meanings. In addition, teachers can occasionally incorporate this technique into reading or talking about the text of stories (e.g., "The monster is catching the boys. He's catching them").

Redirects and Prompted Initiations

Two intervention techniques used in LAP to encourage children's interactions with each other are redirects and prompted initiations. A redirect occurs when the child approaches an adult and makes a request that could be made to another child. For example, a child waiting for a turn on a swing might approach an adult and say, "My turn on the swing." In this situation, the adult would typically redirect the child's initiation by suggesting that the child talk with the individual on the swing. In some cases, additional assistance could be provided in the form of a model (e.g., "Tell Jill, 'It's my turn' "). An alternative situation is that involving a prompted initiation in which the child does not make the initial request to the adult. Instead, the adult initially suggests or prompts the child to approach another child to play or request an item. These redirecting and prompting techniques can assist children with language impairments to learn to initiate interactions and effect change directly instead of relying on an adult as the mediator. In this way, interactions between children are prompted.

Scripted Play

Scripted play is a valuable intervention procedure because it provides opportunities for verbal communication within a meaningful context. A script (Constable, 1986; Nelson, 1981, 1986) is a representation of an event, an ordered sequence of actions organized around a goal and including actors, actions, and props. For example, most people have a script for eating at a restaurant, including the sequence of events of ordering, eating, and paying, and involving people eating, waiters or waitresses, and a cashier. Scripts do allow variations, but generally center around the same goal. There are both similarities and differences in eating at a fast-food restaurant and in having dinner at an expensive restaurant.

Use of Scripts Throughout the Day

The notion of scripts as event representations is used throughout the classroom day in preschools such as LAP. Familiar daily routines, such as arrival time, circle time, and snacktime, develop into scripted event representations for young children. This familiarity acts as a basis upon which language experiences can be built. Children know that they will eat during snacktime; this stimulates discussion of what the daily snack is, who brought it, how it was prepared, and other possible variations on the general snack theme.

In addition to their general use to provide structure for the daily routine, scripts are inherent to the LFC center time. More specifically, each day, a particular dramatic play activity is available for children to select.

Dramatic play activities involve using scripts for such things as everyday events (e.g., grocery shopping, gardening, cooking, cleaning), for certain special events (e.g., vacation, camping, fishing), and for occupations (e.g., mechanic, veterinarian, electrician). This list provides only a small sample of possible dramatic play activities. (Part III of this book provides many more scripted play activity suggestions.)

Dramatic Play Activities

Scripted dramatic play activities are designed to enhance the children's world knowledge and the language that accompanies it. Typically, preschool children require some background, introduction, and priming for the dramatic play script of the day. This is generally provided by a discussion and/or demonstration prior to the actual activity; that is, the roles are introduced, the use of props is demonstrated, and the basic goal(s) are discussed. Children will frequently contribute their existing knowledge of the script during such discussion. The comments "Our cat was sick" and "He got a shot" were heard during the introduction to a visit to the veterinarian play script. After even an initial introduction to a new script, children begin to build a skeletal event representation for a particular activity and carry out a dramatic play script with limited adult direction and/or intervention.

Language Exchanges Between Peers

From the perspective of language intervention, scripted dramatic play activities serve a variety of functions. First, and perhaps foremost, they stimulate language exchanges, particularly exchanges between children. As children assume roles in dramatic play interactions—for example, as customers or cashiers and veterinarians or pet owners—they practice verbal negotiation skills as they exchange essential props. One of the children with typically developing language skills might request the cash register with utterances like, "My turn for the register" or, "Can I have a turn now, please?", while the children with language impairments may begin by making no verbal request at all, then advance to a primitive request such as, "Gimme that," and ultimately arrive at more sophisticated polite forms like, "Can I use that, please?" Hearing the verbal negotiations of typically developing children and practicing with the accurate models provide an optimal learning ground for children with language impairments. An occasional adult model or recast is typically all that is needed to set the wheels of dramatic play negotiations in motion.

In a more general sense, dramatic play activities are central to the facilitation of social interactive skills. More than any other time during the LAP day, the dramatic play activity is built on interaction and is difficult, if not impossible, to carry out without conversational exchange. By nature, dramatic play activities encourage children to initiate conversations with peers and adults and to respond to peer and adult initiations. The familiar, repetitive structure of dramatic play activity scripts enhances the likelihood of interactive success for children with language impairments. After hearing a teacher or peer act as a waiter, saying repeatedly, "Do you want more coffee?", the child with a language impairment can take the waiter role and initiate with, "More coffee?" In this way, the roles and structure of dramatic play scripts assist the social interactive skills of children with language impairments.

Intervention Strategy

Scripted dramatic play activities constitute a key language intervention strategy used in the concentrated normative model of classroom activities. Opportunities for verbal communication about both familiar and unfamiliar objects and events arise during these activities. Children can practice social interactive skills, particularly child–child interactions, in this context, and these activities capitalize on the interactions of children with special needs with their typically developing peers. Also, it is during these activities that children can practice language form as well as function and use. Furthermore, adults can provide focused linguistic input about events and objects of interest to the child during scripted play activities.

IMPLEMENTATION OF INTERVENTION

Intervention goals are to be achieved during preschool activities. As described above, in LAP, intervention procedures include the teacher and/or clinicians using a variety of verbal productions including focused contrasts, modeling, event casts, open questions, expansions, recasts, redirects and prompted initiations, and scripted play. Commands, requests, and test questions can be used to find out a child's present level of performance but are not considered facilitory for acquiring new language forms. Some of these intervention techniques are controlled by the adults in the sense that adults can employ them at any time; others are controlled by the children. For example, an adult can provide a model for a child whenever it is appropriate. However, an adult cannot expand a child's production unless the child has first said something. To that extent, the use of expansions by the adult is under the child's control. The following case study provides an example of intervention techniques and plans for a child attending LAP.

Tom

Three-year-old Tom speaks primarily in one-word utterances. (His mean length of utterance [MLU] is 1.22.) Tom's words are usually intelligible, and he appears to understand much of what is said to him. He is shy when interacting with peers, preferring to watch rather than to play with them. He usually pays attention to the teacher during group activities and responds nonverbally to adult directions.

Standardized Testing

The Peabody Picture Vocabulary Test–Revised (Dunn & Dunn, 1981) requires the child to choose a target picture from four choices. On this test,

Tom achieved a raw score of 10, a standard score equivalent of 78 (mean = 100 +/− 15), and a percentile rank of 7. On the receptive section of the Reynell Developmental Language Scales–U.S. Edition (Reynell & Gruber, 1990), the child is required to listen to a variety of requests and demonstrate his or her understanding through manipulation of toy objects. Tom received a raw score of 31, a standard score of 74 (mean = 100 +/− 15), and a percentile rank of 5. On the expressive section of the Reynell Development Language Scales–U.S. Edition (Reynell & Gruber, 1990), which requires the child to label items, define words, and describe pictures, Tom achieved a raw score of 12 and a standard score below 63, which rates him below the first percentile. On the Goldman-Fristoe Test of Articulation (Goldman & Fristoe, 1969) (administered imitatively), Tom scored at the 28th percentile, which is within low normal limits.

Therapy Goals

Long-term therapy goals for Tom are as follows:

1. To increase vocabulary knowledge
2. To increase MLU
3. To increase appropriate peer interactions

Tom's short-term goals are as follows:

1. By the end of the semester, Tom will understand and produce 20 new nouns and 10 new verbs at a level of 80% correct. (Words will be chosen from classroom themes and activities.)
2a. By the end of the semester, Tom's MLU will increase to 2.5 words as measured by a language sample.
2b. By the end of the semester, Tom will produce the following morphemes at the 80% criterion level: "on," "in," and "-ing." (A language sample will be used for measuring purposes.)
3. By the end of the semester, Tom will increase his initiations and responses to peers as measured by the Social Interactive Coding System (Rice, Sell, & Hadley, 1990).

The goals for Tom, then, are to increase vocabulary knowledge, length and complexity of utterances, and appropriate peer interactions.

Example of a Therapy Plan

An essential factor in planning for intervention in a classroom setting is that the plan be flexible. This is necessary because much of the intervention will be completed during child-centered activities when the adult is following the child's interests. The adult, therefore, cannot be sure which activity will be the focus of the child's attention. Planning for therapy, then, is important in preparing the adult to take advantage of the types of communicative opportunities that might occur in the classroom.

Another factor in planning for therapy is to maintain a focus on a specific child's goals and objectives. By making tentative plans of action based on information about the daily themes and activities, the adult will be more likely to provide appropriate input and note relevant out-

put. Therefore, to incorporate speech and language goals, the adult should do the following:

1. Read curriculum plans for each day of the week, specifically focusing attention on the Language Skills Facilitated section.
2. Identify the target child's speech and language goals, which relate to the week's activities and could be incorporated into daily events.
3. Complete a therapy guide (see Figure 3).

Figure 3 provides an example of a typical therapy guide. The child's target language skills are listed in this guide. Optimum times during the day for intervention are also noted (see When to Emphasize Target Skills). Possible intervention strategies (see How to Emphasize Target Skills) are generated to highlight how these skills will be facilitated. Any special materials are also listed in the guide (see Special Props and/or Materials Needed). Finally, after intervention has begun, notes are made about what actually happened (see Documentation of Progress [What Happened?]). Specific data relating to the objectives, such as longest sentence produced, production of target structures, and peer interaction successes, are of particular interest.

Examples of Therapy During Classroom Activities

Arrival Time

The child in the case study, Tom, is playing with the blocks and farm animals. His teacher describes what Tom is doing. Verbal responses from Tom are invited but not required. A number of specific vocabulary words can be used during the activities. Targeted grammatical structures are italicized in the examples below. In addition, many opportunities for assisting appropriate peer interactions arise.

THERAPY GUIDE

Child: S.B.
Clinician: L.D.
Date: 9/23
Theme: Transportation (Airplane)

Target Language Skill(s):

1. Increase use of specific vocabulary (focus on nouns, verbs, adjectives, and locatives).
2. Increase number of initiations with peers.
3. Increase use of present progressive (-*ing*).

When to Emphasize Target Skills:

During center time, snacktime, outdoor play, and free time.

How to Emphasize Target Skills:

Provide *focused contrasts* and *modeling* to elicit target structures and expand child utterances by:

- *Describing* what he is doing and providing labels for objects, actions, and locations (parallel talk) (e.g.,"D., you're buy*ing* a ticket . . . you are the pilot"; "You are mak*ing* an airplane," "He is fly*ing* the airplane fast,""It is land*ing* on the ground")

- *Joining in* the activities and also describing what the clinician is doing ("I want a *large* coke," "My seatbelt is *on*," "I'm go*ing* to Disneyland")

- *Commenting* on and *expanding* child utterances (e.g., "belt off," "yes, your belt is off," "I can fix it")

- Encourage *requesting* from a peer or teacher during snacktime, art, and sharing time. Encourage peer interaction through sharing the role of pilot or flight attendant. *Redirect* child to peers when appropriate.

Special Props and/or Materials Needed:

Utilize play materials child is using in dramatic play, art, block, or quiet areas.

Documentation of Progress (What Happened?):

[Describe on back of sheet success/failure of therapy procedures.]

- S. used -*ing* form three times (omitted it seven other times for a total correct use of 3/10). The -*ing* structure was modeled by the clinician 20 times during the course of the day.

- By the end of center time, S. used the term "pilot" twice instead of just pointing when he wanted to be the pilot. S. appeared to understand "behind" because he got behind another child on command while waiting for a turn.

- S. verbally initiated two times to an adult during a 10-minute observation.

Figure 3.   An example therapy guide for a child attending LAP. The adults who will be facilitating targeted language skills in the classroom should prepare a therapy plan for each child. Therapy plans should be related to the weekly theme. (From Bunce, B.H., & Watkins, R.W. [1995]. Language intervention in a preschool classroom: Implementing a language-focused curriculum. In M.L. Rice & K.A. Wilcox [Eds.], *Building a language-focused curriculum for the preschool classroom. Vol. I: A foundation for life-long communication* [p.57]. Baltimore: Paul H. Brookes Publishing Co.; reprinted by permission.)

Models:	"You are build*ing* a fence. A big fence. The cows can't get out. The cow is jump*ing*. He is jump*ing* over the fence. He is *on* the ground now."
Focused Contrasts:	"He's not *in* the truck. He's *on* the ground."
Expansions:	When the child says, "Block," the adult could say, "Big block," "Two blocks," "More blocks," or "Blocks *in* tub" depending on child's meaning.
Prompted Initiations:	"Ask M. for a block. Say, 'Block, please.' "

Center Time

Dramatic Play—Veterinarian   Tom is pretending to be the veterinarian and has a toy doctor kit available. Again, a number of specific vocabulary words can be used. Italics highlight the grammatical morphemes targeted for this child.

Models:	"My doggie's sick. Give him a shot," "Is my dog OK?", "Help my dog," and "Thank you for help*ing* my dog."
Expansions:	If the child says, "Hurt," the adult could say, "Doggie is hurt."
Prompted Initiations:	"Go tell B., 'My turn.' "
Open Questions:	If the adult asks "Where can we go?", the child might say "Vet." The adult could then say, "OK, we'll go to the vet" or "We're driv*ing* to the vet." (These are both expansions and acknowledgments.)
Redirects:	If the child says, "Want car," the adult could redirect the child to a peer with, "Tell C., 'Car, please.' "

Art/Science Area   Tom is decorating a valentine bag.

Models:	"Paper is red or pink," "Cutt*ing* out the heart," "You're past*ing*," and "You're putt*ing* it *on* the bag."
Expansions:	If the child says, "Cut," the adult could expand with, "Cutt*ing* the paper."
Prompted Initiations:	The adult could say, "Ask G. Say, 'More glue, please.' "
Open Questions:	The adult might ask, "What color do you want?" When the child points one out, the adult could provide a model, "You want red."

Quiet Area   Tom is working with a puzzle and later gets a book for the clinician to read.

Models:	"You're putt*ing* the sun *on* the top. The dog goes here [pointing to a place on the puzzle]. It's at the bottom of the puzzle."

| *Expansions:* | If the child says, "Pig here," the adult might say, "The pig goes here." |
| *Open Questions:* | The adult could ask, "What's happening?" The child might respond, "Boy ride" and an expansion such as, "Boy is rid*ing* a bike" can then follow. |

Block Area   Tom is playing with blocks and little cars.

| *Models:* | "You're stack*ing* blocks. The blocks are fall*ing*." |
| *Expansions:* | If the child says, "Car hit," the adult might say, "The cars are hitt*ing*." |

Storytime

Storytime is a teacher-directed time during which short stories are read and sometimes acted out. Stories may focus on labeling to present new vocabulary, or they may be adventure stories, which provide an introduction to story grammar. Adventure stories often have the following sequence: 1) character introduction, 2) several events, 3) climax, and 4) resolution. Many children's stories are home–adventure–home stories—the character's adventure begins at home, he or she has some adventures, and then the character returns home and is safe.

Stories with repetitive lines also can be effective in teaching language structure and in helping children predict future events. These stories can provide a way for children to be involved in storytelling. As a line is read repeatedly, the children can join in. Acting out familiar stories helps the children understand a story's sequence and provides a way to demonstrate knowledge of the story's grammar. Use of dialogue from a story can help children produce or practice new sentence structures.

Adult:	Teddy bear, Teddy bear,
	What do you see?
	I see ―――――
	Looking at me.
Child:	"Look me."

Sharing Time

The purpose of sharing time is to teach children how to ask questions. It is also a time during which children can show the class something they brought from their homes. Two children come to the front of the class. One child asks questions about the other child's sharing item. Initially, the children are taught to ask three questions, "What do you have?" "What do you do with it?" and "Where did you get it?" Later additional questions are encouraged. The routine questions are important as they provide support for the child who has limited language, and the routine itself helps both children know what to do and say. More important, these questions can help children learn more information about their environments outside of the classroom. Adults and other children usually respond to someone asking them, "What do you have?" or "What's that?" The children's exposure to new vocabulary is thereby increased, and they have learned one way to initiate interactions.

Transition Times

Transition times can also be used as language-learning opportunities. For example, it is very easy to find out if children understand the use of certain grammatical forms such as the uncontractible copula ("to be" used as a main verb and in situations in which it cannot be contracted to the 's form). One time to do this is when the children are getting ready to go outside. The teacher can ask such questions as, "Who is ready?" Children who are in line with coats on can respond, "I *am*" or, "He *is*." Requests for help in putting on outdoor clothes can be a good time to provide labels for clothing items or body parts: "Put your hand in the mitten," "Let's zip up your coat," "You need your hat to cover your ears," and so forth.

Outside Time

Outside time activities provide many opportunities to model, expand, prompt, and redirect children's verbal productions. Particular emphasis can be placed on teaching a variety of verbs (e.g., run, jump, skip, ride, slide, dig, climb, build) and on prepositions (e.g., in, through, on, down, under, on top of, in front of, behind). Again variation in the complexity of the language can be made: "M. is sliding down the slide" and "S. is riding the bike on the road" versus "Climb ladder" and "Dig in sand." Turn taking can be highlighted during outside time. Prompted initiations such as "Tell J., 'My turn, please' " can help a child begin to negotiate for a turn on a bike or another piece of equipment.

Snacktime

Snacktime also provides many activities to model, expand, prompt, and redirect children's verbal productions. It is also a time to teach politeness (e.g., "Please pass the juice," "May I have more crackers, please?"). Number skills can also be taught. For example, a teacher can say, "You have five crackers. Now you ate one. How many do you have left?", "How many crackers do you have?", or "You can have two more crackers." It is also a time to encourage peer–peer exchanges. This can be done through prompted initiations. If the adult says to the child, "Why don't you ask S. to pass the juice," the child might say to S., "S., please pass the juice"). It can also be accomplished through redirects. The child might say to an adult, "I need more," and the adult can redirect with, "Ask S. to hand you the crackers." Then the child might say to S., "Hand me the crackers, please." Peer-to-peer conversations can also be encouraged by just allowing them to occur. Letting the children sit by their special friends also encourages them to talk to each other.

Group Time

Group time is a teacher-directed activity in which new vocabulary and concepts can be introduced to the children. The lessons may involve matching, labeling, classification, and sequencing activities, or they may involve learning the alphabet and number concepts. During group time children can be supported in their participation to ensure success. Activities can easily be manipulated to allow for different skill levels. For example, one child might be asked to match a pattern sequence of colored blocks (red-blue-red-blue) with the pattern present, while another child might have to produce the pattern from memory.

During the group activities, the teacher uses appropriate language facilitation strategies, which include modeling appropriate vocabulary and structure and prompting and expanding the children's initiations and responses. For a classification activity, the teacher can model the appropriate verbal and nonverbal responses and then have the children perform the appropriate responses with a new item. Using open questions can be effective in helping the children learn to problem-solve or to focus on a specific feature. For example, the teacher might ask, "How can we find out how many ribs Smiley [the skeleton] has?" At least one child usually responds, "Count them." The teacher can then count or have a child help count.

Music Time

Music time is a time to have fun singing and doing rhythm activities with other children. The songs are short and often repetitive so that they are easily learned. The melody and rhythm help in learning the songs. Also, the children can often respond nonverbally by clapping or imitating the teacher's hand motions. Some children first begin to speak when singing or doing fingerplays. For example, in a traditional song such as "Old MacDonald Had a Farm," children can initially participate by just making appropriate animal sounds. Later, they can join in singing the whole song.

SUMMARY

The description of intervention provided in this chapter illustrates how children with specific language impairments can receive a concentrated normative model of intervention within typical preschool activities. Strategies for facilitating language learning in the classroom setting hinge on providing an environment in which many opportunities for natural language use and interaction occur. There must be opportunities for both child–child and adult–child talk. A balance between activities that provide new information should be struck with concepts requiring new responses and those that are routine events supporting and extending old knowledge. Finally, specific language features can be facilitated within naturally occurring conversations by means of the adults' use of focused contrasts, modeling, event casts, open questions, expansions, recasts, redirects and prompted initiations, and scripted play.

II

SAMPLE CURRICULUM

~4~

Developing Your Own Language-Focused Curriculum

The purpose of this chapter is to provide strategies and suggestions for organizing and planning your own language-focused curriculum based on the experience gained from developing such a program at the Language Acquisition Preschool at the University of Kansas. Every program is different and there may be wide variation in the children served, the staff members' training and experience, and the available materials and facilities. Therefore, the curricular ideas and plans presented here may require adaptation so they will fit the needs of your particular program.

A major curricular goal in developing a language-focused curriculum is to provide opportunities for language learning throughout all of the preschool activities (cf. Chapter 1 for elaboration on assumptions underlying the LFC, and Chapter 2 for a description of curricular structure). It is also important to foster the development of the children's social, cognitive, and motor skills. Therefore, in order to meet children's different developmental needs, you will need to plan a variety of activities.

In developing such a curriculum, both long- and short-term planning are important. Long-term planning involves the overall organization of the curriculum and provides a focus for the development of the thematic units. As discussed in Chapter 2, the thematic units in turn provide a framework for daily activities. Short-term planning involves specific details for the implementation of individual activities. This chapter describes in detail how to use some of the planning guides developed for the Language Acquisition Preschool for both long- and short-term LFC planning.

Several important features should be considered when developing a LFC. First, it is important to remember that a major curriculum goal is to provide opportunities for *language learning* throughout the preschool day (cf. Chapters 1 and 2). Second, there should be a *variety of activities* or centers available that require different levels of language usage. For example, dramatic play activities require talking and interacting with others in order to play, whereas block or manipulative activities may require less talking and no interaction with peers. Third, in addition to fostering language learning, activities should provide for the *development of children's social, cognitive, and motor skills*. Fourth, the activities need to be *developmentally appropriate* for 3- to 5-year-old children. Therefore, the activities must allow for differential levels of difficulty and hands-on manipulation. This chapter discusses the planning process in general, then provides guidelines for planning a language-focused curriculum, and, finally, demonstrates how to use the lesson plans in Part III.

PLANNING A LANGUAGE-FOCUSED CURRICULUM

As described in Chapter 2, there are several steps in planning a language-focused curriculum. First, the overall structure of the classroom and schedule of activities must be laid out. Second, there must be provision for activities that are routine and for activities that change daily. Third, plans for the activities that change daily (e.g., dramatic play, art, story, group, music) must be made in an organized format.

To provide the needed organization, a number of planning guides are used. First, a semester (or monthly) calendar is used to note weekly themes and tentative dramatic play activities (see Figure 4). Second, a weekly planning guide lists the activities for the week and notes needed props and supplies (see Figure 5 on p. 57). Third, daily planning guides are completed for each day (see Figure 6 on p. 58). The daily planning guides provide suggestions for the facilitation of language, social, cognitive, and motor skills throughout the classroom activities. Finally, specific lesson or activities plans are developed for the dramatic play, art, and group activities. Curricular examples are provided in Chapter 5.

In order to provide flexibility in developing the weekly curriculum, a listing of various themes and dramatic plays supporting the themes are compiled in Part III. Then, a collection of actual lesson plans for various dramatic play, art, and group activities is provided. The dramatic play activities are organized alphabetically. The art activities are organized according to the major motor skills required (e.g., construction, cutting, drawing, painting, pasting), and the group activities are organized by activity type (e.g., alphabet, phonic, and number skills listed as preacademic). Other activities are filed under matching and labeling (e.g., color or shape recognition), classifying, sequencing, and safety and life skills. Both the art and group activity plans have markings indicating the relative difficulty of the task (e.g., more difficult tasks are marked with an asterisk).

Organizing plans in a master file permits for mixing and matching of activities according to theme. It also allows particular activities to be

SEPTEMBER

Discovering. . .

Theme	Activities	Monday	Tuesday	Wednesday	Thursday
LAP favorites	**Dramatic play**	Water play	House	Fast-food restaurant	Camping
	Art	Water paint	Drawings	Playdough	Cheerio art
	Story	*Rainbow Fish*	*If You Give a Mouse a Cookie*	*Will I Have a Friend?*	*We're Going on a Bear Hunt*
	Group	Things in water	Hot/cold	Letter "A" (apple)	"Blue"
	Music	Five Little Ducks	I'm a Little Teapot	Peanut Butter and Jelly	A Camping We Will Go
Places in the Community	**Dramatic play**	Doctor's office	Beauty/barber shop	Gas station/ garage (mechanic)	Grocery store
	Art	Chalk drawings	Shaving-cream fingerpainting	Water-color painting	Food picture collage
	Story	*Going to the Doctor*	*Count*	*What's Under Your Hood, Orson?*	*Little Fish, Big Fish*
	Group	Body parts	Letter "B" (barber)	Sound sequencing	Big and little
	Music	Hokey Pokey	ABC Song	Johnny Works with One Hammer	I Like to Eat

(continued)

Figure 4. A semester or monthly calendar should be used by program staff to plan weekly themes and activities. A blank version of this form is provided in Appendix B at the end of this book.

Figure 4. *continued*

SEPTEMBER

Discovering. . .

Theme	Activities	Monday	Tuesday	Wednesday	Thursday
Transportation	**Dramatic play**	Airplane	Boats	Cars (racing)	Delivery trucks
	Art	Paper airplanes	Meat tray boats	Vehicle rubbings	Easel paintings
	Story	*We're Taking an Airplane Trip*	*Mr. Gumpy's Outing*	*Wheels*	*The Truck Book*
	Group	Shapes—circle	Same and different	Letter "C" (cookie)	Circle collage
	Music	Airplane Song	Row, Row, Row Your Boat	C is for Cookie	Wheels on the Bus
Community helpers	**Dramatic play**	Construction worker	Veterinarian	Office worker	Firefighter
	Art	Popsicle art	Paper bag puppet	Drawings	Playdough
	Story	*A House Is a House for Me*	*Moses, the Kitten*	*A Letter to Amy*	*The Fire Engine*
	Group	Square	Care of pets	Letter "D" (desk)	Fire safety rules
	Music	Johnny Works with One Hammer	Five Little Monkeys	ABC Song	Hurry, Hurry, Drive the Firetruck

(continued)

Figure 4. *continued*

SEPTEMBER

Discovering. . .

Theme	Activities	Monday	Tuesday	Wednesday	Thursday
Food	**Dramatic play**	Farm	Pizza parlor	Grocery store	House (cooking)
	Art	Cottonball chickens	Pizza	Coffee-filter water color	Macaroni necklaces
	Story	*Our Farmyard*	*The Three Bears*	*Whiskerville Grocery*	*It Looked Like Spilt Milk*
	Group	Square/circle	Act out *The Three Bears*	Fruits/ vegetables	Letter "E" (eat)
	Music	Old MacDonald Had a Farm	I Wish I Were a Pepperoni Pizza	Apples and Bananas	Who Stole the Cookie?

used in more than one thematic unit. For example, an airplane dramatic play activity could be used as part of both transportation and vacation themes. Similarly, specific art and group activities could also be used with more than one thematic unit. Although many of the activity lesson plans are already developed and provided in this volume, program staff members can design their own curricula around the choices they make in planning a particular week's lessons. Furthermore, additional lesson plans can be made by staff members and added to the master file. Stories and songs appropriate to particular themes are not provided in this volume, as each preschool program has its own collection. Daily planning guides are left to the discretion and creativity of program staff, as these guides should vary with the combination of activities chosen. Daily planning guides should be completed to aid in focusing on the development of language, social, cognitive, and motor skills (see Chapter 5 for curricular examples).

The task for staff members in designing a language-focused curriculum, then, is to choose and/or develop the appropriate activities. In order to facilitate the process of planning, blank planning guides and lesson plans are provided in Appendix B at the end of this book. Typically, staff members meet at the beginning of the semester to sketch out possible weekly themes and associated dramatic play activities. Then, during weekly meetings, plans are finalized for the specific dramatic play, art, story, group, and music activities that are to occur during the next week. Specific planning is best done at least a week in advance so that materials can be located and a newsletter can be prepared for families.

The planning process should involve all staff members. At the initial meeting, the members brainstorm ideas for possible themes and a variety of dramatic play activities related to each theme. To be effective, it is important that staff members feel free to make suggestions. Often what one person says will give another person an idea that can then be developed by the group. In addition, suggestions for themes and possible dramatic plays are listed at the beginning of Part III. New themes and dramatic plays developed by the staff members should be added to the guide. After a theme and the dramatic plays are chosen, then the weekly planning guide for a specific week can be completed.

Weekly Planning Guides

The weekly planning guide is an overall plan of activities for the week. Space to indicate the semester and weekly themes and the date is provided at the top of the page. The rest of the form features two matrices, with the types of activities that change daily (i.e., dramatic play, art, story, group, music) listed across the top of one matrix and the days of the week listed along the side (see Figure 5). The format is based on a 4-day per week program but could easily be expanded to 5 days or reduced to 3 days. After the staff members have decided on which days the different dramatic play activities are to occur, then the rest of the matrix is completed by selecting appropriate art, story, group, and music activities to support the thematic unit and dramatic play activities. The second matrix on the form is used to compile a list of props and materials needed for each day of the week. Staff should find this matrix helpful as they prepare and set up each day's activities.

Guidelines for selection of the art and group activities are made more explicit later in this chapter. In general, art activities are chosen so that a variety of art media are used during a particular week (e.g., cutting, painting, pasting, drawing, sculpting). Similarly, group activities are chosen so that the cognitive demands of the activities vary each day (e.g., matching, classifying, problem solving, alphabet and number skills). Difficulty is also a consideration in the choice of art and group activities for a particular week.

Daily Planning Guides

In addition to a weekly planning guide, an overall plan for each day is developed. This daily planning guide provides suggestions for incorporating language, social, cognitive, and motor skills in the day's activities (see Figure 6 and the curricular examples in Chapter 5). This guide is helpful in providing an overall focus for a particular day's activities and for em-

CURRICULUM: WEEKLY PLANNING GUIDE

Semester Theme: Vacations

Weekly Theme: _____ **Week of:** June 13–16

	Dramatic Play	Art	Story	Group	Music
Monday	Airplane	Paper airplanes	*The Trip*	Measuring (how far planes flew)	I'm a Little Airplane
Tuesday	Motel	Water-color painting	*Jake Baked the Cake*	Letter "M"	Going to Kentucky
Wednesday	Beach	Aquariums	*A House for a Hermit Crab*	Color mixing (Mix primary colors to make secondary colors)	Bubble, Bubble, Bubble, POP
Thursday	Amusement park	Mural	*Here We Are*	Sound sequencing	Mickey Mouse Song

Suggested Props and Materials:

Monday	Seatbelts, luggage, tickets, counter, metal detector, rudder, instrument panel, paper, paper clips, markers . . .
Tuesday	TVs, rooms, keys, check-in desk, telephones, restaurant, table, food, pool, brooms, vacuum cleaners, water paints, paper, frames. . .
Wednesday	Sandboxes, beach towels, sunglasses, lifeguard stand, shovels, pails, shells, starfish, tissue paper, fish shapes, yarn (for seaweed), blue cellophane, paper plates . . .
Thursday	Mural paper, bean bag toss, Sit & Spin, concession stand, trampoline, ball toss, clothespin drop, drum (for sound pattern sequencing) . . .

Figure 5.   A weekly planning guide like this sample is used to list activities as well as props and supplies. (From Bunce, B.H., & Watkins, R.W. [1995]. Language intervention in a preschool classroom: Implementing a language-focused curriculum. In M.L. Rice & K.A. Wilcox [Eds.], *Building a language-focused curriculum for the preschool classroom. Vol. I: A foundation for lifelong communication* [p. 63]. Baltimore: Paul H. Brookes Publishing Co.; reprinted by permission.)

CURRICULUM: DAILY PLANNING GUIDE

Theme: <u>Transportation</u>
Week of: <u>September 14, 1993</u>

(Monday)   Tuesday   Wednesday   Thursday

Dramatic Play	Art	Story	Group	Song
Airplane	Paper airplanes	*The Trip*	Circles	I'm a Little Airplane

Language Skills Facilitated

- **Vocabulary** - transportation, airplane, pilot, flight attendant, baggage, suitcase, take-off, landing, seat belt, security check, ticket, seat, passenger, beverage, cockpit . . .

- **Verb Phrase Structures** - fasten your seatbelt, land*s* the plane, *is* land*ing*, land*ed*, *flew* the plane, serv*ed* food, check*ed* baggage, who's going on the plane? I *am* (incontractible auxiliary verb), I*'m* flying (contractible auxiliary) . . .

- **Adjective/Object Descriptions** - large plane, small plane, big suitcase, little bag, carry-on bag, blue ___, red ___, purple ___, . . .

- **Pronouns** - I, you, he, she, we, they, my, your, her, his, our, their, me, us, them

- **Prepositions** - In, on, under, over, near, beneath, next to, beside, around, inside, outside

- **Sounds** - /l/ lands, pilot, fill; /r/ ride, car; /**s**/ sit, talks; /**k**/ carry, ticket, pack; /f/ five, off . . .

Social Skills Facilitated:

- Initiating to peers and adults; responding to questions and requests from peers and adults
- Negotiating with peers for toys and materials
- Group cooperation—waiting for a turn in a group, taking a turn at the appropriate time

Cognitive Skills Facilitated:

- Problem Solving Skills—how to fold paper to make a plane
- Classification Skills—circle shapes
- Sequencing Skills—song, story
- Narrative/Story Structure—adventure

Motor Skills Facilitated:

- **Large Motor**—outdoor play activities: jumping, running, hopping, pedaling, climbing . . .
- **Small Motor**—writing, drawing, glueing, folding . . .

Figure 6.   A daily planning guide like the example shown here should be completed for each preschool day. (From Bunce, B.H., & Watkins, R.W. [1995]. Language intervention in a preschool classroom: Implementing a language-focused curriculum. In M.L. Rice & K.A. Wilcox [Eds.], *Building a language-focused curriculum for the preschool classroom. Vol. I: A foundation for lifelong communication* [p. 56]. Baltimore: Paul H. Brookes Publishing Co.; reprinted by permission.)

phasizing their interrelatedness and their connections to various skills. In LAP, these guides list the activities that change daily (i.e., the dramatic play, art, story, group, and music activities) across the top of the form. Although the routine activities (e.g., calendar time, sharing time) are not listed on the form, staff should realize that the facilitation of language, social, cognitive, and motor skills also takes place during those activities.

Language Skills

On the daily planning guide, under "language skills facilitated," general vocabulary, adjective/object descriptions, verb phrase structures, pronouns, prepositions, and sounds that might be addressed through the specific day's activities are listed. This is not necessarily a complete listing, but is intended as a beginning point for program staff.

General Vocabulary   Nouns and verbs are the primary words listed in the vocabulary section. Words are chosen that relate to the particular dramatic play, art, story, and/or group activities. For example, a mechanic dramatic play might feature words such as *mechanic, battery, engine, tool, wrench, screwdriver, spark plug, fix,* and *repair.* Another example is a camping dramatic play, in which words such as *sleeping bag, tent, campfire, camp, hike,* and *fish* could be chosen.

Verb Phrase Structures   The verb phrase structures category should include a listing of a variety of syntactic forms. The forms chosen should typically include regular and irregular past tense (e.g., *fix/fix**ed**, drive/**drove**)*, third-person singular (e.g., *she repairs*), structures involving the verb "to be" (e.g., **is** *working,* **was** *working, who* **is** *here? I* **am**), and any other targeted structure form for a particular child.

Adjectives/Object Descriptions   In a similar manner, adjective/object descriptions should be chosen to relate to the specific daily activities. For the mechanic dramatic play suggested above, terms such as *big/little car, heavy/light battery,* and *flat tire,* could be listed.

Pronouns   The pronoun section should include a variety of pronouns, such as subjective (e.g., *I, you, he, she, they*), objective (e.g., *me, him, her, them*), and possessive (e.g., *my, her, his, their*) pronouns. Some of the pronouns might be a specific target for a particular day or a particular child. These pronouns could be circled to highlight them.

Prepositions   Prepositional phrases also can be listed on the daily planning guide. Prepositions are important locative terms and can be easily incorporated into many play activities (e.g., the child goes *down* the slide, places the block *in* the truck, or puts the glue *on* the paper).

Sounds   Finally, the target sounds for a particular activity can be noted on the daily planning guide. Several children may have different target sounds; therefore, words containing several target sounds should be listed. If the appropriate words are listed in advance, they are more likely to be incorporated into the spontaneous conversations. It is sometimes difficult to think of words with target sounds on the spur of the moment. Target sounds often include /k/, /s/, /d/, and /l/. Single-syllable words are usually listed with the target sound in the initial or final position. For example, in the mechanic dramatic play, the following sounds and words could be noted: /k/ in car and rack; /s/ in see and gas; /d/ in down and found; and /l/ in lift and fall. Of course, other words and sounds could be targeted.

Other Structures   Other structures, such as question forms, can be listed as well. Question forms are incorporated in sharing time activities (with the children asking and answering), and in the story time or group activities when the teacher usually asks questions and the children answer.

Social Skills

Many of the activities in the classroom foster social skills. Of particular interest during the child-centered activities is helping the children develop skills in initiating and responding to peers and adults, in negotiating with peers for toys and materials, and in taking turns. During teacher-directed activities, children learn group cooperation skills, such as waiting for a turn and then performing before a group. Although these skills are listed under social skills, it must be noted that they also involve language skills. Even if the initiation or response by a child is nonverbal, the child must still understand the language used during the interaction. In other words, social and language skills are closely intertwined.

Cognitive Skills

Three different kinds of cognitive skills are noted on the daily guide. Problem solving, classifying, and sequencing skills relate to general classroom activities as well as to particular group activities.

Problem Solving   Problem-solving skills can be facilitated in many different ways during many different activities. For example, during play with puzzles, the child may have a problem with a particular piece. The teacher may watch and then encourage the child to note features of the puzzle piece that might help, suggesting that two yellow colors might go together or that the piece is upside down. During dramatic play activities, there may be some difficulty that the children must address. Teachers can demonstrate how to problem-solve by listing the steps in a solution. For example, during the mechanic dramatic play, the teacher could say something like, "This wheel won't stay on. . . . Maybe I can put the bigger screw in." . . . "Now it fits . . . but I must tighten the nut so it won't fall out." Another way to encourage problem solving is to set up the problem and then pause so that the children can suggest solutions. For example, in an art activity, the problem can be that there are not enough pairs of scissors (or markers, paint, or paper). The teacher might wait to see if the children can solve the problem themselves. If they do not solve the problem, then a comment such as, "There are not enough scissors to go around. What can we do?" can be made. If the children do not suggest that they can share, the teacher can say to two children, "When we do not have enough, we share" or, "We can see if there are more in the cupboard." During group activities, there are many opportunities to problem-solve. For example, during an alphabet lesson, the problem can be to find words that start with a particular sound. During a fire safety lesson, the problem can be what numbers to dial for help. Other problem-solving group activities might involve science, when the children watch and then try to explain or predict the outcome. Although children can demonstrate solutions to problems nonverbally, problem-solving activities have the potential to involve language.

Classifying   Being able to classify items according to a criterion is an important cognitive skill. The ability to form classifications requires several other skills. First, the child must be able to match items so that likeness or sameness can be identified on some dimension. Second, the child needs to be able to note differences. In addition, the differences need to be the crucial contrasts. For example, bananas and corn could be in the same category if the classification was based on color. However, if the task was to differentiate between fruits and vegetables, then they would be in different categories.

In the preschool classroom, there are many opportunities for using classification skills. For example, children can classify colors, shapes, and sizes of objects during play with blocks and other manipulatives, during art projects, and during group activities. During dramatic play activities, different items could be classified according to a specific category. For example, children could help choose the items found at a fast-food restaurant, a gas station, or the doctor's office. Although classifying objects can be done nonverbally, language can aid in understanding tasks. Nonverbal classification usually relies on perception (e.g., color, size, shape) to form categories. Many other categories are formed based on their verbal label (e.g., vegetables, furniture, farm animals); therefore, language can be crucial in understanding and delineating categories.

Sequencing   Another cognitive task concerns the ability to follow a sequence or to create a sequence by putting items in a certain order. Sequencing involves recognition of what comes first and then what follows. Sequencing underlies classroom activities. The class schedule follows a sequence, and art activities often have a sequence (e.g., first you cut, then you paste; first you dip your brush in the water, then in paint, and then on the paper). Some dramatic play activities follow a sequence (e.g., grocery store). Stories often follow a predictable sequence with a beginning, a build-up to a climax, and then a resolution. Songs also follow a sequence. Language itself is sequential. There are rules regarding the sequence of sounds, words, and phrases. Language also can help maintain or define a sequence. Words such as "first," "middle," and "last" often define a particular order.

Motor Skills

Motor activities can be divided into those that involve gross (large) motor skills and those that use fine (small) motor skills.

Gross Motor Skills   Outside time activities typically involve gross motor skills. The activities might include walking, running, sliding, jumping, climbing, pedaling, bouncing, throwing, digging, and so forth. Other activities might include group games, such as "Duck, Duck, Goose." In addition to providing enjoyment for the children, objectives for gross motor activities are to provide appropriate exercise, to improve the children's coordination skills, to facilitate turn-taking skills, and to encourage cooperative play.

As the children play on the playground equipment or in group games, they not only use their muscles but also employ language and social skills. Children may have to take turns in order to play on or with the playground toys or equipment. They may have to negotiate when they get their turn (e.g., "my turn's next," "after you ride the bike, I get it"). Outdoor play is a good time for children to understand and use a variety of verbs (e.g., *bounce, turn, run, ride, slide, dig, roll*). It is also a good place to learn about a variety of prepositions (e.g., *in* the tunnel, *down* the slide, *under* the house, *below* the pole).

Fine Motor Skills   Fine motor skills are facilitated in a variety of classroom activities, particularly the art activities. Specific skills to be facilitated include the following: 1) using a pincer grip, 2) using a dominant hand (some preschool-age children are still in the process of choosing a dominant hand), 3) learning to cross the midline, 4) learning to cut with scissors, and 5) learning other skills requiring eye–hand coordination. When playing with paintbrushes, markers, crayons, or chalk, the children learn to use a pincer grip and to employ the appropriate eye–hand coordination to make pictures or designs. Cutting and pasting activities may require different fine motor coordination skills. Other classroom activities that use fine motor skills include stacking small blocks, putting Lego toys together, drawing on the chalkboard, pouring juice, and so forth. Activities that facilitate fine motor skills can also facilitate language skills. For example, children can learn a variety of verbs in connection with activities requiring fine motor skills (e.g., cutting, drawing, painting, pasting, pouring). Many fine motor activities also provide opportunities for children to negotiate for turns and to play cooperatively (see the discussion under Art Activity Plans).

GUIDELINES FOR THEMES AND ACTIVITIES

Themes and Dramatic Play Activities

The main consideration in choosing a theme, whether for the year or the semester, is that it be broad enough to incorporate a variety of weekly themes. "Discovery," "Investigating," and "Our World" are examples of themes that allow for a range of more specific thematic units. The weekly thematic units form the backbone of the LFC.

Several factors must be considered in choosing weekly themes and associated dramatic play activities. *First, the themes used at the beginning of the school year should involve dramatic play activities that are familiar to the children.* Familiar activities are easier for the children to enjoy because they understand how to "play" the different roles; novel or less familiar activities should be introduced later in the school year after the children have adjusted and made friends. Familiar activities allow the children to use known structures in the unknown or unfamiliar setting of school.

For the first day of a school year or the first day following a vacation, staff should plan activities that involve water play. Water play tends to be calming and fun for the children and eases the transition back to school. The theme for the first week of school might be "Discovering the Classroom" or "Classroom Favorites" and include dramatic play activities such as "Bathing Babies," "Doctor's Office," "Farm" (involving sand play and tractors), and "Grocery Store."

A second important factor in planning weekly themes is to choose themes with a variety of potential dramatic play activities. A "Winter" theme may be hard to sustain for an entire week. Although shredded newspaper can be used to represent snow and plastic dropcloths can be made into a skating rink, one day of paper all over the floor is usually enough. A more general theme involving "Seasons" might be easier to sustain, and would still allow for one day devoted to winter snow and skating activities.

A third guideline for selecting weekly themes is to be careful not to choose themes that require frequent repetition of a particular dramatic play. As a general rule, try not to repeat a dramatic play activity more than once every 4 months. The children become bored with a dramatic play if it is repeated too often. Also, for dramatic play activities that are being repeated, it is helpful to add new props. For example, a drive-up window can be added to the basic fast-food restaurant layout to add a new dimension to the children's play. Often there are many potential dramatic plays that could be selected for a particular theme so that too much repetition is not a problem (see pp. 135–137 for a listing of suggested themes and dramatic play activities).

Fourth, when selecting themes and dramatic plays to support the themes, consider the different types of dramatic play activities (see Chapter 2 for a discussion of types of dramatic play activities). Dramatic play activities vary depending on whether they revolve around a *central* type of activity (e.g., a doctors' office where there can be several "doctors" and "nurses" doing similar activities revolving around a central theme that does not depend on a specific sequence), whether they have a *sequence* of repeated activities (e.g., a picnic or grocery store scenario where the activity has a defined sequence and there is a need to restart the sequence, such as packing up the picnic basket and going back to the starting point), or whether they consist of a variety of *related* activities (e.g., a craft fair where each activity stands alone and individual activities can be interchanged [There is no one central activity that defines the dramatic play. There could be bead stringing, paper weaving, paper folding, Play-Doh sculpture, or any of several other activities at a craft fair.]). If the dramatic play activity involves a sequence, then the adults need to be prepared to help the children restart the activity. This may mean restocking the shelves of the grocery store or repacking the picnic basket in order to begin the activity all over again. *A helpful rule of thumb is to limit the number of heavily sequential dramatic play activities to one per week because of the need for adult monitoring and action.* The dramatic play activities in Part III are marked according to whether they involve central, sequential, or related activities.

Finally, themes that involve difficult concepts are better developed during the second semester after the children are familiar with the school routine. For example, a "Seasons" theme is better developed in the second semester than earlier in the year because understanding time concepts can be difficult. An "Exploration" theme, for which the dramatic play activities might involve exploring space, trekking through a jungle, or working in a submarine, stretches the children's understanding and imagination and may need extensive support from the adults.

"Foods" is an example of a theme well chosen for a week early in the fall semester. Possible dramatic plays might be playing house (with cooking as a major activity), fast-food restaurant, grocery store, and fishing (including boat and water play). All of these activities, with the possible exception of fishing, are relatively familiar to children. With the addition of water play to the fishing activity, the children will participate even if they are unsure about the fishing activity. Later in the fall, a farm or harvest dramatic play activity might be appropriate. The day on which a particular dramatic play activity occurs is generally an arbitrary decision. The reasoning for a particular choice might concern prop availability, the desire to have a water table activity scheduled, or the schedule of a parent volunteer who will do a cooking demonstration. Sometimes the sequence of the dramatic play activities is important in the development of the theme; however, often the sequence may depend more on staff convenience. For example, if several programs are using the same props, then each program might use a different dramatic play sequence that week so that one program could use the grocery store props, another does a cooking activity, another does the fishing activity, and so forth. Group planning is particularly important if more than one program is involved.

Activity Plans

Once a weekly theme is chosen and the daily activities have been tentatively selected, then daily lesson or activity plans reflecting that theme are developed. Lesson plans are needed for activities that change daily—specifically, dramatic play, art, story, group, and music activities. Routine activities such as snacktime and outside time also sometimes reflect the theme (e.g., having pizzas for snack on a day when the dramatic play is "pizza parlor," playing with the gas pump outside when the dramatic play activity is "mechanic").

Dramatic Play Activity Plans

Lesson plans for the dramatic play activities include the following four main objectives:

1. To increase the children's knowledge and use of new vocabulary
2. To increase the children's use of a variety of syntactic constructions
3. To encourage peer interaction
4. To expand the children's conceptual knowledge of the world

In order to achieve these objectives, the dramatic play activities provide opportunities to learn and use many different vocabulary words pertaining to a variety of settings and occupations (e.g., words pertaining to flying in an airplane, words used in an office or at a gas station). The wholistic nature of dramatic play activities allows the children to be surrounded by the particular vocabulary of an activity in a context that supports understanding it. Similarly, the activities allow for the use of a variety of syntactic structures. As they play, children may need to talk about things in the present, future, or past. They may need to use a variety of pronouns, prepositional phrases, or question structures. Many of the activities require peer negotiation of turns with a particular prop and other peer interactions to enact the dramatic play (e.g., "My turn to be the pilot"; "I wanted to be next"; "Hamburger, please"; "Okay, do you want ketchup on it?"). Also, as the children enact a role or scene, they begin to understand some of the features needed in "real" world situations and in this way they expand their world knowledge. For example, in an airplane scenario, children learn that passengers need tickets, luggage goes through a metal detector, and food and drinks are served to passengers. They also learn about the different roles of crew members.

In order to implement the objectives listed above, lesson plans should focus on providing general descriptions of the dramatic play activity, setting, props, roles involved, and possible verbal productions needed for the activity (see Figure 7 and the examples in Part III). In addition, the adults' roles in facilitating language development should be outlined in the lesson plans.

General Description and Setting   The general description of the activity gives a quick overview of what is to be done. Because every school's available space for dramatic play activities will be different, only general suggestions can be given here. However, the layout can be very simple. For example, a grocery store can consist of an area with shelves of plastic food, cardboard containers, and cans arranged in aisles with a table holding a cash register. The inside of an airplane might consist of an arrangement of chairs with "seatbelts" (men's ties tied to a chair), a dashboard (pilot's cockpit equipment), and a cart for the flight attendant's use. A playhouse (e.g., Playskool wooden playhouse) becomes a rocket ship, a wagon train, a ticket office, or a drive-up window of a fast-food restaurant. Sometimes the transformation is helped by strategic use of cardboard or turning the house on its side. A play stove, refrigerator, sink, and tables can be part of a house or of a restaurant kitchen.

Props   Once the basic layout is detailed in the lesson plan, other props should be suggested to add to the dramatic play activity. For example, hats can be worn to indicate which children are the fast-food restaurant workers and which are the customers. Sometimes toys that are facsimiles of real items can be used as props (e.g., pretend pizza, hamburgers, and french fries, toy cash registers, doctor kits). However, having toy facsimiles is not required. Simple but effective props can be made out of commonly available objects. For example, hair dryers made out of toilet paper rolls and cottage cheese containers are as effective as plastic models. Similarly, fishing poles made from large paintbrushes and strings with magnets on the end can be used instead of plastic fishing poles. Paper fish are caught using the magnets because large paper clips are attached to the fish. Children can also help create their own props. For example, binoculars can be made by taping two toilet paper rolls together and attaching a yarn "strap."

ACTIVITY PLAN

Dramatic Play: Airplane   **Date:** _____

Type of Activity: (Central)   Sequential   Related

Objectives: 1. To learn new and employ familiar vocabulary
                   2. To learn new and employ a variety of syntactic constructions
                   3. To interact with peers
                   4. To sequence familiar routines
                   5. To expand conceptual knowledge of the world

General Description of Activity

Introduce activity by reading the book *Going on an Airplane Trip.* An airplane trip involves purchasing a ticket, checking baggage at the counter, going through security check, and finally finding a seat on the plane. Seatbelts must be fastened for take-off. Food and beverages are served by flight attendants. When you arrive baggage needs to be reclaimed at the baggage area. Carry-on luggage can be stored under a seat.

Setting

- Airport
- Ticket office or counter
- Airplane facsimile (chairs arranged in rows behind a "cab" where a play dashboard is set up)
- Kitchen
- Cockpit
- Baggage claim area (optional)
- Metal detector (optional)

Props

- Tickets
- Chairs with seatbelts (men's ties can be used for seatbelts)
- Dashboard
- Luggage
- Food and drinks
- Trays
- Carts
- Dolls

Roles

- Pilot and co-pilot
- Flight attendants
- Passengers
- Clerks at the ticket counter
- Security people

(continued)

Figure 7.   Activity plans should be completed for the dramatic play, art, and group centers. A sample dramatic play activity plan is shown here. (From Bunce, B.H., & Watkins, R.W. [1995]. Language intervention in a preschool classroom: Implementing a language-focused curriculum. In M.L. Rice & K.A. Wilcox [Eds.], *Building a language-focused curriculum for the preschool classroom. Vol. I: A foundation for lifelong communication* [pp. 65–66]. Baltimore: Paul H. Brookes Publishing Co.; reprinted by permission.)

Figure 7. *continued*

Verbal Productions

Level of linguistic complexity varies with the role or competence of the child playing the role.

- "We're coming in for a landing so fasten your seat belts" or "Plane's landing."
- "Do you want a beverage?" or "Drink, please."
- "May I see your ticket?" or "Ticket?"

Adult Facilitory Role

The adult's role is to assist the children in the role play and to help expand their language use. Emphasis on different structures and/or vocabulary may be necessary depending on the individual child's needs and abilities. The adult(s) may provide focused contrasts, model appropriate scripts, ask open questions, expand or recast the child's productions, redirect a child to request items from another child, or provide confirming feedback to a particular child.

Props can be stored in cardboard or plastic boxes. It is helpful to label the boxes with the particular theme(s) so that the props can be used often. This labeling is also helpful because additional props can be added to the boxes as dramatic play activities are extended. Some props (e.g., plastic food) are used in a variety of dramatic play activities (e.g., grocery store, cooking at home, restaurant). For these props, it is better to label boxes with lists of items rather than particular dramatic play names.

Roles It is important to have at least four different roles for each dramatic play in order to ensure different interactions among peers (cf. roles listed on the dramatic play lesson plans in Part III). For some dramatic plays, it is not difficult to develop four roles (e.g., fast-food restaurant has a cook, cashier, customer, and clean-up crew member; a doctor's office has a receptionist, doctor, nurse, and patient). For other dramatic play activities, it is more difficult to devise four roles. For these dramatic plays, it may be possible to set up four areas of related activities. For a scientist dramatic play, different activities such as looking through a microscope, using a magnifying glass, mixing colored water, or experimenting with magnets might be arranged.

Verbal Productions A crucial feature of the dramatic play activities is that they allow participation of children with varying degrees of linguistic competency. However, in order to participate in the activities, some verbal interaction is usually required. Children who use one- and two-word utterances can participate in the dramatic play along with children who routinely produce much longer utterances. The children with less language competency can "practice" using their language skills in a highly motivating activity. At the same time, they can listen to the language used by the others and observe contextual markers.

Adults' Roles The adults need to support interactions among the children by modeling appropriate productions. Some of the modeling can be accomplished when introducing the activity to the children (see Chapter 2). Essentially, the introductions involve actual role play, stories, or video clips of the activity to demonstrate possible scripts and actions. Adults also can support the interactions in the dramatic play by assuming a role, commenting on the actions of others, or beginning an activity and then turning the crucial prop over to a child. Specific language stimulation techniques are described in Chapter 3 of this volume (see also Bunce & Watkins, 1995). These techniques include focused contrasts, modeling, event casts, open questions, expansions, recasts, redirects and prompted initiations, and scripted play.

Art Activity Plans

General objectives for art lesson plans are the following:

1. To encourage creativity
2. To foster development of fine motor skills
3. To encourage turn taking
4. To foster conversation between peers and adults

In order to achieve these objectives, different types of art activities are planned that allow for a range of creativity and employ different motor skills and materials.

The art activities may require the use of shared materials, or they may be a shared project that requires negotiation. The art activities also may require help from an adult or older child, thus encouraging conversation. The conversation at the art table may involve free exchanges or routinized phrases such as, "Pass the markers, please" or, "Scissors, please." The children with lower levels of linguistic competency may be able to participate in the art activities by using just a few phrases. In this way, the context of the art activity promotes communication.

In order to implement the art activity objectives, a general lesson plan is used that describes the art activity and lists the necessary supplies (see Figure 8 and the examples in Part III). The description outlines how the project is to be completed. Sometimes, a sample project or a diagram is included in the plans.

In planning for a particular week, several factors should be considered. *First, the activity needs to involve the child's creation and be something the child enjoys doing.* It is the process that is important, not necessarily the product. An occasional teacher-directed art activity resulting in a particular product may be necessary (e.g., a present for parents, a prop for a dramatic play); however, these heavily teacher-directed art projects should be kept to a minimum.

Second, the children's skill level and needs are of major concern. If a classroom involves 3- to 5-year-old children, then activities need to encompass a range of abilities so that the 3-year-olds as well as the 5-year-olds can do the activity. Even if the classroom has only one age group, children's skill levels vary, so it is important to have activities that can be done by all of the children. It is also important that the activity facilitate motor development, particularly for children who have difficulty in this area. (An occupational therapist can offer specific suggestions for children who have major fine motor impairments.)

Third, art projects that involve several steps may be more appropriate during the latter part of the semester or year rather than in the first month or so. Delaying more complicated projects allows time for the

children to develop their direction-following and motor abilities. The delay also allows time for the teacher to assess the children's skill level and design activities in which the children can be successful and enjoy completing the project.

Fourth, there should be a balance among the activities so that the children are not, for example, painting every day. It may be helpful to or-

ART ACTIVITY PLAN

Art: ___Aquariums___   **Date:** _____

Objectives: 1. To foster creativity
                   2. To foster small motor development (e.g., drawing, painting, cutting, *pasting* skills)
                   3. To increase vocabulary knowledge
                   4. To practice turn-taking skills
                   5. To converse with peers and adults

General Plan:

White glue is smeared to the bottom half of a paper plate using a Popsicle stick or a cotton swab. Sand is sprinkled onto the glue to form the bottom of the "ocean." The children then glue different items that could be under the sea, such as fish, sharks, and seaweed, on the plate but above the sand. The plate is then wrapped in blue plastic wrap to represent the water and to create an aquarium effect.

Supplies Needed:

- Paper plates
- White glue
- Popsicle sticks or cotton swabs
- Sand
- Fish cut-outs
- Seaweed (green construction paper or green yarn)
- Blue plastic wrap

Figure 8.   A sample art activity plan.

ganize the art activity plans with regard to the type of art medium and/or fine motor skill used in the activity (e.g., painting, cutting).

In Part III, the art activities are organized in the following categories and listed alphabetically: construction, cutting, drawing, painting, and pasting. The construction category usually involves a 3-dimensional object (e.g., making an animal out of Play-Doh or an airplane out of paper) and may involve two or more of the other categories in the formation of the object. An asterisk on the art activity plan indicates an activity that may be difficult for some children or, in general, may require adult assistance to complete. Two asterisks on an art activity plan indicate a more difficult art project. It is suggested that these lesson plans be used late during the first semester or during the second semester.

Group Activity Plans

General objectives for the group activity plans are the following:

1. To foster listening skills
2. To increase conceptual knowledge
3. To teach appropriate group interaction skills
4. To practice turn taking

Also, embedded in the activities is a focus on language skills. Children will learn new vocabulary, hear a variety of syntactic structures, and have opportunities to respond or ask questions. In order to achieve these objectives, a variety of concepts are presented during group time. Some of the concepts involve preacademic readiness skills, such as alphabet and number skills or safety/life skills (e.g., fire safety rules). Other concepts involve basic skills such as being able to match or label items, form classifications, and/or identify or place items in a sequence. The group activities are teacher directed and as such require the children to pay attention to the teacher in a group setting. This requires the children to focus on the teacher's presentation rather than the teacher following the interests of individual children. Much of this focus is accomplished through listening. The activities are taught so that there is active participation by the children. As different children perform required actions, others can watch and learn. Usually the children cannot all have a turn at the same time, so they get practice in waiting for their turn.

In order to implement the objectives for group activities, the group activity plan outlines an introductory activity, suggestions for group participation, and a summary or transition activity. In addition, the materials needed for the activity are listed (see Figure 9 and the examples in Part III).

In planning for the group activity, some of the same factors that were outlined previously also apply to the group activities. *First, the children's skill levels need to be considered when developing the lesson plans.* Some of the group activities are more difficult to understand than others and, therefore, should be presented after the children have adjusted to the routine of listening to the adults and waiting their turn.

Second, some activities are based on earlier-developing concepts and so these lessons should be presented later in the semester or year.

GROUP ACTIVITY PLAN

Group: Float/sink   **Date:** _____

Objectives:
1. To foster listening skills
2. To increase conceptual knowledge
3. To teach appropriate group interaction skills
4. To practice turn taking

Introduction:

Fill a clear plastic container with water. Put a boat that floats in the water. Then say, "The boat is floating." Next, put a penny in the water and watch it sink. Have a child come up and identify the object that floats.

Group Participation:

Have the children come up one at a time and choose an object. Have each of them predict whether it will sink or float. Then let them put it in the water and the class should judge whether they are correct or not. Repeat the activity with different objects until all of the children have had a chance to put an object in the water.

Summary/Transition Activity:

Have the children try to tell why an object will float or sink. Show them that some things that are big and some that are small sink. Try to get the children to note that why an object floats depends on the material the object is made of, rather than the size.

Materials Needed:

- A clear plastic container filled with water
- Objects that will float (e.g., boats, corks, plastic spoon)
- Objects that will sink (e.g., screw, metal spoon)

Figure 9. A sample group activity plan.

For example, classification of different shapes might follow lessons on specific shapes.

Third, whenever possible, the lesson plans should be structured so that there are differential response demands. This variation of response demands allows for children with different levels of competency to be able to participate. It also provides a model for the children for whom the concepts are completely new. For example, one child may be required to do a matching task with circle shapes, another to label a circle shape, and still another child might have to find an object that is round. All of these responses could be part of a lesson on circles.

Fourth, there should be a balance among the kinds of concepts being addressed each week. For example, one day of the week might address preacademic skills, such as alphabet or number concepts. Another day might involve matching or sequencing skills, and another might focus on classification of items or on safety or life skills issues (e.g., fire safety rules, learning one's address).

In Part III, the group activities have been organized into the following categories: 1) labeling and matching, 2) classification, 3) sequencing,

4) safety and life skills, and 5) preacademics. Most of the group activity plans in Part III include suggestions for ways to simplify the activity demands so that all of the children can respond successfully. Nevertheless, some of the activities are more appropriate after the children have become adjusted to the group format and are marked with an asterisk to indicate a more advanced difficulty level. Activities for each week typically involve a focus on an alphabet letter, a labeling or matching activity, a classification activity, and either a sequencing or safety/life skills activity. Number concepts are addressed earlier in the day through the calendar activity and during snacktime (or whenever appropriate), as described in Chapter 2. Later in the year, a group activity focusing on the writing of numbers or simple addition/subtraction concepts can be presented. Color concepts are also embedded throughout the daily activities. In addition, one color is highlighted each month by having the children wear that color on Thursdays. The primary colors are the focus in the fall semester and the secondary colors during the spring semester (i.e., September is "blue" month, October is "yellow" month, November and December are "red" months, January is "orange" month, February is "purple" month, and March is "green" month). Additional colors such as pink, brown, or black can be addressed in other months. Sometimes, a specific group activity will involve the labeling, matching, mixing, or classification of colors.

Story Formats

Formal activity plans for story reading are not provided in this volume; however, the format described here could be used. The format consists of the children gathering around the teacher who then reads or tells a story. Pictures that accompany the narration are shown either as the teacher reads or following the reading of each page. Occasionally, the story may be acted out by the children after the reading or telling. Often, the teacher will ask one or two questions about the story at the end of the reading as a summary activity. The type of question can be varied depending on the specific child's linguistic competency. For example, a *what* question is typically easier to respond to than a *why* question (cf. Blank, Rose, & Berlin, 1978, for a discussion of different levels of questions).

Specific objectives for the story activity are the following:

1. To foster listening skills
2. To enjoy and develop knowledge of different types of stories
3. To foster sequencing skills
4. To learn new vocabulary
5. To foster development of emergent literacy skills, such as predicting what will happen, left to right orientation, and print awareness

Several factors govern the choice of a particular story for a particular day. *First, the story is chosen with regard to the weekly theme. Second, the complexity of the story is a consideration, with simpler stories chosen earlier in the year and more complex ones later. Third, the type of story may also be a factor.* Usually there is variation in the kinds of stories read so that the stories for 1 week are not all labeling stories, adventure stories, fairy tales, or stories with a repetitive line.

In planning the weekly curriculum, it is helpful to have already organized the books available according to specific themes or dramatic play activities. In LAP, a file system is used wherein titles of books are written on 3" × 5" cards and placed under different theme and/or dramatic play categories. The same book might be listed under several categories. For example, *Brown Bear, Brown Bear, What Do You See?* (Martin & Carle, 1967) could be listed under the theme "Senses" (for the sense of sight) or under "Animals." The books could also have a code on them indicating the type of story (e.g., labeling, repetitive line, adventure, fairy tale, rhyming, no-word book). This file card system could be developed over a year as the weekly curriculum is planned. Also, whenever new books are purchased, they should be categorized immediately.

Music Formats

As with story reading, no formal activity plans are provided in this volume for music activities; however, a format such as the one described here could be employed. The children sit in a half circle around the teacher. The teacher tells the children the title of the song and then starts to sing it. If the children know the song, they join in singing. If the song is new, it is sung by the teacher with the children listening. Sometimes the song is introduced via a recording. The song is then repeated, with the children joining in whenever possible. Each day one song could reflect the weekly theme. Other songs that may or may not be related to the theme could then be sung. These songs may be favorites of the children or songs from previous weeks. The teacher should have a variety of songs available; however, sometimes the children might choose the songs to be sung. Occasionally one child might perform a song for the class and sometimes teach it to the others.

Specific objectives for the music activity are the following:

1. To foster the enjoyment of music
2. To encourage the development of rhythm and movement
3. To encourage participation in a choral activity with repetitive refrains
4. To practice sequencing of sounds, words, and phrases
5. To learn how to vary intonation and prosody
6. To understand terms such as loud/soft and fast/slow as they relate to music

Music activities also support the development of the ability to predict what will come next based on intonation or melody. The support from the melody, the repetitive nature of many of the songs, and the joint singing by others helps children with limited linguistic ability become active participants. Sometimes it is through music activities that children first begin to respond verbally. Music activities are important in the preschool classroom because they foster the development of linguistic, cognitive, motor, and social skills.

Several factors are considered in choosing the songs for a particular day. *First, a song is chosen that relates to the theme. Second, the songs should appeal to and be enjoyed by the children. Third, the level of difficulty may govern the choice of the particular song—that is, songs with complicated rhythms, melodies, movements, or long verses may not be appropriate early in the semester. Fourth, the type of concept being taught in other settings may affect the choice of songs.* For example, if knowledge of body parts is the focus of the group activity, then a song such as "Heads, Shoulders, Knees, and Toes" might be sung.

In planning the curriculum, it is helpful to have a list of possible songs from which to choose. One way to do this is to have different children's songbooks available during planning time. Another way to organize is to have a card file with the songs categorized according to themes. It is also helpful to categorize the songs as involving movement, having repetitive refrains, pertaining to particular holidays, and including particular concepts (e.g., numbers, colors, shapes).

SUMMARY

As described in this chapter, several levels of planning are necessary in developing a language-focused curriculum. Long-range planning involves choosing a semester (or yearly) theme and then sketching out a semester (or year) of possible weekly themes. This long-range planning provides an overall sequence to the development of the curriculum. The short-term planning provides the specific details of how to implement the curriculum. For activities that change daily these plans include the weekly planning guide, the daily planning guide, and the daily activity plans. (General plans and information on routine classroom activities are addressed in Chapter 2.) The weekly planning guide provides a quick overview of the week's activities and the supplies needed. The daily planning guide provides the focus on language, social, cognitive, and motor skills important to the development of the 3- to 5-year-old child. The daily activity plans provide information on how to implement a particular lesson.

Providing guidelines for the selection and implementation of specific themes and daily activities was the focus of the remainder of this chapter. These guidelines addressed each activity (i.e., dramatic play, art, group, story, and music) separately. Specific issues to consider when selecting an activity were outlined. In general, the guidelines addressed issues regarding the goals of an activity, the levels of difficulty, the sequence of an activity, and the achievement of a balance in the types of activities chosen. Guidelines for implementation included how to introduce an activity, how to encourage child participation to meet the goals of the activity, and how to organize the plans and supplies.

~5~

Curricular Examples

As described in Chapters 2 and 4, the language-focused curriculum is developed around thematic units that support children's growth in language, social, cognitive, and motor skills. Some of the activities are routine and are not addressed here (see Chapter 2). Other activities change daily and require specific planning. As described in Chapter 4, a number of planning aids are used. Specifically, semester or monthly calendars can be used to plan weekly themes and activities. The weekly planning guide lays out the overall plan of action for the week, delineating the dramatic play, art, story, group, and music activities. The daily planning guide specifies how each day's activities might facilitate the language, social, cognitive, and motor skills of the children (e.g., specific vocabulary and structures are noted). Finally, specific activity (lesson) plans are developed for implementing the dramatic play, art, and group activities. Blank planning guides are supplied in Appendix B at the end of this book.

In this chapter, the "Discovering . . ." theme is planned in a series of monthly calendars spanning 4 months. Then examples used in the Language Acquisition Preschool are provided to illustrate the curriculum planning for 2 weeks. The planning is based on a 4-day week. The first week's theme is entitled "Discovering Places" and the second week's theme is "Discovering Transportation."

Discovering. . .

Theme	Activities	Monday	Tuesday	Wednesday	Thursday
LAP favorites	**Dramatic play**	Water play	House	Fast-food restaurant	Camping
	Art	Water paint	Drawings	Playdough	Cheerio art
	Story	*Rainbow Fish*	*If You Give a Mouse a Cookie*	*Will I Have a Friend?*	*We're Going on a Bear Hunt*
	Group	Things in water	Hot/cold	Letter "A" (apple)	"Blue"
	Music	Five Little Ducks	I'm a Little Teapot	Peanut Butter and Jelly	A Camping We Will Go
Places in the Community	**Dramatic play**	Doctor's office	Beauty/barber shop	Gas station/ garage (mechanic)	Grocery store
	Art	Chalk drawings	Shaving-cream fingerpainting	Water-color painting	Food collage
	Story	*Going to the Doctor*	*Count*	*What's Under Your Hood, Orson?*	*Little Fish, Big Fish*
	Group	Body parts	Letter "B" (barber)	Sound sequencing	Big and little
	Music	Hokey Pokey	ABC Song	Johnny Works with One Hammer	I Like to Eat

(continued)

SEPTEMBER

Discovering. . .

Theme	Activities	Monday	Tuesday	Wednesday	Thursday
Transportation	**Dramatic play**	Airplane	Boats	Cars (racing)	(Delivery) Trucks
	Art	Paper airplanes	Meat tray boats	Vehicle rubbings	Easel paintings
	Story	*We're Taking an Airplane Trip*	*Mr. Gumpy's Outing*	*Wheels*	*The Truck Book*
	Group	Shapes—circle	Same and different	Letter "C" (cookie)	Circle collage
	Music	Airplane Song	Row, Row, Row Your Boat	C is for Cookie	Wheels on the Bus
Community helpers	**Dramatic play**	Construction worker	Veterinarian	Office worker	Firefighter
	Art	Popsicle art	Paper bag puppet	Drawings	Play-dough
	Story	*A House Is a House for Me*	*Moses, the Kitten*	*A Letter to Amy*	*The Fire Engine*
	Group	Square	Care of pets	Letter "D" (desk)	Fire safety rules
	Music	Johnny Works with One Hammer	Five Little Monkeys	ABC Song	Hurry, Hurry, Drive the Firetruck

(*continued*)

SEPTEMBER

Discovering. . .

Theme	Activities	Monday	Tuesday	Wednesday	Thursday
Food	**Dramatic play**	Farm	Pizza parlor	Grocery store	House (cooking)
	Art	Cottonball chickens	Pizza	Coffee-filter water color	Macaroni necklaces
	Story	*Our Farmyard*	*The Three Bears*	*Whiskerville Grocery*	*It Looked Like Spilt Milk*
	Group	Square/circle	Act out *The Three Bears*	Fruits/ vegetables	Letter "E" (eat)
	Music	Old MacDonald Had a Farm	I Wish I Were a Pepperoni Pizza	Apples and Bananas	Who Stole the Cookie?

OCTOBER

Discovering. . .

Theme	Activities	Monday	Tuesday	Wednesday	Thursday
Vacation	**Dramatic play**	Airplane	Motel	Amusement park	Boat (cruise ship)
	Art	Kites	Postcards	Mickey Mouse ears	Easel painting
	Story	*Going on a Plane*	*Ira Sleeps Over*	*Where the Wild Things Are*	*At the Seaside*
	Group	Sound patterns	Loud/soft	"Yellow"	Letter "F"
	Music	Going to Kentucky	Rock'a-bye Baby	It's a Small World	Five Little Speckled Frogs
Senses	**Dramatic play**	Hair salon	TV studio	Health clinic	Bakery (make cookies)
	Art	Cornstarch	Water-color painting	Faces	Play-Doh (scented)
	Story	*Here Are My Hands*	*Bear Shadow*	*Don't Interrupt*	*The Gingerbread Man*
	Group	Feely bag	Video	Sound lotto	Letter "G"
	Music	Heads, Shoulders, Knees, and Toes	Teddy Bear, Teddy Bear, Touch the Ground	If You're Happy (Shout Hooray)	ABC Song

(*continued*)

OCTOBER

Discovering. . .

Theme	Activities	Monday	Tuesday	Wednesday	Thursday
Fall	**Dramatic play**	Fall clean-up	Fall sports	Harvest (farm)	State fair
	Art	Leaf rubbings	Chalk pictures	Collage	Doghouse and dog prints
	Story	*Red Leaf, Yellow Leaf*	*Who's Counting?*	*The Little Red Hen*	*Raccoons and Ripe Corn*
	Group	Classify leaves	Number recognition	Letter "H"	Farm/zoo animals
	Music	Five Little Leaves	Take Me Out to the Ballgame	Way Down Yonder in the Paw, Paw Patch	Five Little Ducks
Places	**Dramatic play**	School	Laundromat	Doctor/hospital	Fitness center
	Art	Popcorn letters	Water-color painting	Doctor kit collage	Play-Doh
	Story	*Grover Goes to School*	*Just a Mess*	*Jenny's in the Hospital*	*Jamal's Busy Day*
	Group	Shape (triangle)	Unifix blocks	Emergency information	Letter "I" (inches)
	Music	ABC Song	Mulberry Bush	Brush Your Teeth	Teddy Bear, Teddy Bear, Touch the Ground

(continued)

OCTOBER

Discovering. . .

Theme	Activities	Monday	Tuesday	Wednesday	Thursday
Halloween	**Dramatic play**	Grocery store	Construction (house)	Decorate a Halloween house	Halloween party and parade
	Art	Chalk drawings	Pumpkin pictures (shapes)	Ghosts and skeletons	(no art)
	Story	*Clifford's Halloween*	*Monsters Don't Scare Me*	*Trick or Treat Little Critter*	*The Halloween Performance*
	Group	Carve a pumpkin	Letter "J"	Bones in a skeleton	Trick-or-treat safety
	Music	Did You Ever See a Pumpkin?	Five Little Pumpkins	Three Little Witches	Medley of Halloween songs

Discovering. . .

Theme	Activities	Monday	Tuesday	Wednesday	Thursday
Things big kids do	**Dramatic play**	Care of cars (Car wash)	Newspaper carrier	Fast-food restaurant worker	Babysitter
	Art	Shape pictures	Newspaper collage	Bird feeders	Fingerpainting
	Story	*Red Light, Green Light*	*Curious George Rides a Bike*	*Gregory, the Terrible Eater*	*Just Me and My Little Sister*
	Group	Writing a 2	Write class newsletter	Letter "K"	Addresses
	Music	Twinkle Twinkle, Traffic Light	Extra, Extra, Read All About It	Apples and Bananas	Ring Around the Rosie
Animals	**Dramatic play**	Farm animals	Zoo animals	Pets (vet)	Rodeo
	Art	Easel painting	Animal rubbings	Popsicle cages	Lacing
	Story	*The Cow that Went Oink*	*Zoo Song*	*Good Dog, Carl*	*Is Your Mama a Llama?*
	Group	Act out *The Cow that Went Oink*	Zoo/farm animals	Writing a 3	Letter "L"
	Music	Had a Little Rooster	Five Little Monkeys	BINGO	Sillies

(continued)

NOVEMBER

Discovering. . .

Theme	Activities	Monday	Tuesday	Wednesday	Thursday
Ways to take care of our world	**Dramatic play**	Park clean-up (picnic)	Utility worker	Hospital	Sanitation worker (recycling)
	Art	Bird feeders	String paintings	Teddy bear outline	Collage (magazine)
	Story	*Are You My Mother?*	*Katy and the Big Snow*	*Teddy Bear Cures a Cold*	*The Berenstain Bears Don't Pollute*
	Group	Color patterns	Letter "M"	"Red"	Recycle
	Music	Raindrops and Lemondrops	Clap Your Hands	Heads, Shoulders, Knees, and Toes	Clean-Up
Homes	**Dramatic play**	Castles	Teepee	Our house	Thanksgiving
	Art	Crowns	Tissue-paper art	Water-color painting	
	Story	*Cinderella*	*The Legend of Bluebonnet*	*Friendships First Thanksgiving*	
	Group	Alphabet grab bag	Letter "N"	Addresses	
	Music	London Bridge	Funny Bunny	Two Little Houses	

(continued)

NOVEMBER

Discovering. . .

Theme	Activities	Monday	Tuesday	Wednesday	Thursday
Different explorers	**Dramatic play**	Pioneers	Astronauts (space)	Divers (under the sea)	Forest rangers (camping)
	Art	Play-Doh	Glitter finger paint	Aquariums	Easel painting
	Story	*And You Can Be the Cat*	*My First Book About Space*	*Big Al*	*Chipmunk Song*
	Group	Writing a 4	Things that fly	Shapes (rectangle)	Letter "O"
	Music	Down in the Meadow	Raincloud Song	All the Little Fishies	Two Little Blackbirds

DECEMBER

Discovering. . .

Theme	Activities	Monday	Tuesday	Wednesday	Thursday
Occupations	**Dramatic play**	Mechanic	Police officer	Grocery clerk	Scientist
	Art	Chalk drawings	Badges	Veggie prints	Marble painting
	Story	*Working Hard with the Mighty Loader*	*Play It Safe*	*Do You Like Kayla?*	*I Was Walking Down the Road*
	Group	Empty/full	Letter "P"	Writing a 5	Ice cube melt
	Music	Johnny Works with One Hammer	ABC Song	On Top of Spaghetti	Raindrops and Lemondrops
Seasons	**Dramatic play**	Fall (fix-up)	Winter fun	Spring (garden)	Summer (beach)
	Art	Water-color painting	Snowflakes	Kites	Sand pictures
	Story	*Apples and Pumpkins*	*Snow Day*	*Big Sarah's Little Boots*	*A House for Hermit Crab*
	Group	Letter "Q"	Classify clothes	It's spring	Loud/soft
	Music	Building Song	Jingle Bells	Little Ducky Duddle	Five Little Fishies

(*continued*)

DECEMBER

Discovering. . .

Theme	Activities	Monday	Tuesday	Wednesday	Thursday
Hobbies	**Dramatic play**	Craft fair	Fishing/picnic	Car racing	Sports
	Art	Painted rocks	Tissue-paper fish	Vehicle rubbings	drawings
	Story	*What Rhymes with Snake?*	*Brown Bear, Brown Bear, What Do You See?*	*Go Dog Go*	*Cross-Country Cat*
	Group	Letter "R"	Unifix blocks	Seatbelt safety	All about balls
	Music	Where is Thumbkin?	Five Little Fishies	Traffic Light Song	If You're Happy
At the mall	**Dramatic play**	Department store	Pizza parlor	Pet store	Toy store
	Art	Catalog collage	Crayon-wash pizzas	Pet drawings	Teddy bear pictures
	Story	*Try on a Shoe*	*Bread, Bread, Bread*	*Scallywag*	*Corduroy*
	Group	Letter "S"	Follow/give directions	What does __ eat?	Act out *Corduroy*
	Music	Something in My Pocket	I Wish I Were a Pepperoni Pizza	I Have a Little Turtle	Going on a Bear Hunt

(continued)

DECEMBER

Discovering. . .

Theme	Activities	Monday	Tuesday	Wednesday	Thursday
The elements	**Dramatic play**	Camping (fire)	Garden (earth)	Boat (water)	Rocket/space (air)
	Art	Red fingerpaint	Play-Doh (brown)	Water paint	Kites
	Story	*Who Said Red?*	*The Giving Tree*	*Boats*	*Goodnight, Moon*
	Group	Shapes (diamond)	Letter "T"	Float/sink	Sound sequencing
	Music	A Camping We Will Go	ABC Song	Little Green Frog	The Rocket Song

CURRICULUM: WEEKLY PLANNING GUIDE

Semester Theme: Discovering. . .

Weekly Theme: Places in the Community   **Week of:** _____

	Dramatic Play	Art	Story	Group	Music
Monday	Doctor's office	Chalk drawings	*Going to the Doctor*	Body parts	Hokey-Pokey
Tuesday	Beauty/barber shop	Shaving-cream fingerpainting	*Count*	Letter "B"	ABC Song
Wednesday	Gas station/Garage	Water-color painting	*What's Under Your Hood, Orson?*	Sound sequencing	Johnny Works with One Hammer
Thursday	Grocery store	Food collage	*Big Fish, Little Fish*	Big and little	I Like to Eat

Suggested Props and Materials:

Monday	*Dramatic play:* Doctor/nurse kits, including toy stethoscope, thermometer, syringes, and bandages; dolls, examining tables, desk, telephone . . . *Art:* Chalk, black paper *Group:* Doll or skeleton
Tuesday	*Dramatic play:* "Salon" chairs, desk, appointment book, curlers, combs (with children's names), pretend shampoo, sink, dolls, pretend hair dryers, smocks . . . *Art:* Shaving cream, smocks, boards for shaving-cream pictures *Group:* List of "B" words, pictures and objects that begin with letter "B"
Wednesday	*Dramatic play:* Tools, pretend car lift, pretend car with battery, battery checker, gas pumps, road outlined with tape, desk, telephone . . . *Art:* Water-color paints, brushes, paper *Group:* Drum
Thursday	*Dramatic play:* Plastic fruits and vegetables, pretend canned goods, bakery items, milk and egg cartons, carts, cash register, money, grocery bags . . . *Art:* Magazines, scissors, glue sticks, paper *Group:* Big and little items (e.g., big apple, little apple, big car, little car, etc.)

CURRICULUM: DAILY PLANNING GUIDE

Theme: Discovering places
Week of: _____

(Monday)   Tuesday   Wednesday   Thursday

Dramatic Play	Art	Story	Group	Music
Doctor's office	Chalk drawings	Going to the Doctor	Body parts	Hokey Pokey

Language Skills Facilitated:

- **Vocabulary:** doctor, nurse, paramedic, ambulance, stethoscope, thermometer, fever, cast, x-ray, oxygen, accident, vehicle, arm, leg, ankle, bandage, forehead . . .

- **Verb Phrase Structures:** *is* carrying the stretcher, *drove* the ambulance, ride*s*, examine*s*, *gave* oxygen, set*s* the leg . . .

- **Adjective/Object Descriptions:** broken leg, big ambulance, loud siren

- **Pronouns:** I, you, he, she, we, they, my, your, her, his, our, their, me, us, them

- **Prepositions:** I, you, he, she, we, they, my, your, her, his, our, their, me, us, them

- **Sounds:** /k/ *c*arry, do*c*tor, bro*k*e; /s/ *s*et, in*s*ide, u*s*, ambulan*c*e . . .

Social Skills Facilitated:

- **Initiating to peers and adults, responding to questions and requests from peers and adults**

- **Negotiating with peers for toys and materials**

- **Group cooperation:** waiting for a turn in a group, taking a turn at the appropriate time

Cognitive Skills Facilitated:

- **Problem-Solving Skills:** what a doctor does

- **Classification Skills:** things in a doctor's office, body parts

- **Sequencing Skills:** story and songs

Motor Skills Facilitated:

- **Large Motor Skills:** outdoor play activities—jumping, running, hopping, pedaling, climbing . . .

- **Small Motor Skills:** writing, *drawing*, glueing . . .

DRAMATIC PLAY ACTIVITY PLAN

Dramatic Play: Doctor's office   **Date:** _____

Type of Activity: (Central)   Sequential   Related

Objectives: 1. To learn new, and employ familiar, vocabulary
2. To learn new, and employ a variety of, syntactic constructions
3. To interact with peers
4. To sequence familiar routines
5. To expand conceptual knowledge of the world

General Description of Activity

A doctor's office with several examination rooms and a waiting room is set up. People call the receptionist and make appointments. When it is time for their appointments, they go into the examination room with the doctor. He or she examines them by looking into the mouth, ears, and eyes; checking reflexes; checking muscle tone; listening with the stethoscope; and so forth. A patient might have a broken bone that needs to be X-rayed, set in a cast, and wrapped with a bandage.

Settings

- Several examination rooms
- Waiting room
- Patients' "homes"

Props

- Table with a telephone and appointment book
- Several tables or mats to represent examination rooms
- Doctor kits
- Bandages
- "X-ray" machine
- Telephone in area representing patients' "homes"

Roles

- Doctor
- Nurse
- Receptionist
- Patient
- Parent

Verbal Productions

Level of linguistic complexity varies with the role or competency of the child playing the role.

- "Open your mouth, please" or "Open mouth."
- "Where does it hurt?" or "Hurt?"
- "I don't feel good. My tummy hurts" or "I sick."

Adult Facilitory Role

The adult's role is to facilitate in the role play and to help expand language use. Emphasis on different sounds, structures, and/or vocabulary may be necessary, depending on the child's needs and abilities. The adult(s) may model appropriate scripts, ask open questions, expand or recast a child's productions, redirect a child to request items from another child, use a modification of a cloze procedure to provide contrastive feedback, or provide confirmative feedback to a particular child.

ART ACTIVITY PLAN

Art: <u>Chalk drawings</u>　　　　　　　　　**Date:** _____

Objectives:　1.　To foster creativity
　　　　　　　　2.　To foster small motor development (*drawing*, painting, cutting, pasting, etc.)
　　　　　　　　3.　To increase vocabulary knowledge
　　　　　　　　4.　To practice turn-taking skills
　　　　　　　　5.　To converse with peers and adults

General Plan

The children are given black construction paper, and they can use white chalk to draw pictures on it. Some of the children might like to draw X-ray pictures by making line drawings of skeleton-like people. Some of the X-ray pictures could be of "broken" arms and then could be incorporated into the dramatic play. (The artists could be the "radiologists.") Other children might want to draw general pictures that have nothing to do with the X-ray idea.

Supplies Needed

- Black construction paper
- White chalk
- Chalk of other colors
- Chalk fixative (to be sprayed on the drawings to keep the pictures from smudging)

GROUP ACTIVITY PLAN

Group: Body parts   **Date:** _____

Objectives: 1. To foster listening skills
2. To increase conceptual knowledge
3. To teach appropriate group interaction skills
4. To practice turn taking

Introduction

Children are seated in a semicircle around the teacher. The teacher holds up a doll (or skeleton) and asks one child to "Point to the doll's arm." After that child has pointed to a doll's arm, the teacher then says, "Today we are going to find different body parts on the doll (or skeleton) or on ourselves."

Group Participation

Other children then find the doll's (or skeleton's) body parts (wrist, toes, head, eyes, etc.). For each body part, a child comes up and points to a "body part" on him- or herself. The child can then label the part indicated or can choose another child to provide the label verbally. The activity is ended by playing a guessing game (I'm thinking of a body part that you use to *"point."* What is it?) When children guess correctly, the teacher holds up a picture of the appropriate body part.

Summary/Transition Activity

The teacher holds up the doll (or skeleton) again and quickly has the children shout out the label as he or she points to the hair, eyes, arm, hand, leg, toes, and so forth. Then the children put away their chairs and get ready for music.

Materials Needed

- Doll (or skeleton)
- Pictures of different body parts

CURRICULUM: DAILY PLANNING GUIDE

Theme: Discovering places

Week of: _____

Monday (Tuesday) Wednesday Thursday

Dramatic Play	Art	Story	Group	Music
Beauty/barber shop	Shaving-cream fingerpainting	*Count*	Letter "B"	ABC Song

Language Skills Facilitated:

- **Vocabulary:** comb, brush, hair, wash, cut, set, curl, dry, blow dry, fix, shave, shaving cream, emery board, customer, appointment . . .

- **Verb Phrase Structures:** curl*s* her hair, *is* curl*ing*, curl*ed*; dr*ies*, *is* dry*ing*, dr*ied*, will dry; cut*s*, *is* cutt*ing*, cut . . .

- **Adjective/Object Descriptions:** soft/hard __, wet/dry hair, cold/hot __, long/short hair, rough/smooth __

- **Pronouns:** I, you, he, she, we, they, my, your, her, his, our, their, me, us, them

- **Prepositions:** in, on, under, over, near, beneath, next to, beside, around, inside, outside

- **Sounds:** /k/ *c*ut, ba*ck*; /s/ *s*et, cut*s*; /S/ *sh*ave, bru*sh*; /l/ *l*ong, cur*l* . . .

Social Skills Facilitated:

- **Initiating to peers and adults, responding to questions and requests from peers and adults**

- **Negotiating with peers for toys and materials**

- **Group cooperation:** waiting for a turn in a group, taking a turn

Cognitive Skills Facilitated:

- **Problem-Solving Skills:** how to fix hair

- **Classification Skills:** things found in a beauty shop

- **Sequencing Skills:** alphabet song, story

Motor Skills Facilitated:

- **Large Motor Skills:** outdoor play activities—jumping, running, hopping, pedaling, climbing

- **Small Motor Skills:** writing, *drawing*, glueing . . .

94

DRAMATIC PLAY ACTIVITY PLAN

Dramatic Play: Beauty/barber shop   **Date:** _____

Type of Activity: (Central)   Sequential   Related

Objectives:
1. To learn new, and employ familiar, vocabulary
2. To learn new, and employ a variety of, syntactic constructions
3. To interact with peers
4. To sequence familiar routines
5. To expand conceptual knowledge of the world

General Description of Activity

A beauty/barber shop is a place where people get their hair shampooed, cut, dried, and styled. In a hair salon, they also might get a manicure and in a barber shop, a shave. Children can use their fingers in a cutting motion to pretend to cut hair.

Settings

- Salon chair (use a high chair for dolls to sit in)
- Chairs (for children)
- Sink to "wash" hair
- Reception area with telephone, appointment book, and pencil or crayon
- Barber chair
- Manicurist table

Props

- Curlers and clips
- Combs (put children's names on the combs so they use only theirs, and disinfect at the end of play)
- Mirrors
- Fingernail polish bottles (filled with water)
- Pretend shampoo and conditioner
- Pretend hair spray
- Pretend hair dryer (made out of two toilet paper rolls and a cottage cheese container, with a twisted pipe cleaner to represent the cord)
- Plastic chips (razors)
- Shaving cream
- Smocks (typically used when the children paint)
- Pretend nail polish remover
- Nail files
- Towels
- Toy cash register
- Pretend money

Roles

- Customers
- Receptionist
- Beautician
- Barber
- Manicurist

Verbal Productions

Level of linguistic complexity varies with the role or competency of the child playing the role.

- "I'm washing her hair" or "Wash hair."
- "Do you want your hair to be cut?"
- "Your hair is wet" or "Wet."
- "Cut my hair, please or "Cut hair."
- "He is shaving" or "He shaved."

Adult Facilitory Role

The adult's role is to facilitate role play and to help expand language use. Emphasis on different sounds, structures, and/or vocabulary may be necessary depending on the child's needs and abilities. The adult(s) may model appropriate scripts, ask open questions, expand or recast a child's productions, redirect a child to request items from another child, use a modification of a cloze procedure to provide contrastive feedback, or provide confirmative feedback to a particular child.

ART ACTIVITY PLAN

Art: Shaving-cream fingerpainting   **Date:** _____

Objectives: 1. To foster creativity
2. To foster small motor development (drawing, *painting*, cutting, pasting, etc.)
3. To practice turn-taking skills
4. To converse with peers and adults

General Plan

A dab of shaving cream is placed on each child's formboard. The children use their hands and fingers to smear the shaving cream all over the board and then use their fingers to draw and write in the shaving cream. They can make designs, draw pictures, or write letters and numbers. They can also use Popsicle sticks, paintbrushes, or other tools to draw in the shaving cream.

Supplies Needed

- Shaving cream
- Formboards (one per child)
- Popsicle sticks
- Paintbrushes (one per child)
- Other tools for drawing in the shaving cream

GROUP ACTIVITY PLAN

Group: Letter "B" _____ **Date:** _____

Objectives: 1. To foster listening skills
               2. To increase knowledge of the alphabet and sounds
               3. To teach appropriate group interaction skills
               4. To practice turn taking

Introduction

The teacher writes an upper- and lowercase letter "B" on the blackboard (or on poster paper) and gives several examples of words that begin with "B," emphasizing the /b/ or "buh" sound at the beginning of the words. (The teacher may hold up pictures of objects (or objects themselves) with names that begin with "B.") The teacher then directs the children's attention to the alphabet picture displays around the room.

Group Participation

The teacher asks if anyone's name begins with "B" (e.g., Betty, Bob). Those children write the letter "B" on the blackboard (or poster paper). Two or three other children are given the opportunity to write the letter "B" on the blackboard. If necessary, staff help the children write the letter. As the children write the uppercase letter "B," the teacher provides verbal guidance: "Start at the top and draw a straight line down. Go back to the top and make a half circle to the middle of the line. Now, make another half circle from the middle to the bottom of the line." Some of the other children can practice writing a "B" in the air with their fingers (or use individual chalkboards). The teacher then asks the children to think of words that begin with "B" and writes the words on the blackboard, drawing quick sketches (when possible) of the suggested words. If a child suggests a word that does not begin with "B," he or she is told, "No, that begins with a ____" and the sound is compared to the "B" sound. Pictures or objects representing "B" words can be provided as prompts for children who do not know any words so that they can participate. (Cards can be handed out at the beginning of the lesson or as the lesson proceeds.) Additional words can be sought in a picture dictionary if the class has difficulty arriving at words that begin with "B."

Summary/Transition Activity

After about 10–15 words have been suggested, the teacher reviews the words, emphasizing the "B" sound.

Materials Needed

- Blackboard and chalk
- Pictures of objects (or objects themselves) with names that begin with "B"
- Alphabet picture displays
- Picture dictionary (or an alphabet video dictionary)
- Poster paper and markers (optional)
- Individual chalkboards (optional)

CURRICULUM: DAILY PLANNING GUIDE

Theme: Discovering places

Week of: Gas station/

Monday   Tuesday   Wednesday   Thursday

Dramatic Play	Art	Story	Group	Music
Gas station/ garage (mechanic)	Water-color painting	*What's Under Your Hood, Orson?*	Sound sequencing	Johnny Works with One Hammer

Language Skills Facilitated:

- **Vocabulary:** gas, gas pump, car, truck, oil, tire, fix, mechanic, hood, attendant, tools, wrench, screw driver, flat tire, battery . . .

- **Verb Phrase Structures:** driv*es*, *is* driv*ing*, drove; pump*s*, *is* pump*ing*, pump*ed*; *has, have, had; does, do, did*

- **Adjective/Object Descriptions:** big/little truck, hard/easy to fix, flat tire, slow/fast car . . .

- **Pronouns:** I, you, he, she, we, they, my, your, her, his, our, their, me, us, them

- **Prepositions:** In, on, under, over, near, beneath, next to, beside, around, inside, outside

- **Sounds:** /r/ *r*un, ca*r*; /g/ *g*as, ru*g*; /s/ *s*ave, ga*s* . . .

Social Skills Facilitated:

- **Initiating to peers and adults, responding to questions and requests from peers and adults**

- **Negotiating with peers for toys and materials**

- **Group cooperation:** waiting for a turn in a group, taking a turn

Cognitive Skills Facilitated:

- **Problem-Solving Skills:** what is needed to fix a car

- **Classification Skills:** matching sound patterns—same–different comparisons

- **Sequencing Skills:** songs, story

Motor Skills Facilitated:

- **Large Motor Skills:** outdoor play activities—jumping, running, hopping, pedaling, climbing

- **Small Motor Skills:** writing, drawing, glueing, *painting* . . .

DRAMATIC PLAY ACTIVITY PLAN

Dramatic Play: Gas station/garage (mechanic)   **Date:** _____

Type of Activity: (Central)   Sequential   Related

Objectives: 1. To learn new, and employ familiar, vocabulary
2. To learn new, and employ a variety of, syntactic constructions
3. To interact with peers
4. To sequence familiar routines
5. To expand conceptual knowledge of the world

General Description of Activity

A gas station or garage is a place where vehicles can be repaired, gassed up, or tuned up. The oil in the car may need to be changed or the battery recharged. People can call ahead and make appointments. In one area, a receptionist/cashier desk is arranged. Another area can have a wooden or cardboard facsimile of a car with a hood that opens so that the mechanics can work under the hood if needed. Also, blocks or a vehicle erector set may be arranged in one area to build cars. An optional activity is to have a parts counter or store.

Setting

- Garage/repair shop
- Desk
- Cashier's station
- Gas pumps
- Car lift (cardboard blocks holding a plastic truck high enough for a child to slide under)
- Parts counter or store (optional)

Props

- Appointment book and pencil or crayon
- Toy cash register
- Pretend money
- Hoses for pumps
- Car with hood, which can be made out of cardboard
- Dashboard
- Tools
- Pretend battery
- Pretend computer
- Pretend cans for oil change
- Play telephones
- Pretend parts to sell (optional)

Roles

- Mechanics
- Customers
- Receptionist
- Sales clerk
- Cashier

Verbal Productions

Level of linguistic complexity varies with the role or competency of the child playing the role.

- "May I please have the wrench?" or "Wrench, please."

- "Please start the car now" or "Start."

- "My car needs a new battery" or "Battery."

Adult Facilitory Role

The adult's role is to facilitate role play and to help expand language use. Emphasis on different sounds, structures, and/or vocabulary may be necessary depending on the child's needs and abilities. The adult(s) may model appropriate scripts, ask open questions, expand or recast a child's productions, redirect a child to request items from another child, or use a modification of a cloze procedure to provide contrastive feedback, or provide confirmative feedback to a particular child.

ART ACTIVITY PLAN

Art: Water-color painting   **Date:** _____

Objectives: 1. To foster creativity
2. To foster small motor development (drawing, *painting*, cutting, pasting, etc.)
3. To increase vocabulary knowledge
4. To practice turn-taking skills
5. To converse with peers and adults

General Plan

White construction paper, water-color paintboxes, and paintbrushes are laid out on the art tables. Tubs of water to clean the brushes are placed above the paper. The children put on smocks and sit down at the art tables. Each child selects a brush, wets it, and chooses a paint color. The children then paint on the paper, rinsing the brush before selecting new colors. The children can paint collages of colors or animals, people, houses, flowers, and so forth.

Supplies Needed

- White construction paper
- Water-color paintboxes
- Paintbrushes
- Tubs of water
- Smocks
- Drying racks or counter space

GROUP ACTIVITY PLAN

Group: Sound sequencing   **Date:** _____

Objectives: 1. To foster listening skills
2. To increase the ability to recognize and sequence patterns
3. To teach appropriate group interaction skills
4. To practice turn taking

Introduction

A drum is placed in front of the children. The teacher taps out a simple pattern while the children listen. The teacher then repeats the pattern while they listen again. One child is invited to come up to the front of the class and try to make the same pattern. (The child can be helped if necessary so that the sound pattern matches.)

Group Participation

A different pattern is played and another child tries to match it. This continues until all the children have had at least one turn. The patterns can vary from two short taps to complicated patterns involving a series of taps grouped in two or three sequences. For example, one pattern might be tap-tap-pause-tap. Another might be tap-tap-tap-pause-tap-tap. Still another might be tap-pause-tap-tap-tap. Other sample patterns include the following:

- Tap-tap-pause-tap-tap
- Tap-tap-tap-pause-tap
- Tap-pause-tap-tap
- Loud tap-pause-soft tap
- Loud tap-loud tap-pause-soft tap-soft tap

Variation

- A keyboard can be used to set a rhythm.
- The children may clap the rhythms.

Summary/Transition Activity

The teacher reviews that the day's activity involved matching patterns and then plays a rhythm from a song that is to be sung during music time.

Materials Needed

- Drum
- Keyboard (optional)

CURRICULUM: DAILY PLANNING GUIDE

Theme: Discovering places

Week of: _____

Monday   Tuesday   Wednesday   (Thursday)

Dramatic Play	Art	Story	Group	Music
Grocery store	Food collage	*Little Fish, Big Fish*	Big and little	I Like to Eat

Language Skills Facilitated:

- **Vocabulary:** groceries, cart, cereal, shop, checker, buy, sell, bag, sack, shelf, money, change . . .

- **Verb Phrase Structures:** eats, is eating, ate, has eaten; pushes, is pushing, pushed; buys, bought, checks, is checking, checked

- **Adjective/Objective Descriptions:** big/little bag, full/empty shelf

- **Pronouns:** I, you, he, she, we, they, my, your, her, his, our, their, me, us, them

- **Prepositions:** In, on, under, over, near, beneath, next to, beside, around, inside, outside

- **Sounds:** /S/ shelf, push; /k/ cart, sack; /s/ sell, carts . . .

Social Skills Facilitated:

- **Initiating to peers and adults, responding to questions and requests from peers and adults**

- **Negotiating with peers for toys and materials**

- **Group cooperation:** waiting for a turn in a group, taking a turn

Cognitive Skills Facilitated:

- **Problem-Solving Skills:** what to buy, how to glue objects

- **Classification Skills:** big/little

- **Sequencing Skills:** songs, story

Motor Skills Facilitated:

- **Large Motor Skills:** outdoor play activities—jumping, running, hopping, pedaling, climbing

- **Small Motor Skills:** writing, drawing, glueing . . .

DRAMATIC PLAY ACTIVITY PLAN

Dramatic Play: Grocery store _____ **Date:** _____

Type of Activity: Central   (Sequential)   Related

Objectives: 1. To learn new, and employ familiar, vocabulary
2. To learn new, and employ a variety of, syntactic constructions
3. To interact with peers
4. To sequence familiar routines
5. To expand conceptual knowledge of the world

General Description of Activity

The children pretend to be grocery shopping. They can make a list, take their "children" with them, choose the items on the list to put in their carts, pay, sack, and go home. Other children can be the grocery store workers. Some keep the shelves stocked, and others are checkers and baggers.

Setting

- Grocery store
- Shelves and aisles
- Check-out stand
- Customers' homes

Props

- Shelves
- Canned goods and other food items
- Fruit and vegetable area
- Pretend cash register
- Pretend money
- Pretend coupons
- Shopping carts
- Grocery bags
- Pencil and paper for making lists
- Table for checkout area

Roles

- Shoppers
- Cashiers
- Stockers
- Baggers

Verbal Productions

Level of linguistic complexity varies with the role or competency of the child playing the role.

- "Will that be all? Your total is $5" or "All? Five!"
- "Milk, please" or "Milk."
- "Do you have any cereal?" or "Want cereal."

Adult Facilitory Role

The adult's role is to facilitate role play and to help expand language use. Emphasis on different sounds, structures, and/or vocabulary may be necessary depending on the child's needs and abilities. The adult(s) may model appropriate scripts, ask open questions, expand or recast a child's productions, redirect a child to request items from another child, use a modification of a cloze procedure to provide contrastive feedback, or provide confirmative feedback to a particular child.

ART ACTIVITY PLAN

Art: Food collage   **Date:** _____

Objectives:
1. To foster creativity
2. To foster small motor development (drawing, painting, *cutting*, *pasting*, etc.)
3. To increase vocabulary knowledge
4. To practice turn-taking skills
5. To converse with peers and adults

General Plan

Children cut out pictures of food from magazines or newspaper advertisements. The children then glue these pictures on round white paper plates (or construction paper) to make food collages. Children can choose from a variety of different food pictures. Older children can be helped to make pictures of the different food groups.

Supplies Needed

- Magazines (with pictures of food)
- Newspapers (food ads)
- White paper plates or construction paper
- Scissors
- Glue (or paste)
- Illustrations of the different food groups (optional—for older children)

GROUP ACTIVITY PLAN

Group: Big and little

Date: _____

Objectives:
1. To foster listening skills
2. To increase conceptual knowledge
3. To teach appropriate group interaction skills
4. To practice turn taking

Introduction

A big tub and a little tub are placed in front of the children. The teacher holds up a big object and a little object (e.g., a big toy horse and a little toy horse). The teacher then puts the big object in the big tub and the little object in the little tub. He or she then tells the children they are going to help sort some objects into big and little items.

Group Participation

The teacher holds up other items that are the same except for size and has different children put the items in the two tubs. They tell why they put the items where they did. ("I put it there because it is a big ____ or a little ____.") The class proceeds through several item pairs. A variety of sizes are available so the children begin to understand that it is the comparison between the items that determines whether something is big or little. (For later lessons, the terms large and small may be used.)

Summary/Transition Activity

Two children come to the front of the classroom and the rest of the children say who is big and who is little. The child who is little then sits down. Another child who is taller than the "big" child comes up. Then, the children decide who is bigger. Finally, an adult stands by the last child and asks who is bigger? (Another way would be to have the big child sit down and place a doll by the little child and ask, "Now who is bigger?") The teacher should be careful not to choose the smallest child in the class or a child who is particularly sensitive about his or her size.

Materials Needed

- Big tub
- Little tub
- Ten pairs of items of different sizes
- Doll (optional)

CURRICULUM: WEEKLY PLANNING GUIDE

Semester Theme: Discovering . . .

Weekly Theme: Transportation _____ **Week of:** _____

	Dramatic Play	Art	Story	Group	Music
Monday	Airplane	Paper airplanes	*We're Taking an Airplane Trip*	Circles	Airplane Song
Tuesday	Boats	Meat tray boats	*Mr. Gumpy's Outing*	Same and different	Row, Row, Row Your Boat
Wednesday	Cars (racing)	Car rubbings	*Wheels*	Letter "C"	C is for Cookie
Thursday	(Delivery) Trucks	Easel paintings	*The Truck Book*	Circle collage	Wheels on the Bus

Suggested Props and Materials:

Monday	*Dramatic play:* Dashboard for cockpit, airplane facsimile, chairs with "seatbelts," counter, tickets, suitcases, dishes, carts, trays . . . *Art:* Paper, markers, paper clips *Group:* Tape to make circles, circle cutouts
Tuesday	*Dramatic play:* Water table, wading tub, boats, miniature people, fishing poles (with magnets), paper fish (with paper clips) . . . *Art:* Styrofoam meat trays, Popsicle sticks, triangles, glue sticks *Group:* Five object pairs that are exactly the same, 10 other objects (e.g., dolls, balls, cars, blocks)
Wednesday	*Dramatic play:* Toy cars, ramps, race tracks, "garage," tape on floor for roads . . . *Art:* Paper, vehicle shapes, black crayons with paper removed (to be used in rubbing motion) *Group:* Cards with pictures of words that begin with "C," chalk, chalkboard, picture dictionary
Thursday	*Dramatic play:* Boxes (to be tied on as child becomes a delivery truck), small paper plates to be steering wheels, warehouse, "goods," gas stations, taped roads . . . *Art:* Easel, easel paper, brushes, tempera paint *Group:* Paper circles, poster paper with clown figure drawn hidden by construction paper, glue

CURRICULUM: DAILY PLANNING GUIDE

Theme: Transportation

Week of: _____

(Monday) Tuesday Wednesday Thursday

Dramatic Play	Art	Story	Group	Music
Airplane	Paper airplanes	*We're Taking an Airplane Trip*	Shapes—circle	Airplane Song

Language Skills Facilitated:

- **Vocabulary:** transportation, airplane, pilot, flight attendant, baggage, suitcase, take-off, landing, seat belt, security check, ticket, seat, passenger, beverage, cockpit . . .

- **Verb Phrase Structures:** fasten your seatbelt; land*s* the plane, *is* land*ing*, land*ed*; *flew* the plane; serv*ed* food; check*ed* baggage; who*'s* going on the plane? I *am* (uncontractible auxiliary verb), I*'m* flying (contractible auxiliary) . . .

- **Adjective/Objective Descriptions:** large plane, small plane, big suitcase, little bag, carry-on bag, blue __, red__, purple __ . . .

- **Pronouns:** I, you, he, she, we, they, my, your, her, his, our, their, me, us, them

- **Prepositions:** in, on, under, over, near, beneath, next to, beside, around, inside, outside

- **Sounds:** /l/ *l*ands, pi*l*ot, fi*ll*; /r/ *r*ide, ca*r*; /s/ *s*it, talk*s*; /k/ *c*arry, ti*ck*et, pa*ck*; /f/ *f*ive, o*ff* . . .

Social Skills Facilitated:

- **Initiating to peers and adults, responding to questions and requests from peers and adults**

- **Negotiating with peers for toys and materials**

- **Group cooperation:** waiting for a turn in a group, taking a turn

Cognitive Skills Facilitated:

- **Problem-Solving Skills:** how to fold paper to make an airplane

- **Classification Skills:** circle shapes

- **Sequencing Skills:** song, story

110

Motor Skills Facilitated:

- **Large Motor Skills:** outdoor play activities—jumping, running, hopping, pedaling, climbing

- **Small Motor Skills:** writing, drawing, glueing, *folding* . . .

DRAMATIC PLAY ACTIVITY PLAN

Dramatic Play: Airplane   **Date:** _____

Type of Activity: (Central)   Sequential   Related

Objectives:
1. To learn new, and employ familiar, vocabulary
2. To learn new, and employ a variety of, syntactic constructions
3. To interact with peers
4. To sequence familiar routines
5. To expand conceptual knowledge of the world

General Description of Activity

An airplane trip involves purchasing a ticket, checking baggage at the counter, going through a security check, and finally finding a seat on the airplane. Seatbelts must be fastened for take-off. Food and beverages are served by flight attendants. Upon arrival, baggage needs to be reclaimed at the baggage area. Carry-on luggage can be stored under a seat.

Setting

- Airport
- Ticket office or counter
- Airplane facsimile (chairs arranged in rows behind a "cab," where a play dashboard is set up)
- Kitchen
- Cockpit
- Baggage claim area (optional)
- Metal detector (optional)

Props

- Tickets
- Chairs with seatbelts (men's ties can be used for seatbelts)
- Dashboard
- Luggage
- Food and drinks
- Trays
- Carts
- Dolls
- Pretend money
- Dishes

Roles

- Pilot and copilot
- Flight attendants

- Passengers
- Clerks at the ticket counter
- Security people

Verbal Productions

Level of linguistic complexity varies with the role or competency of the child playing the role.

- "We're coming in for a landing so fasten your seatbelts" or "Plane's landing."
- "Do you want a drink?" or "Drink, please."
- "May I see your ticket?" or "Ticket?"

Adult Facilitory Role

The adult's role is to facilitate role play and to help expand language use. Emphasis on different structures and/or vocabulary may be necessary depending on the child's needs and abilities. The adult(s) may model appropriate scripts, ask open questions, expand or recast a child's productions, redirect a child to request items from another child, use a modification of a cloze procedure to provide contrastive feedback, or provide confirmative feedback to a particular child.

ART ACTIVITY PLAN

Art: Paper airplanes   **Date:** _____

Objectives:
1. To foster creativity
2. To foster small motor development (drawing, painting, cutting, *folding*, etc.)
3. To increase vocabulary knowledge
4. To practice turn-taking skills
5. To converse with peers and adults

General Plan

A paper airplane is begun by decorating the paper. Drawings or different colors and stickers can be used. The 8½-inch × 11-inch sheet of paper (different dimensions can be used) is then folded to make an airplane.

To make the airplane, follow these instructions:

1. Fold the paper in half lengthwise.
2. Fold a top edge down until it is even with the folded bottom to form a triangle shape.
3. Turn the paper over and fold the other side the same way so that one third of the paper is slanted and ending in a point.
4. Clip a paper clip to the point of the triangle. (A paper clip is used on the "nose" of the airplane to hold the plane together and to provide appropriate weight so the airplane will fly.)
5. Fold the rest of the top edge even with the bottom fold and make a crease.
6. Let go of the paper so it sticks out to make a wing.
7. Turn the paper over and fold the other side in the same way.

The paper airplane is then ready to fly. (Other paper folding can be done to form other styles of airplanes.)

Supplies Needed

- 8½-inch × 11-inch paper
- Markers or crayons
- Stickers (optional)
- Paper clips

GROUP ACTIVITY PLAN

Group: Shapes—circle   **Date:** _____

Objectives:
1. To foster listening skills
2. To increase conceptual knowledge
3. To teach appropriate group interaction skills
4. To practice turn taking

Introduction

Using colored tape, a large circle and a small circle are made on the floor in front of the children. Tracing around each shape with an index finger, the teacher names each circle as large or small. The teacher then holds up a cardboard circle (many are available) and says, "This is a circle—a large circle. I'm going to put it in the large circle area."

Group Participation

One at a time the children are then asked to place a cardboard circle in either the large or small circle area. Some of the children are asked to make circles in the air.

Note

Having two circle areas (large and small) allows the teacher to make different types of requests. One child can be asked to label the shape as a circle and helped to place it in the appropriate outline. Another child can be asked to identify the large circle and focus on both the shape and size of a cut-out. The activity, then, can be used to review the concept of large and small while the new concept of shapes is introduced.

Summary/Transition Activity

A circle cut-out and a square cut-out are held up and the children are asked to choose the circle. Then a circle cut-out and a triangle cut-out are held up and again the children are asked to identify the circle.

Variation

Similar activities can be done to introduce squares, and then triangles.

Materials Needed

- Colored tape
- Circle cut-outs in a variety of sizes
- Square cut-out
- Triangle cut-out

CURRICULUM: DAILY PLANNING GUIDE

Theme: Transportation

Week of: _____

Monday   (Tuesday)   Wednesday   Thursday

Dramatic Play	Art	Story	Group	Music
Boats	Meat tray boats	*Mr. Gumpy's Outing*	Same and different	Row, Row, Row Your Boat

Language Skills Facilitated:

- **Vocabulary:** sink, float, water, fish, boat, liner, rowboat, shark, sea, ocean, waves, swim, triangle, three sides . . .

- **Verb Phrase Structures:** *is* fish*ing*; catch*es*; float*ed*; *swam*; *has* a fish, *has gone* sailing; *rode* in a boat; who *is* going fishing, I *am* (uncontractible auxiliary); who *is* the biggest, I *am* (uncontractible copula) . . .

- **Adjective/Object Descriptions:** big __, little __, high water, low water, tiny __, green __, blue __ . . .

- **Pronouns:** I, you, he, she, we, they, my, your, her, his, our, their, me, us, them

- **Prepositions:** in, on, under, over, near, beneath, next to, beside, around, inside, outside

- **Sounds:** /f/ *f*ish; /s/ *s*ail, boat*s*; /l/ *l*ittle, pai*l*; /r/ *r*ow boat, fa*r*; /k/ *c*atch, sin*k*; /sh/ *sh*ip, fi*sh*

Social Skills Facilitated:

- **Initiating to peers and adults, responding to questions and requests from peers and adults**

- **Negotiating with peers for toys and materials**

- **Group cooperation:** waiting for a turn in a group, taking a turn

Cognitive Skills Facilitated:

- **Problem-Solving Skills:** what sinks and what floats

- **Classification Skills:** things that sink or float

- **Sequencing Skills:** songs

Motor Skills Facilitated:

- **Large Motor Skills:** outdoor play activities—jumping, running, hopping, pedaling, climbing . . .

- **Small Motor Skills:** writing, drawing, glueing, *fingerpainting* . . .

DRAMATIC PLAY ACTIVITY PLAN

Dramatic Play: Boats   **Date:** _____

Type of Activity: (Central)   Sequential   Related

Objectives:
1. To learn new, and employ familiar, vocabulary
2. To learn new, and employ a variety of, syntactic constructions
3. To interact with peers
4. To sequence familiar routines
5. To expand conceptual knowledge of the world

General Description of Activity

Children learn that boats are used on the water to travel from one place to another, and people often fish from boats. Toy boats, toy people, and toy sea animals can be used in the water table to represent boats on an ocean. A fishing boat area can be set up so that children can catch "fish." A cardboard box could be used to make a submarine for a boat that goes under the water. The activity could be extended by having a picnic and "cooking" the fish.

Setting

- Water table—filled with water
- Wading pool—filled with water
- Boat facsimile
- Fishing area—designated by blue cloth or a taped off area

Props

- Toy boats
- Toy people
- Various rubber sea animals (e.g., seals, whales, sharks, fish)
- Wooden or cardboard boat
- Blue satin sheet (optional)
- Paper fish (with paper clips attached)
- Fishing poles (with magnets attached to catch the fish)
- Pails
- Pretend grill (to cook the fish)
- Picnic items (basket, food, paper plates, utensils)

Roles

- Fishermen and women
- Captain of the boat
- Operator(s) of the toy boats, toy people, and toy animals

Verbal Productions

Level of linguistic complexity varies with the role or competency of the child playing the role.

- "I caught a fish" or "Fish."
- "My boat can float with all these people in it" or "My boat."
- "I'm the captain. You sit here" or "You sit."
- "It's sinking" or "Sink."

Adult Facilitory Role

The adult's role is to facilitate role play and to help expand language use. Emphasis on different sounds, structures, and/or vocabulary may be necessary depending on the child's needs and abilities. The adult(s) may model appropriate scripts, ask open questions, expand or recast a child's productions, redirect a child to request items from another child, use a modification of a cloze procedure to provide contrastive feedback, or provide confirmative feedback to a particular child.

ART ACTIVITY PLAN

Art: Meat tray boats _____ **Date:** _____

Objectives: 1. To foster creativity
2. To foster small motor development (drawing, painting, cutting, *pasting*, etc.)
3. To increase vocabulary knowledge
4. To practice turn-taking skills
5. To converse with peers and adults

General Plan

Styrofoam meat trays are placed on the art table along with Popsicle sticks, stickers or other decorations, construction paper, and glue. The children can decorate the trays. The pre-cut triangle-shape construction paper is glued to the stick to make a sail. The stick is then pushed into the middle of the styrofoam tray. The boat can be sailed in the lake (water table or tub filled with water).

Supplies Needed

- Styrofoam meat trays
- Popsicle sticks
- Stickers or other decorations
- Precut construction paper triangles
- Glue (or paste)
- Water table or tub filled with water (optional—the "lake")

GROUP ACTIVITY PLAN

Group: Same and different   **Date:** _____

Objectives: 1. To foster listening skills
2. To increase conceptual knowledge
3. To teach appropriate group interaction skills
4. To practice turn taking

Introduction

The teacher holds up two objects that are exactly the same and talks about what is the same about them. He or she then puts them into one "pile" or tub and holds up two new objects that are different from each other (e.g., a car and a boat). The teacher labels these as different and puts them in another "pile" or tub.

Group Participation

The teacher continues to present pairs of objects to the children and have each child decide whether a pair of objects is the same or different and place the objects in the appropriate pile or tub. The class should start out with objects that are exactly the same or are quite different from each other. Then, the class proceeds to objects that vary somewhat but that can still be labeled the same (e.g., different color cars). The teacher should focus on the fact that items can be the same even when they are alike in some ways, but are not necessarily alike in every way and explain that often things are the same if they can be labeled with the same word (e.g., cars).

Summary/Transition Activity

The teacher reviews the meaning of the words: *same* describes things that are alike in some way, and *different* describes things that are not alike.

Materials Needed

- Five exactly matched pairs of objects
- Ten other objects (e.g., cars, dolls, boats, balls)
- Two tubs (optional)

CURRICULUM: DAILY PLANNING GUIDE

Theme: Transportation
Week of: _____

Monday   Tuesday   (Wednesday)   Thursday

Dramatic Play	Art	Story	Group	Music
Cars (racing)	Vehicle rubbings	*Wheels*	Letter "C"	C is for Cookie

Language Skills Facilitated:

- **Vocabulary:** transportation, vehicle, car, track, ramp, garage, truck, win, lose, flag, start, finish, wheels, square . . .

- **Verb Phrase Structures:** go*es* fast, win*s* the race, crash*ed* the car, push*ed* it, *was* rac*ing*, start*s*, stopp*ed*, *won*, *were* los*ing*

- **Adjective/Object Descriptions:** race car, fast __, slow __, big/little __, yellow flag, checkered flag

- **Pronouns:** I, you, he, she, we, they, my, your, her, his, our, their, me, us, them

- **Prepositions:** in, on, under, over, near, beneath, next to, beside, around, inside, outside

- **Sounds:** /r/ *r*ace, sta*r*te*r*, *c*a*r*; /s/ *s*ee, mi*sses*, ra*c*e; /**sh**/ *sh*ape, fini*sh*; blends—*fl*ag, *tr*uck, *st*art

Social Skills Facilitated:

- **Initiating to peers and adults, responding to questions and requests from peers and adults**

- **Negotiating with peers for toys and materials**

- **Group cooperation:** waiting for a turn in a group, taking a turn

Cognitive Skills Facilitated:

- **Problem-Solving Skills:** how to set up tracks

- **Classification Skills:** vehicles/ nonvehicles

- **Sequencing Skills:** song, racing the cars, art

Motor Skills Facilitated:

- **Large Motor Skills:** outdoor play activities—jumping, running, hopping, pedaling, climbing . . .

- **Small Motor Skills:** writing, drawing, glueing, *rubbing* . . .

122

DRAMATIC PLAY ACTIVITY PLAN

Dramatic Play: <u>Cars (racing)</u>   **Date:** _____

Type of Activity: Central   Sequential   (Related)

Objectives: 1. To learn new, and employ familiar, vocabulary
               2. To learn new, and employ a variety of, syntactic constructions
               3. To interact with peers
               4. To sequence familiar routines
               5. To expand conceptual knowledge of the world

General Description of Activity

Tracks for cars to race on, areas for cars to be worked on, and areas for spectators are arranged for the car race. For this dramatic play, small Hot Wheel or Matchbox cars and tracks are used. Several tracks and cars are laid out, and children play the roles of drivers, mechanics, timers, and spectators. The activity could be expanded to include concession stands. (Electric tracks could also be used, particularly for children with physical disabilities so they could press the switches.) Cars can be raced by having children release two cars simultaneously and watch as they race down the tracks, which are elevated on one end.

Settings

- Three or four different track areas (one track area with two tracks elevated on one end and other tracks that form circles or ovals)
- Garage or pit area
- Spectator area
- Portable slide elevated on one end (optional—another track)
- Concession stand (optional)

Props

- Assortment of toy cars
- Tracks
- Electric tracks (optional)
- Checkered flag
- Play stop watch
- Tools (e.g., wrench, screwdriver, pretend batteries)
- Chairs for spectators
- Pretend drink machine
- Cups
- Pretend cotton candy (optional)

Roles

- Drivers
- Mechanics
- Timers or judges
- Spectators
- Concession stand workers

Verbal Productions

Level of linguistic complexity varies with the role or competency of the child playing the role.

- "Get your cars ready" or "Ready."
- "Your car needs a new engine" or "New car."
- "That car went very fast" or "Fast car."
- "I fixed it" or "Fix."

Adult Facilitory Role

The adult's role is to facilitate role play and to help expand language use. Emphasis on different structures and/or vocabulary may be necessary depending on the child's needs and abilities. The adult(s) may model appropriate scripts, ask open questions, expand or recast a child's productions, redirect a child to request items from another child, use a modification of a cloze procedure to provide contrastive feedback, or provide confirmative feedback to a particular child.

ART ACTIVITY PLAN

Art: Vehicle rubbings   **Date:**

Objectives:
1. To foster creativity
2. To foster small motor development (drawing, painting, cutting, pasting, *rubbing*, etc.)
3. To increase vocabulary knowledge
4. To practice turn-taking skills
5. To converse with peers and adults

General Plan

Various outlines of vehicles are cut out of cardboard. The children place these cut-outs under newsprint or tracing paper. Holding the chalk at both ends, children rub a crayon (with paper covering removed) over the paper, back and forth until the shape is slowly revealed. A variety of other cut-outs can be used to add to the picture.

Supplies Needed

- Precut cardboard vehicle cut-outs
- Newsprint or tracing paper
- Crayons (paper removed)
- Container to hold crayons
- Other cut-outs

GROUP ACTIVITY PLAN

Group: Letter "C"   **Date:** _____

Objectives: 1. To foster listening skills
2. To increase knowledge of the alphabet (C)
3. To teach appropriate group interaction skills
4. To practice turn taking

Introduction

The children are seated in a circle. The capital letter "C" and the lower case "c" are written on the blackboard. The teacher tells the children that there is something special about the letter "C." It has *two* sounds. Sometimes it says "kuh" and sometimes it says "sss." The teacher gives several examples of words that begin with "C." The teacher encourages the children to begin to look at the various alphabet pictures around the room.

Group Participation

The teacher asks if anyone's name starts with "C" (e.g., Carl). A child whose name begins with "C" comes to the blackboard and writes the letter "C" on the board. (If no one's name starts with "C," then the teacher has the leader-for-the-day come up.) Other children can practice writing "C" in the air with their fingers. The children are then asked if they can think of words that begin with "C." These words are written, and in some cases quick pictures of the suggested words are drawn on the blackboard. If a child suggests a word that does not begin with "C," he or she is told, "No, that begins with a __" and the sound is compared to "Kuh" or "sss."

If a child suggests a word that begins with "K," tell the child that the word starts with "K," but that "K" makes the same sound as one of the "C" sounds. (Do the same if a child suggests an "s" word.)

Picture cards of some C words could be available to hand out to children who do not know any words so that they can participate. A picture dictionary can be made available so that the teacher/children can look up more words that begin with "C."

Summary/Transition Activity

After about 10–15 words have been suggested, the teacher reviews the words, emphasizing the "kuh" or "sss" sound. An alternative to writing or drawing the words on a blackboard is to use large poster paper that can be kept for later review. The children should then get ready for music time.

Materials Needed

- Blackboard and chalk
- Alphabet pictures
- Picture cards with "C" words
- Picture dictionary
- Poster paper
- Markers
- Individual chalkboards (optional)

CURRICULUM: DAILY PLANNING GUIDE

Theme: Transportation

Week of: _____

Monday   Tuesday   Wednesday   (Thursday)

Dramatic Play	Art	Story	Group	Music
(Delivery) Trucks	Easel paintings	*The Truck Book*	Circle collage	Wheels on the Bus

Language Skills Facilitated:

- **Vocabulary:** delivery truck, warehouse, goods, load, gas station, gas pump, road, highway, ramp, park, slow, fast, rectangle . . .

- **Verb Phrase Structures:** load*s*; *was* stack*ing*; unload*ed*; deliver*s*; gas*es* up; back*ed* up; *drove*; who stopp*ed*?, I *did* . . .

- **Adjective/Object Descriptions:** big __, little __, heavy __, light __ . . .

- **Pronouns:** I, you, he, she, we, they, my, your, her, his, our, their, me, us, them

- **Prepositions:** in, on, under, over, near, beneath, next to, beside, around, inside, outside

- **Sounds:** /**k**/ *k*ey, ti*ck*et, tru*ck*; /**r**/ *r*oad, na*rr*ow, deliver; /**s**/ *s*end, out*s*ide, ga*s*; **blends**—*s*low, *s*tack, *tr*ip . . .

Social Skills Facilitated:

- **Initiating to peers and adults, responding to questions and requests from peers and adults**

- **Negotiating with peers for toys and materials**

- **Group cooperation:** waiting for a turn in a group, taking a turn

Cognitive Skills Facilitated:

- **Problem-Solving Skills:** how to load a truck

- **Classification Skills:** shapes

- **Sequencing Skills:** songs, story

Motor Skills Facilitated:

- **Large Motor Skills:** outdoor play activities—jumping, running, hopping, pedaling, climbing, painting . . .

- **Small Motor Skills:** writing, drawing, *painting* . . .

DRAMATIC PLAY ACTIVITY PLAN

Dramatic Play: (Delivery) Trucks   **Date:** _____

Type of Activity: (Central)   Sequential   Related

Objectives:
1. To learn new, and employ familiar, vocabulary
2. To learn new, and employ a variety of, syntactic constructions
3. To interact with peers
4. To sequence familiar routines
5. To expand conceptual knowledge of the world

General Description of Activity

Children learn that delivery trucks pick up goods and transport them to new locations and the goods are often stored in a warehouse. In this case, the children take turns being the trucks. As each child takes a turn being the truck, the trailer (a cardboard box) is tied around his or her waist. The children back up to the warehouse (Playskool house or other designated area). Other children load them up and then they drive around the room following the road (delineated by masking tape) until they reach the place where they are to unload (bookcases). An extension of this activity is to add a store area to receive the goods, police officers on motorcycles to make sure the drivers drive safely, or a gas station where they must gas up their trucks.

Settings

- Warehouse
- Loading areas
- Roads
- Various stores
- Gas station (optional)

Props

- Masking tape (to mark the road)
- Cardboard boxes
- Small lids or paper plates (steering wheels)
- Variety of goods (fruits and vegetables, toys, books, etc.)
- Motorcycles (optional—made from yardsticks with paper circles attached to both ends)
- Hose (optional—for gas)
- Pretend road signs
- Pad and pencil or crayon (to note shipments)
- Pretend money
- Cash register
- Police hat (optional)

Roles

- Drivers
- Warehouse workers
- Unloaders
- Store clerks
- Gas station/garage attendants (optional—see p. 196)
- Police officers (optional—see p. 226)

Verbal Productions

Level of linguistic complexity varies with the role or competency of the child playing the role.

- "I am ready to be loaded. Give me those boxes" or "Load up."
- "I want a table delivered tomorrow" or "Need a table."
- "You were going too fast. Here's your ticket" or "Too fast. Here's ticket."
- "Back your truck up . . . a little more . . . stop" or "Back up."

Adult Facilitory Role

The adult's role is to facilitate role play and to help expand language use. Emphasis on different structures and/or vocabulary may be necessary depending on the child's needs and abilities. The adult(s) may model appropriate scripts, ask open questions, expand or recast a child's productions, redirect a child to request items from another child, use a modification of a cloze procedure to provide contrastive feedback, or provide confirmative feedback to a particular child.

ART ACTIVITY PLAN

Art: Easel paintings   **Date:** _____

Objectives:
1. To foster creativity
2. To foster small motor development (drawing, *painting*, cutting, pasting, etc.)
3. To increase vocabulary knowledge
4. To practice turn-taking skills
5. To converse with peers and adults

General Plan

Easel boards are set up with two to four different colors of tempera paint in the painting cups. Each cup has its own paintbrush. (It is helpful to have cup covers with holes in them for the brushes. As the brushes are dipped into the paint and then pulled through the holes, some of the excess paint is removed.) Large sheets of paper are clipped to the easelboards.

The children put on their smocks and then paint shapes, objects, or anything else they want on large sheets of paper. Sometimes children will paint pictures and then experiment by painting other colors on top. Staff might have the children tell about their paintings. The painting can later be labeled for display. (The children should decide whether they want their paintings displayed.) An area should be designated for drying the pictures. A wooden clothes rack can be used to dry the pictures.

Notes

- It is helpful to place the easels over plastic or newspaper so that the drips won't stain the floor.
- This is a large muscle activity, particularly appropriate for children 3 years and older.

Supplies Needed

- Easels
- Easel boards
- Tempera paint (two to four colors per easel)
- Cups to hold the paint (one per color of paint)
- Large paintbrushes (one per color of paint)
- Large sheets of paper
- Smocks
- 12-inch × 18-inch or 18-inch × 24-inch paper
- Wooden rack or other area for drying
- Plastic or newsprint to place under the easels

GROUP ACTIVITY PLAN

Group: Circle collage   **Date:**

Objectives: 1. To foster listening skills
2. To increase conceptual knowledge
3. To teach appropriate group interaction skills
4. To practice turn taking

Introduction

The teacher holds up a piece of construction paper cut in the shape of a circle. She asks the children, "What shape is this?" After they respond "circle," she pastes the circle onto a big piece of poster board (at the bottom of the poster board a figure is drawn but is covered so that the children cannot see the person). The teacher then passes out one paper circle to each child.

Group Participation

The teacher asks one child what shape they have. When they say "circle," they can come up and past the circle onto the poster board. To make the activity more difficult for some children, have them label both color and shape or size and shape (have them compare their circle to another child's and decide if it is a big or little circle). After all of the children have pasted their circles, draw lines from each circle down to the figure's hand so that it looks as if the person is holding a lot of balloons. Remove the paper hiding the figure and show the children the collage.

Summary/Transition Activity

Count the number of circle (balloons) the clown is holding. Have the children put their chairs away and prepare for music.

Materials Needed

- Eighteen construction paper circles (different sizes and colors)
- Glue stick or paste
- Large poster paper with clown figure drawn at the bottom but covered
- Marker

~III~

ACTIVITY PLANS

The outline below provides a summary of the guidelines to be used in planning a language-focused curriculum. The guidelines focus on the selection of themes and the development of lesson plans for the dramatic play, art, and group activities. For specific elaboration on the guidelines, see Chapter 4.

OVERVIEW OF GUIDELINES

1. Choose a general **semester (or yearly) theme**.
2. Choose a **weekly theme** that meets the following requirements:
   - Can be sustained for a week (dramatic play activities adequate in number to support theme)
   - Is familiar to the children (particularly at the beginning of the year; later children's knowledge can be extended by having less familiar activities)
   - Does not require repeating a dramatic play activity more than once a month

- Requires no more than one sequential dramatic play activity (e.g., grocery store, picnic) per week

3. Choose **weekly dramatic play activities** that meet the following criteria:

   - Support the theme
   - Have at least four roles or related activities
   - Have appropriate props (or props that are easily made)
   - Allow different levels of participation
   - Are appealing and motivating to the children
   - Involve varying types of activities (i.e., central, sequential, related)
   - Include only one sequential activity per week

4. Choose **weekly art activities** that meet the following criteria:

   - Support the theme
   - Encourage creativity
   - Allow different levels of participation
   - Vary in art medium and materials employed
   - Emphasize process over product
   - Have varied motor skill demands or can be adapted to accommodate a variety of skill levels
   - Do not involve multiple steps (until later in the semester or year)

5. Choose **weekly group activities** that meet the following criteria:

   - Support the theme
   - Provide a balance among types of concepts addressed (e.g., classification, matching, sequencing, preacademic, safety)
   - Allow different levels of participation and skill levels

6. Choose **stories** that meet the following criteria:

   - Support the theme
   - Provide variation in type of story (e.g., fairy tale, adventure, labeling, repetitive line)
   - Appeal to children

7. Choose **music** that

   - Supports the theme and/or concepts being taught (e.g., color, shape, number)
   - Appeals to children
   - Provides movements or hand motions when appropriate
   - Varies in difficulty

USING PART III

As mentioned previously, this planning guide is designed to provide ideas and suggestions for planning a language-focused curriculum. The focus should be on making the preschool program interactive by incorporating suggested themes and activity plans, which are available for use at the staff's discretion. Staff can choose themes and particular dramatic play, art, and group activities to form the basis of the preschool day. However, because each preschool staff will have different needs and resources, the guides provided here are not comprehensive. In particular, it is suggested that staff develop their own daily plan that fits with their particular needs (see Chapter 5 for a 2-week curricular example). The following are suggestions for using the plans in this part:

1. Choose a weekly theme from the list provided on pages 135–137 (or develop a theme and add it to list), and note dramatic play activities associated with the theme.
2. Choose appropriate dramatic play activities from the listing on page 141, where

    -   Activities are listed alphabetically.
    -   More difficult dramatic plays are marked with an asterisk.

3. Choose appropriate art activities from the listing on page 141, where

    -   Activities are listed alphabetically according to type (i.e., construction, cutting, drawing, painting, pasting).
    -   More difficult activities are marked with asterisk.

4. Choose appropriate group activities from the listing on page 143, where

    -   Activities are listed in the following order: matching/labeling, classification, sequencing, life skills and safety, and preacademics.
    -   More difficult activities are marked with an asterisk.

5. Complete the daily planning guide in a manner appropriate to the setting (see the curricular examples in Chapter 5).
6. Collect all lesson plans for 1 week and file with weekly plan for easy access by all staff members. (Plans should be replaced in the planning guide when staff are finished with them.)

WEEKLY THEMES

THEMES	RELATED DRAMATIC PLAYS
Animals	Circus Farm Gardening Pet store/veterinarian Rodeo Jungleland/safari Scientist (bugs and birds) Zoo/zookeeper
Caring for ourselves, our world, and others	Babysitter Fishing/picnic Police officer Sanitation worker
Community helpers	Construction/repair Doctor/nurse Firefighter Library Newspaper carrier Paramedic Police officer Post office Sanitation worker Teachers Utility worker Veterinarian
Different homes	Camping Cinderella/castle House/apartment
The elements (air, earth, water, fire)	Sports (bubbles, balls, balloons, kites) Beach/gardening Firefighter Water play, boats, fishing
Exploring (explorers)	Boats Camping Fishing Jungleland/safari Pioneers Space travel
Family and friends	Amusement park Camping Sports House/apartment
Fill'er up (things that can be filled)	Mechanic Sports (balls/balloons) Water play

Hobbies	Camping
	Car racing
	Craft fair
	Fishing/picnic
	Pet store
	Sports
Investigating foods	Fast-food restaurant
	Fishing/picnic
	Grocery store
	Harvest (farm or garden)
	Pizza parlor
Occupations	Airplane
Places people go	Amusement park
Places people work	Car racing
	Department store
	Doctor/nurse
	Farm
	Grocery store
	Hair salon/barbershop
	Health clinic
	House/apartment
	Laundromat
	Library
	Mechanic (gas station)
	Motel
	Office worker
	Paramedic
	Pet store
	Restaurant
	School (bus)
	Zoo/zookeeper
Safety	Doctor/nurse
	Firefighter
	Mechanic (gas station)
	Police officer
	Utility worker
Seasons (fall, winter, spring, summer)	Harvest
	Cleaning, gardening
	Vacation, water play
Senses	Concert in the park—sound
	Fast-food restaurant—taste and smell
	Hair salon/barbershop—touch
	Pizza parlor—taste and smell
	Science—sound
	Water play—touch

Things big kids do	Babysitter
	Fast-food
	Newspaper carrier
	Swimming
Transportation	Airplane
	Boats
	Car racing
	Cruise ship
	Mechanic (gas station)
	School
	Space travel
	Trucks (delivery)
Vacations	Airplane
	Amusement park
	Beach
	Camping
	Cruise ship
	Jungleland/safari
	Motel
	Sports
	Water play

DRAMATIC PLAY ACTIVITIES

Airplane   148
* Amusement park   150

Babysitter   152
Beach   154
Beauty/barber shop   156
Boats   158

Camping   160
Car wash   162
Car (racing)   164
* Cinderella/castle   166
Circus   168
Cleaning (spring/fall)   170
* Concert/art in the park   172
Construction/repair   174
* Crafts fair   176
* Cruise ship   178

(Delivery) Trucks   246
* Department store   180
Doctor's office   182

Farm   184
Fast-food restaurant   186
Firefighter   188
Fishing/picnic   190
Fitness center   192

Gardening   194
Gas station/garage (mechanic)   196
Grocery store   198

Harvest (farm or garden)   200
Health clinic   202
House/apartment   204

* Jungleland/safari   206

Laundromat   208
* Library   210

Motel   212

* Newspaper carrier   214

Office worker   216

Paramedic   218
Pet store   220
* Pioneers   222
Pizza parlor   224
Police officer   226
Post office   228

Rodeo   230

* Sanitation worker   232
School (bus)   234
Scientist (bugs and birds)   236
* Scientist (water and air)   238
* Space travel   240
Sports   242

Television studio   244
Trucks (delivery)   246

* Utility worker   248

Veterinarian   250

Water play   252
Winter fun   254

Zoo/zookeeper   256

The activities listed here are marked according to their level of difficulty. Activities without any asterisks are considered the easiest, and activities with one asterisk * are considered somewhat difficult and may not be appropriate for the beginning of the school year or semester.

ART ACTIVITIES

The activities listed here are marked according to their level of difficulty. Activities without any asterisks are considered the easiest; activities with one asterisk * are considered somewhat difficult and children may need adult guidance; and activities with two asterisks ** are the most difficult so children will need adult guidance.

GROUP ACTIVITIES

The activities listed here are marked according to their level of difficulty. Activities without any asterisks are considered the easiest, and activities with one asterisk * are considered somewhat difficult and may not be appropriate for the beginning of the school year or semester.

DRAMATIC PLAY ACTIVITIES

DRAMATIC PLAY ACTIVITY PLAN

Dramatic Play: Airplane   **Date:** _____

Type of Activity: (Central)   Sequential   Related

Objectives: 1. To learn new, and employ familiar, vocabulary
2. To learn new, and employ a variety of, syntactic constructions
3. To interact with peers
4. To sequence familiar routines
5. To expand conceptual knowledge of the world

General Description of Activity

An airplane trip involves purchasing a ticket, checking baggage at the counter, going through a security check, and finally finding a seat on the airplane. Seatbelts must be fastened for take-off. Food and beverages are served by flight attendants. Upon arrival, baggage needs to be reclaimed at the baggage area. Carry-on luggage can be stored under a seat.

Settings

- Airport
- Ticket office or counter
- Airplane facsimile (chairs arranged in rows behind a "cab," where a play dashboard is set up)
- Kitchen
- Cockpit
- Baggage claim area (optional)
- Metal detector (optional)

Props

- Tickets
- Chairs with seatbelts (men's ties can be used for seatbelts)
- Dashboard
- Luggage
- Food and drinks
- Trays
- Carts
- Dolls
- Pretend money
- Dishes

Roles

- Pilot and copilot
- Flight attendants
- Passengers
- Clerks at the ticket counter
- Security people

Verbal Productions

Level of linguistic complexity varies with the role or competency of the child playing the role.

- "We're coming in for a landing so fasten your seatbelts" or "Plane's landing."
- "Do you want a drink?" or "Drink, please."
- "May I see your ticket?" or "Ticket?"

Adult Facilitory Role

The adult's role is to facilitate role play and to help expand language use. Emphasis on different structures and/or vocabulary may be necessary depending on the child's needs and abilities. The adult(s) may model appropriate scripts, ask open questions, expand or recast a child's productions, redirect a child to request items from another child, use a modification of a cloze procedure to provide contrastive feedback, or provide confirmative feedback to a particular child.

DRAMATIC PLAY ACTIVITY PLAN

Dramatic Play: Amusement park   **Date:** _____

Type of Activity: (Central)   Sequential   Related

Objectives: 1. To learn new, and employ familiar, vocabulary
2. To learn new, and employ a variety of, syntactic constructions
3. To interact with peers
4. To sequence familiar routines
5. To expand conceptual knowledge of the world

General Description of Activity

An amusement park has several rides and other activities in which the children can participate. In this dramatic play, the children often circulate among activities. Often there are concession stands where they can "purchase" items such as hot dogs. Some families bring picnics to the park, and some parks have trains for transportation from one area to another.

Settings

- Various rides (e.g., Sit & Spin, mini-trampolines)
- Ticket office
- Concession areas

Props

- Tickets
- Bowling ball and pins
- Bean-Bag Toss
- Pretend roller coaster (made from boxes)
- Target board and balls with Velcro adhesive so they stick to the target
- Pretend food (e.g., hot dogs, sodas, ice cream, cotton candy)
- Two cash registers
- Pretend money

Roles

- Customers
- Park workers (to run the games and the rides)
- Ticket sellers
- Concession stand workers

Verbal Productions

Level of linguistic complexity varies with the role or competency of the child playing the role.

- "I want a ride on the roller coaster, please" or "Want ride."
- "She needs a ticket" or "Ticket?"
- "It's his turn" or "Turn, please."

Adult Facilitory Role

The adult's role is to facilitate role play and to help expand language use. Emphasis on different structures and/or vocabulary may be necessary depending on the child's needs and abilities. The adult(s) may model appropriate scripts, ask open questions, expand or recast a child's productions, redirect a child to request items from another child, use a modification of a cloze procedure to provide contrastive feedback, or provide confirmative feedback to a particular child.

DRAMATIC PLAY ACTIVITY PLAN

Dramatic Play: Babysitter   **Date:** _____

Type of Activity: (Central)   Sequential   Related

Objectives:
1. To learn new, and employ familiar, vocabulary
2. To learn new, and employ a variety of, syntactic constructions
3. To interact with peers
4. To sequence familiar routines
5. To expand conceptual knowledge of the world

General Description of Activity

A babysitter takes care of babies and children. A babysitter feeds and bathes children, reads them stories, plays with them, takes them for walks, puts them to bed, and so forth.

Settings

- House(s)
- Park (optional)

Props

- Play stove
- Play refrigerator
- Tables and chairs
- Highchairs
- Cupboards, dishes, utensils, and bottles
- Pretend food
- Beds, blankets, and pillows
- Dolls
- Dolls' clothes
- Books
- Baby carriage
- Play bathtub
- Wash cloths and towels
- Pretend soap
- Bath toys (e.g., rubber duck)

Roles

- Babysitters
- Children
- Babies
- Parents

Verbal Productions

Level of linguistic complexity varies with the role or competency of the child playing the role.

- "It's time for bed, now" or "Bed, now."
- "The baby needs a bottle. Please get it from the table" or "Bottle!"
- "First, I'll read you the story, and then you go to bed" or "Story, bed"

Adult Facilitory Role

The adult's role is to facilitate role play and to help expand language use. Emphasis on different structures and/or vocabulary may be necessary depending on the child's needs and abilities. The adult(s) may model appropriate scripts, ask open questions, expand or recast a child's productions, redirect a child to request items from another child, use a modification of a cloze procedure to provide contrastive feedback, or provide confirmative feedback to a particular child.

DRAMATIC PLAY ACTIVITY PLAN

Dramatic Play: Beach _____ **Date:** _____

Type of Activity: Central   Sequential   (Related)

Objectives: 1. To learn new, and employ familiar, vocabulary
2. To learn new, and employ a variety of, syntactic constructions
3. To interact with peers
4. To sequence familiar routines
5. To expand conceptual knowledge of the world

General Description of Activity

A day at the beach usually involves playing with sand near a water or pretend water area. Small plastic pools can be filled with sand, and some seashells can be buried in the sand so that the children can dig for them. Other activities include playing sand volleyball, laying out on towels to get a tan, and riding in boats. A concession stand area or boardwalk may also be set up. Pretend surf boards made from cardboard could be used. Fishing from a boat could also be done.

Settings

- Blue sheet (or other demarcation) to represent a lake or filled water table
- Small plastic pools filled with sand
- Volleyball area with a taped line to represent the net
- Concession stand(s) or boardwalk
- Lifeguard stand

Props

- Pails and shovels
- Seashells
- Boats (boxes or rubber rafts)
- Lifejackets (plastic painting smocks worn backward)
- Fishing poles (with magnets attached to catch fish)
- Fish (with paper clips attached)
- Surf boards (pieces of sturdy cardboard)
- Megaphone (for lifeguard)
- Towels
- Pretend sunscreen
- Balloons (for use as volleyballs)
- Pretend food
- Pretend soda fountain (box lid with levers)
- Dishes
- Cash registers

Roles

- Sand diggers
- Sunbathers
- Surfers
- Beach vendors
- Customers
- Volleyball players
- Lifeguards
- Boat riders/fishermen and women

Verbal Productions

Level of linguistic complexity varies with the role or competency of the child playing the role.

- "Hit the balloon to me" or "Hit it."
- "I found a pretty shell" or "My shell."
- "He is riding the surf board and he didn't fall" or "Ride"
- "There's a shark! Get out!" or "Shark!"
- "She wants the shovel now" or "Her turn."
- "He will get an ice cream cone, and I will have a coke" or "Cone."

Adult Facilitory Role

The adult's role is to facilitate role play and to help expand language use. Emphasis on different structures and/or vocabulary may be necessary depending on the child's needs and abilities. The adult(s) may model appropriate scripts, ask open questions, expand or recast a child's productions, redirect a child to request items from another child, use a modification of a cloze procedure to provide contrastive feedback, or provide confirmative feedback to a particular child.

DRAMATIC PLAY ACTIVITY PLAN

Dramatic Play: Beauty/barber shop   **Date:** _____

Type of Activity: (Central)   Sequential   Related

Objectives:
1. To learn new, and employ familiar, vocabulary
2. To learn new, and employ a variety of, syntactic constructions
3. To interact with peers
4. To sequence familiar routines
5. To expand conceptual knowledge of the world

General Description of Activity

A beauty/barber shop is a place where people get their hair shampooed, cut, dried, and styled. In a hair salon, they also might get a manicure and in a barber shop, a shave. Children can use their fingers in a cutting motion to pretend to cut hair.

Settings

- Salon chair (use a high chair for dolls to sit in)
- Chairs (for children)
- Sink to "wash" hair
- Reception area with telephone, appointment book, and pencil or crayon
- Barber chair
- Manicurist table

Props

- Curlers and clips
- Combs (put children's names on the combs so they use only theirs, and disinfect at the end of play)
- Mirrors
- Fingernail polish bottles (filled with water)
- Pretend shampoo and conditioner
- Pretend hair spray
- Pretend hair dryer (made out of two toilet paper rolls and a cottage cheese container, with a twisted pipe cleaner to represent the cord)
- Plastic chips (razors)
- Shaving cream
- Smocks (typically used when the children paint)
- Pretend nail polish remover
- Nail files
- Towels
- Toy cash register
- Pretend money

Roles

- Customers
- Receptionist
- Beautician
- Barber
- Manicurist

Verbal Productions

Level of linguistic complexity varies with the role or competency of the child playing the role.

- "I'm washing her hair" or "Wash hair."
- "Do you want your hair to be cut?" or "Cut?"
- "Your hair is wet" or "Wet."
- "Cut my hair, please" or "Cut hair."
- "He is shaving" or "He shaved."

Adult Facilitory Role

The adult's role is to facilitate role play and to help expand language use. Emphasis on different sounds, structures, and/or vocabulary may be necessary depending on the child's needs and abilities. The adult(s) may model appropriate scripts, ask open questions, expand or recast a child's productions, redirect a child to request items from another child, use a modification of a cloze procedure to provide contrastive feedback, or provide confirmative feedback to a particular child.

DRAMATIC PLAY ACTIVITY PLAN

Dramatic Play: Boats _____ **Date:** _____

Type of Activity: (Central)   Sequential   Related

Objectives:
1. To learn new, and employ familiar, vocabulary
2. To learn new, and employ a variety of, syntactic constructions
3. To interact with peers
4. To sequence familiar routines
5. To expand conceptual knowledge of the world

General Description of Activity

Children learn that boats are used on the water to travel from one place to another and people often fish from boats. Toy boats, toy people, and toy sea animals can be used in the water table to represent boats on an ocean. A fishing boat area can be set up so that children can catch "fish." A cardboard box could be used to make a submarine or a boat that goes under the water. The activity could be extended by having a picnic and "cooking" the fish.

Settings

- Water table—filled with water
- Wading pool—filled with water
- Boat facsimile
- Fishing area—designated by blue cloth or a taped off area

Props

- Toy boats
- Toy people
- Various rubber sea animals (e.g., seals, whales, sharks, fish)
- Wooden or cardboard boat and submarine
- Paper fish (with paper clips attached)
- Fishing poles (with magnets attached to catch the fish)
- Pails
- Pretend grill (to cook the fish)
- Picnic items (basket, food, paper plates, utensils)
- Blue satin sheet (optional)

Roles

- Fishermen and women
- Captain of the boat
- Operator(s) of the toy boats, toy people, and toy animals

Verbal Productions

Level of linguistic complexity varies with the role or competency of the child playing the role.

- "I caught a fish" or "Fish."
- "My boat can float with all these people in it" or "My boat."
- "I'm the captain. You sit here" or "You sit."
- "It's sinking" or "Sink."

Adult Facilitory Role

The adult's role is to facilitate role play and to help expand language use. Emphasis on different sounds, structures, and/or vocabulary may be necessary depending on the child's needs and abilities. The adult(s) may model appropriate scripts, ask open questions, expand or recast a child's productions, redirect a child to request items from another child, use a modification of a cloze procedure to provide contrastive feedback, or provide confirmative feedback to a particular child.

DRAMATIC PLAY ACTIVITY PLAN

Dramatic Play: Camping _____ **Date:** _____

Type of Activity: (Central) Sequential Related

Objectives: 1. To learn new, and employ familiar, vocabulary
2. To learn new, and employ a variety of, syntactic constructions
3. To interact with peers
4. To sequence familiar routines
5. To expand conceptual knowledge of the world

General Description of Activity

Families sometimes go camping while traveling away from home. They might camp at a lake, in the mountains, or in a camping area. The people might sleep in tents or under the stars in sleeping bags. They might cook their food over a wood fire or pack a lunch and go hiking or fishing. The class might establish a "ranger station" so families can get maps to tell them where to camp.

Settings

- Campground
- Lake
- Mountains
- Hiking area
- Ranger station

Props

- Tent(s)
- Sleeping bags
- Campfire (wooden blocks)
- Grill
- Picnic items (e.g., basket, food, paper plates, utensils)
- Marshmallows (cottonballs on sticks)
- Boats
- Fishing poles (with magnets attached to catch the fish)
- Fish (with paper clips attached)
- Backpacks
- Maps
- Pretend forest animals (e.g., bears, raccoons, rabbits)

Roles

- Campers (family members)
- Fishermen and women
- Hikers
- Ranger

Verbal Productions

Level of linguistic complexity varies with the role or competency of the child playing the role.

- "I am packing a lunch for the picnic" or "Picnic."
- "Let's unroll our sleeping bags" or "Let's sleep."
- "Fix the tent, please" or "My turn, please."
- "John is walking too fast" or "Too fast."
- "You missed the trail" or "Missed it."

Adult Facilitory Role

The adult's role is to facilitate role play and to help expand language use. Emphasis on different structures and/or vocabulary may be necessary depending on the child's needs and abilities. The adult(s) may model appropriate scripts, ask open questions, expand or recast a child's productions, redirect a child to request items from another child, use a modification of a cloze procedure to provide contrastive feedback, or provide confirmative feedback to a particular child.

DRAMATIC PLAY ACTIVITY PLAN

Dramatic Play: Car wash _____ **Date:** _____

Type of Activity: (Central)   Sequential   Related

Objectives: 1. To learn new, and employ familiar, vocabulary
2. To learn new, and employ a variety of, syntactic constructions
3. To interact with peers
4. To sequence familiar routines
5. To expand conceptual knowledge of the world

General Description of Activity

People take their cars to a car wash to get them washed. Some car washes are automatic—the car is driven through and washed by machines. Boxes with both tops and bottoms cut off and with paper wheels attached to the sides can be the cars. The cars can be "driven" by the children who hold onto both sides of the box. At other car washes the customers use a hose to wash their cars by hand. The set up can be part of a gas station scenario or it can be an individual dramatic play setting. It might also be part of a car dealership dramatic play where the workers must keep the new cars clean.

Settings

- Car wash (a large open box with crêpe paper streamers hanging from the opening so the "cars" can be driven through the box and it emerges "washed")
- Hand car wash with hose area
- Road (marked by masking tape)
- Office
- Gas station (optional)
- Car dealership (optional)

Props

- Cars (medium-size boxes with the tops and bottoms cut off and paper wheels attached to the sides)
- Sponges
- Hoses (cardboard tubes)
- Pretend vacuum
- Pretend air pump
- Pretend soap
- Cash registers
- Pretend money
- Gas pumps (optional for gas station)
- Toy cars (optional for car dealership)
- Masking tape (to mark the road)

Roles

- Car wash attendants
- Drivers
- Customers
- Cashier
- Gas station attendant (optional for gas station)
- Salespersons (optional for car dealership)

Verbal Productions

Level of linguistic complexity varies with the role or competency of the child playing the role.

- "I want my car washed" or "Wash car."
- "My car sure is dirty" or "Dirty."
- "This car is next in line" or "Next."
- "It costs $5 to go through" or "$5, please."
- "She needs a new car" or "Need a car."

Adult Facilitory Role

The adult's role is to facilitate role play and to help expand language use. Emphasis on different structures and/or vocabulary may be necessary depending on the child's needs and abilities. The adult(s) may model appropriate scripts, ask open questions, expand or recast a child's productions, redirect a child to request items from another child, use a modification of a cloze procedure to provide contrastive feedback, or provide confirmative feedback to a particular child.

DRAMATIC PLAY ACTIVITY PLAN

Dramatic Play: Cars (racing)   **Date:** _____

Type of Activity: Central   Sequential   (Related)

Objectives: 1. To learn new, and employ familiar, vocabulary
2. To learn new, and employ a variety of, syntactic constructions
3. To interact with peers
4. To sequence familiar routines
5. To expand conceptual knowledge of the world

General Description of Activity

Tracks for cars to race on, areas for cars to be worked on, and areas for spectators are arranged for the car race. For this dramatic play, small Hot Wheel or Matchbox cars and tracks are used. Several tracks and cars are laid out, and children play the roles of drivers, mechanics, timers, and spectators. The activity could be expanded to include concession stands. (Electric tracks could also be used, particularly for children with physical disabilities so they could press the switches.) Cars can be raced by having children release two cars simultaneously and watch as they race down the tracks, which are elevated on one end.

Settings

- Three or four different track areas (one track area with two tracks elevated on one end and other tracks that form circles or ovals)
- Garage or pit area
- Spectator area
- Portable slide elevated on one end (optional—another track)
- Concession stand (optional)

Props

- Assortment of toy cars
- Tracks
- Electric tracks (optional)
- Checkered flag
- Play stop watch
- Tools (e.g., wrench, screwdriver, pretend batteries)
- Chairs for spectators
- Pretend drink machine
- Cups
- Pretend cotton candy (optional)

Roles

- Drivers
- Mechanics
- Timers or judges
- Spectators
- Concession stand workers

Verbal Productions

Level of linguistic complexity varies with the role or competency of the child playing the role.

- "Get your cars ready" or "Ready."
- "Your car needs a new engine" or "New car."
- "That car went very fast" or "Fast car."
- "I fixed it" or "Fix."

Adult Facilitory Role

The adult's role is to facilitate role play and to help expand language use. Emphasis on different structures and/or vocabulary may be necessary depending on the child's needs and abilities. The adult(s) may model appropriate scripts, ask open questions, expand or recast a child's productions, redirect a child to request items from another child, use a modification of a cloze procedure to provide contrastive feedback, or provide confirmative feedback to a particular child.

DRAMATIC PLAY ACTIVITY PLAN

Dramatic Play: Cinderella/castle   **Date:** _____

Type of Activity: (Central)   Sequential   Related

Objectives:
1. To learn new, and employ familiar, vocabulary
2. To learn new, and employ a variety of, syntactic constructions
3. To interact with peers
4. To sequence familiar routines
5. To expand conceptual knowledge of the world

General Description of Activity

The story about Cinderella or a more generic "king, queen, prince, and princess" activity may be enacted. In any case, one or two castles are needed. The children can dress up in fancy clothes and jewelry, wear crowns and hold scepters, go to a ball, ride on horses or in a carriage, sit on thrones, and so forth.

Settings

- Castles (including moats and drawbridges)
- Ballroom
- Roads (marked with masking tape)
- Throne room

Props

- Torn clothes
- Fancy clothes
- Jewelry
- Crowns
- Scepters
- Horses
- Carriages (stick horses and a box)
- Thrones
- Slippers (for Cinderella)
- Music

Roles

- Cinderella
- Stepmother
- Stepsisters
- Fairy godmother
- King
- Queen
- Prince

- Carriage drivers
- Knights
- Ball attendants

Verbal Productions

Level of linguistic complexity can vary with the role or competency of the child playing the role.

- "I don't have a dress. I can't go" or "No dress. Can't go."
- "May I have this dance?" or "Dance?"
- "Lift the drawbridge. We want in" or "Want in."
- "We danced a long time. It was fun" or "Dance. Fun."

Adult Facilitory Role

The adult's role is to facilitate role play and to help expand language use. Emphasis on different structures and/or vocabulary may be necessary depending on the child's needs and abilities. The adult(s) may model appropriate scripts, ask open questions, expand or recast a child's productions, redirect a child to request items from another child, use a modification of a cloze procedure to provide contrastive feedback, or provide confirmative feedback to a particular child.

DRAMATIC PLAY ACTIVITY PLAN

Dramatic Play: Circus _____ **Date:** _____

Type of Activity: Central   Sequential   (Related)

Objectives:
1. To learn new, and employ familiar, vocabulary
2. To learn new, and employ a variety of, syntactic constructions
3. To interact with peers
4. To sequence familiar routines
5. To expand conceptual knowledge of the world

General Description of Activity

A circus involves animal acts, clown acts, and acts of daring (e.g., tumbling, trick horseback riding, being on a trapeze). At the circus, children can watch the show, participate in the acts, or sell food and souvenirs. There may be parades, side shows, and a carnival strip.

Settings

- Circus rings/stages (Three hula hoops can be the rings.)
- Circus train/cages for animals
- Balance beam area
- Amusement area
- Spectator area
- Concession stand area
- Side show area (e.g., fortune teller's tent)

Props

- Stuffed animals
- Hula hoops
- Circus train or animal cages (made from boxes)
- Balance beam
- Clown costumes and wigs
- Other costumes and jewelry
- Deck of cards (for the fortune teller)
- Musical instruments (for the parade)
- Microphone (toilet-paper roll)
- Pretend food and drinks (e.g., cotton candy, ice cream, popcorn, hot dogs)
- Pretend cash register

Roles

- Animals
- Animal trainers
- Ring master
- Trapeze artists
- Other performers
- Audience members
- Concession workers
- Fortune teller

Verbal Productions

Level of linguistic complexity varies with the role or competency of the child playing the role.

- "Here he is, the great Bobby, doing his marvelous magic act!" or "Bobby do magic."
- "The lion is jumping through the hoop" or "Jump!"
- "She is walking on the balance beam" or "Walking."
- "He eats the ice cream fast" or "Eat ice cream."

Adult Facilitory Role

The adult's role is to facilitate role play and to help expand language use. Emphasis on different structures and/or vocabulary may be necessary depending on the child's needs and abilities. The adult(s) may model appropriate scripts, ask open questions, expand or recast a child's productions, redirect a child to request items from another child, use a modification of a cloze procedure to provide contrastive feedback, or provide confirmative feedback to a particular child.

DRAMATIC PLAY ACTIVITY PLAN

Dramatic Play: Cleaning (spring/fall) _____ **Date:** _____

Type of Activity: Central   Sequential   (Related)

Objectives:
1. To learn new, and employ familiar, vocabulary
2. To learn new, and employ a variety of, syntactic constructions
3. To interact with peers
4. To sequence familiar routines
5. To expand conceptual knowledge of the world

General Description of Activity

Spring (or fall) cleaning involves taking down or putting up window screens, washing windows, and fixing roofs. General spring (or fall) cleaning includes straightening shelves and cupboards, fixing walls, and putting things back neatly.

Settings

- House(s) with removable screens and roof (Playskool toys or handmade constructions from cardboard boxes)
- Household cupboards
- Play refrigerator
- Play stove and sink
- Extra room additions (cardboard added to extend house)

Props

- Window "screens"
- Cleaning supplies (e.g., mop, broom, dust pan, rags, vacuum cleaner)
- Shelves
- Pretend tools

Roles

- Mother
- Father
- Children
- Cleaning crew
- Roofer

Verbal Productions

Level of linguistic complexity varies with the role or competency of the child playing the role.

- "Could I please use that mop when you're finished?" or "Mop, please."
- "These windows need to be washed" or "Window dirty."
- "We fixed the roof with new shingles" or "Fix roof."

Adult Facilitory Role

The adult's role is to facilitate role play and to help expand language use. Emphasis on different structures and/or vocabulary may be necessary depending on the child's needs and abilities. The adult(s) may model appropriate scripts, ask open questions, expand or recast a child's productions, redirect a child to request items from another child, use a modification of a cloze procedure to provide contrastive feedback, or provide confirmative feedback to a particular child.

DRAMATIC PLAY ACTIVITY PLAN

Dramatic Play: Concert/art in the park   **Date:** _____

Type of Activity: Central   Sequential   (Related)

Objectives: 1. To learn new, and employ familiar, vocabulary
2. To learn new, and employ a variety of, syntactic constructions
3. To interact with peers
4. To sequence familiar routines
5. To expand conceptual knowledge of the world

General Description of Activity

A day in the park might include an outdoor concert and an art show. The children can play musical instruments or sell their art. The children could also go on a picnic, walk their dogs, or buy pretend food at a concession stand.

Settings

- A gazebo, or bandshell for the band (marked off with masking tape)
- Art exhibit area
- Concession stands
- Picnic area

Props

- Music stand
- Musical instruments
- Microphones
- Baton (for the director)
- Chairs for audience
- Easels or tables to display arts and crafts
- Pretend food and picnic basket
- Pretend cash register
- Pretend money
- Lemonade (The children can have a real lemonade stand.)
- Stuffed dogs
- Leashes

Roles

- Band members
- Director
- Audience members
- Art exhibit customers
- Artists
- Performance artists (e.g., mimes)
- Concession stand workers

Verbal Productions

Level of linguistic complexity varies with the role or competency of the child playing the role.

- "Bobby will sing the 'ABC Song'" or "Here's Bobby!"
- "Look at this one—lots of red! Would you like to buy it?" or "Buy this one."
- "He played the music too loudly!" or "Too loud."

Adult Facilitory Role

The adult's role is to facilitate role play and to help expand language use. Emphasis on different structures and/or vocabulary may be necessary depending on the child's needs and abilities. The adult(s) may model appropriate scripts, ask open questions, expand or recast a child's productions, redirect a child to request items from another child, use a modification of a cloze procedure to provide contrastive feedback, or provide confirmative feedback to a particular child.

DRAMATIC PLAY ACTIVITY PLAN

Dramatic Play: Construction/repair _____ **Date:** _____

Type of Activity: Central   Sequential   (Related)

Objectives: 1. To learn new, and employ familiar, vocabulary
2. To learn new, and employ a variety of, syntactic constructions
3. To interact with peers
4. To sequence familiar routines
5. To expand conceptual knowledge of the world

General Description of Activity

A construction/repair dramatic play involves putting together different materials to make buildings. A variety of materials can be used. One area can be set up for constructing buildings with Lego or other blocks. Another area can be designated for a new addition to the playhouse (using big boxes). A third area can utilize play bricks and boxes to make another house. The children can problem-solve how to construct houses or apartments by rearranging the boxes, bricks, and blocks. (Some of the houses could be doll size, while others could be big enough for the children to play in).

Houses may also need to be repaired. The roof can be replaced by making "shingles" out of paper bag strips. The strips could be laid on top of cardboard. (The children may be reminded to start at the outer edge and overlay the shingles so that "rain" will roll off the roof, not under the shingles.) The children can put new siding on a house by using strips of colored paper and glue, and wallpaper can be put on the inside of houses.

Settings

- Street (marked with masking tape) lined with houses made from a variety of materials (e.g., blocks, cardboard houses)

Props

- Playhouse
- Cardboard box additions that can be taped to the Playskool house
- Lego blocks
- Blocks
- Play bricks
- Paper strips of various colors for roof or siding
- Glue
- Tools (e.g., plastic hammers, wrenches, saws, screw drivers, screws)
- Tool belts
- Pegs for pounding (wooden clothespins that can be pounded into cardboard)
- Play hard hats
- Masking tape
- Telephones

Roles

- Carpenters
- Architects
- Home owners
- Other construction workers

Verbal Productions

Level of linguistic complexity varies with the role or competency of the child playing the role.

- "I'm building a big house" or "Me build house."
- "We need to make that side higher. Call the carpenter" or "Higher."
- "Look, I pounded the nail into the wall" or "Look."

Adult Facilitory Role

The adult's role is to facilitate role play and to help expand language use. Emphasis on different structures and/or vocabulary may be necessary depending on the child's needs and abilities. The adult(s) may model appropriate scripts, ask open questions, expand or recast a child's productions, redirect a child to request items from another child, use a modification of a cloze procedure to provide contrastive feedback, or provide confirmative feedback to a particular child.

DRAMATIC PLAY ACTIVITY PLAN

Dramatic Play: Crafts fair   **Date:** _____

Type of Activity: Central   Sequential   (Related)

Objectives: 1. To learn new, and employ familiar, vocabulary
             2. To learn new, and employ a variety of, syntactic constructions
             3. To interact with peers
             4. To sequence familiar routines
             5. To expand conceptual knowledge of the world

General Description of Activity

For an arts and crafts fair, a variety of activities are set up so that the children can make and sell their crafts. The children can string beads and/or macaroni for necklaces, fold paper into paper fans, weave with paper, paint pictures, do marble painting (i.e., marbles are dipped in paint and are allowed to roll back and forth on paper that has been placed in a shoe box lid), draw pictures, make stencils, and so forth. Other children can be customers—some of whom may make purchases while others merely browse. Concession stands may be available as well. Pretend cash registers are needed to make change. A band may play as well.

Settings

- Booths for the different craft exhibits
- Concession stands

Roles

- Crafts people
- Customers (Dolls may be included for children.)
- Concession stand workers
- Band members (optional)

Props

- Beads or macaroni and strings
- Marbles, box lids, and paint
- Construction paper (for folding fans)
- Construction paper strips (for paper weaving)
- Paint, paintbrushes, and paper
- Cups
- Pretend soda pop dispenser
- Pretend cotton candy or popcorn
- Play cash registers

Verbal Productions

Level of linguistic complexity varies with the role or competency of the child playing the role.

- "Look! Please buy my special necklace. I worked hard to make it," "Look!" or "Buy this?"
- "I am making a ____" or "I made a ____."
- "What are you making?" or "What doing?"

Adult Facilitory Role

The adult's role is to facilitate role play and to help expand language use. Emphasis on different structures and/or vocabulary may be necessary depending on the child's needs and abilities. The adult(s) may model appropriate scripts, ask open questions, expand or recast a child's productions, redirect a child to request items from another child, use a modification of a cloze procedure to provide contrastive feedback, or provide confirmative feedback to a particular child.

DRAMATIC PLAY ACTIVITY PLAN

Dramatic Play: Cruise ship   **Date:** _____

Type of Activity: (Central)   Sequential   Related

Objectives:
1. To learn new, and employ familiar, vocabulary
2. To learn new, and employ a variety of, syntactic constructions
3. To interact with peers
4. To sequence familiar routines
5. To expand conceptual knowledge of the world

General Description of Activity

When people go on a cruise ship, they sleep in cabins, eat at tables arranged like a restaurant, participate in a variety of activities such as swimming, playing shuffleboard, sunbathing, and buying things at the gift store. There are many people who work on a ship, including the captain, the purser, waiters and waitresses, the gift store salespeople, and the cruise ship doctor.

Settings

- Ship (large cardboard box that has been unfolded to form a "shell" around the classroom's kitchen area)
- Kitchen
- Helm
- Cabins (mats)
- Dining area
- Gift store
- Shuffleboard area
- Sunbathing area
- Pool area
- Water

Props

- Tickets
- Gang plank
- Suitcases
- Mats
- Tables
- Pretend food
- Shuffleboard sticks and pieces
- Sunscreen
- Sunglasses
- Jewelry (for the gift store)
- Dishes

- Pots and pans
- Rudder
- Captain's hat

Roles

- Passengers
- Captain
- Purser
- Waiters and waitresses
- Gift shop salespeople
- Ship's doctor

Verbal Productions

Level of linguistic complexity varies with the role or competency of the child playing the role.

- "He spotted a shark" or "Shark!"
- "I got an eight on the shuffleboard game" or "Eight."
- "He is swimming in the ocean" or "He swimming."
- "I am the captain. You must board now" or "Go now."
- "That's my suitcase" or "Mine."
- "She is turning the wheel fast" or "Fast."

Adult Facilitory Role

The adult's role is to facilitate role play and to help expand language use. Emphasis on different structures and/or vocabulary may be necessary depending on the child's needs and abilities. The adult(s) may model appropriate scripts, ask open questions, expand or recast a child's productions, redirect a child to request items from another child, use a modification of a cloze procedure to provide contrastive feedback, or provide confirmative feedback to a particular child.

DRAMATIC PLAY ACTIVITY PLAN

Dramatic Play: Department store _____ **Date:** Date _____

Type of Activity: (Central)   Sequential   Related

Objectives: 1. To learn new, and employ familiar, vocabulary
2. To learn new, and employ a variety of, syntactic constructions
3. To interact with peers
4. To sequence familiar routines
5. To expand conceptual knowledge of the world

General Description of Activity

In a department store, the children can choose from a variety of items, including many clothes. They can try on the clothes and then purchase them. Store clerks are needed to help the customers in purchasing the clothes and in hanging up clothes that are tried on but not purchased. Cashiers take the customers' money and/or credit cards.

Settings

- Department store
- Counters and racks
- Shelves and other display areas
- Dressing rooms
- Check-out area
- Elevator (optional)

Props

- Clothes, including shoes, belts, and ties
- Hangers
- Purses
- Mirror
- Pretend cash register
- Pretend money
- Pretend credit cards

Roles

- Clerks
- Customers (Dolls may be included for children.)
- Janitors
- Cashiers

Verbal Productions

Level of linguistic complexity varies with the role or competency of the child playing the role.

- "This dress is too big. I need a smaller size" or "Too big."
- "He is working at the cash register now" or "He there."
- "She has had a long turn. I want a turn now" or "My turn."

Adult Facilitory Role

The adult's role is to facilitate role play and to help expand language use. Emphasis on different structures and/or vocabulary may be necessary depending on the child's needs and abilities. The adult(s) may model appropriate scripts, ask open questions, expand or recast a child's productions, redirect a child to request items from another child, use a modification of a cloze procedure to provide contrastive feedback, or provide confirmative feedback to a particular child.

DRAMATIC PLAY ACTIVITY PLAN

Dramatic Play: Doctor's office   **Date:** _____

Type of Activity: (Central)   Sequential   Related

Objectives:
1. To learn new, and employ familiar, vocabulary
2. To learn new, and employ a variety of, syntactic constructions
3. To interact with peers
4. To sequence familiar routines
5. To expand conceptual knowledge of the world

General Description of Activity

A doctor's office with several examination rooms and a waiting room is set up. People call the receptionist and make appointments. When it is time for their appointments, they go into the examination room with the doctor. He or she examines them by looking into the mouth, ears, and eyes; checking reflexes; checking muscle tone; listening with the stethoscope; and so forth. A patient might have a broken bone that needs to be X-rayed, set in a cast, and wrapped with a bandage.

Settings

- Several examination rooms
- Waiting room
- Patients' "homes"

Props

- Table with a telephone and appointment book
- Several tables or mats to represent examination rooms
- Doctor kit collage (see p. 311)
- Bandages
- "X-ray" machine and chalk pictures (X-rays) (see p. 290)
- Telephone in area representing patients' "homes"

Roles

- Doctor
- Nurse
- Receptionist
- Patient
- Parent

Verbal Productions

Level of linguistic complexity varies with the role or competency of the child playing the role.

- "Open your mouth, please" or "Open mouth."
- "Where does it hurt?" or "Hurt?"
- "I don't feel good. My tummy hurts" or "I sick."

Adult Facilitory Role

The adult's role is to facilitate in the role play and to help expand language use. Emphasis on different sounds, structures, and/or vocabulary may be necessary, depending on the child's needs and abilities. The adult(s) may model appropriate scripts, ask open questions, expand or recast a child's productions, redirect a child to request items from another child, use a modification of a cloze procedure to provide contrastive feedback, or provide confirmative feedback to a particular child.

DRAMATIC PLAY ACTIVITY PLAN

Dramatic Play: Farm _____ **Date:** _____

Type of Activity: (Central)   Sequential   Related

Objectives:
1. To learn new, and employ familiar, vocabulary
2. To learn new, and employ a variety of, syntactic constructions
3. To interact with peers
4. To sequence familiar routines
5. To expand conceptual knowledge of the world

General Description of Activity

A farm often has animals such as cows, horses, pigs, and chickens. Different crops also may be grown on a farm. Some farms are dairy farms. Depending on the teacher's focus, different types of activities can be designed around the farm theme. For example, if the focus is on animals, then a barn and corral areas are needed. If the focus is on plants, then an area with soil in which to "plant" can be provided. For a focus on farm machinery, pretend tractors and other machinery should be available. A harvesting focus requires a variety of pretend crops. (Painted Ping-Pong balls can become apples to be harvested, particularly if Velcro can be attached so the balls will stick to a cardboard tree.)

Settings

- Farm house (Playskool house or dismantled cardboard boxes)
- Barn (Playskool house or dismantled cardboard boxes)
- Field (marked with masking tape or pretend fences)
- Planting area (a wading pool filled with sand or soil)

Props

- Pretend tractor
- Pretend machinery
- "Cow" to be milked (Latex gloves filled with milky water)
- Horses (yardsticks)
- Blocks for fencing
- Different farm animals (stuffed animals resembling horses, chickens, pigs, etc.)
- Hats
- Pretend seeds
- Scarecrow
- Trees (with removable Ping-Pong balls for fruit)

Roles

- Farmer(s)
- Farmer's helper(s)
- Different animals (The children can pretend to be animals.)
- Tractor operator
- Other machinery operators
- Milker (optional)
- Fruit pickers (optional)

Verbal Productions

Level of linguistic complexity varies with the role or competency of the child playing the role.

- "It's my turn to feed the chickens" or "Feed chickens."
- "I plowed the field and then planted the corn" or "I plowed the field."
- "He is milking the cow" or "Milk cow."

Adult Facilitory Role

The adult's role is to facilitate role play and to help expand language use. Emphasis on different structures and/or vocabulary may be necessary depending on the child's needs and abilities. The adult(s) may model appropriate scripts, ask open questions, expand or recast a child's productions, redirect a child to request items from another child, use a modification of a cloze procedure to provide contrastive feedback, or provide confirmative feedback to a particular child.

DRAMATIC PLAY ACTIVITY PLAN

Dramatic Play: Fast-food restaurant   **Date:** _____

Type of Activity: (Central)   Sequential   Related

Objectives: 1. To learn new, and employ familiar, vocabulary
2. To learn new, and employ a variety of, syntactic constructions
3. To interact with peers
4. To sequence familiar routines
5. To expand conceptual knowledge of the world

General Description of Activity

At a fast-food restaurant, people order food at a counter from a posted list of items. The cashiers ring up the food order on a cash register, the prepared food is then placed on a tray or in a bag. The food is paid for and either consumed on site or taken to be eaten somewhere else. Common food items are hamburgers, hot dogs, chicken sandwiches, roast beef sandwiches, french fries, salads, pizza, and so forth. Drinks may include soda pop, milk, coffee, milkshakes, and so forth. Often dishes and utensils are made of plastic or Styrofoam. People sit at tables or booths and usually bus their own dishes.

Settings

- Counter (or facsimile)
- Kitchen
- Eating area (booths or tables and chairs)
- Drive-up window (optional)

Props

- Cash register(s)
- Pretend money
- Dishes (plastic or Styrofoam)
- Soda pop dispenser (box lid with pretend levers)
- Posted menu
- Variety of pretend food (e.g., hamburgers, french fries)
- Pretend "Happy Meals" (small boxes with little toys and pretend food inside)
- Paper bags
- Trays
- Dolls
- Walkie-talkie for the drive-through cashier
- Pretend cars

Roles

- Customers
- Cooks
- Cashiers
- Janitors
- Drive-through cashier

Verbal Productions

Level of linguistic complexity varies with the role or competency of the child playing the role.

- "May I take your order?" or "Yes?"
- "I want a hamburger, french fries, and a Coke" or "Coke, please."
- "He is cooking the french fries now" or "Cooking, now."

Adult Facilitory Role

The adult's role is to facilitate role play and to help expand language use. Emphasis on different structures and/or vocabulary may be necessary depending on the child's needs and abilities. The adult(s) may model appropriate scripts, ask open questions, expand or recast a child's productions, redirect a child to request items from another child, use a modification of a cloze procedure to provide contrastive feedback, or provide confirmative feedback to a particular child.

DRAMATIC PLAY ACTIVITY PLAN

Dramatic Play: Firefighter _____ **Date:** _____

Type of Activity: Central (Sequential) Related

Objectives: 1. To learn new, and employ familiar, vocabulary
2. To learn new, and employ a variety of, syntactic constructions
3. To interact with peers
4. To sequence familiar routines
5. To expand conceptual knowledge of the world

General Description of Activity

A firefighter puts out fires. He or she stays at the firehouse and must be ready at a moment's notice to man the fire engine and rush to a fire. A siren is used to warn traffic to get out of the way so the firefighters can get to the fire. Children play firefighter by staying at a "firehouse," sliding down a pole, then getting in the "fire engine," arriving at the fire, and putting it out. Then they have to put the equipment away and go back to the firehouse. (When possible, real firefighters might come to the classroom to talk about their jobs and show their equipment.)

Settings

- Firehouse
- Dispatch office
- Houses (made from dismantled cardboard boxes)
- Roads (marked with masking tape)

Props

- Fire engine (made from boxes with cardboard tubes for hoses)
- Pretend fire hydrants
- Mats for beds
- Pole (optional)
- Hats and other uniform paraphernalia (Rubber painting smocks can be used for fireproof jackets.)
- Pretend telephones
- Microphones (toilet-paper rolls)
- Sirens (flashlights with siren)

Roles

- Firefighters
- Fire chief
- Fire engine driver
- Home owners
- Dispatch officers

Verbal Productions

Level of linguistic complexity varies with the role or competency of the child playing the role.

- "I'm the fire chief" or "Chief."
- "My house is on fire. Come to 124 Lawrence Street" or "Fire! Come!"
- "It's my turn to drive the truck" or "Turn, please."
- "We are sleeping at the firehouse in case there is a fire" or "Sleeping here."

Adult Facilitory Role

The adult's role is to facilitate role play and to help expand language use. Emphasis on different structures and/or vocabulary may be necessary depending on the child's needs and abilities. The adult(s) may model appropriate scripts, ask open questions, expand or recast a child's productions, redirect a child to request items from another child, use a modification of a cloze procedure to provide contrastive feedback, or provide confirmative feedback to a particular child.

DRAMATIC PLAY ACTIVITY PLAN

Dramatic Play: Fishing/picnic _____ **Date:** _____

Type of Activity: Central   (Sequential)   Related

Objectives: 1. To learn new, and employ familiar, vocabulary
2. To learn new, and employ a variety of, syntactic constructions
3. To interact with peers
4. To sequence familiar routines
5. To expand conceptual knowledge of the world

General Description of Activity

Children can pack their fishing equipment and a picnic basket and go to a lakeside park. There they can fish, cook what they catch, and eat their picnic lunch. When they are finished, they can clean up, pack up their supplies, and go home. (The adults need to be aware that the lake will need to be restocked and the picnic basket repacked so that the activity can continue.)

Settings

- Park
- Lake (blue sheet or a wading pool)
- Boat (Playskool house or dismantled cardboard box—optional)
- Bait shop (optional)

Props

- Fishing poles (with magnets attached to catch fish)
- Fish (with paper clips attached)
- Pretend bait
- Pretend cash register (optional—at the bait shop)
- Pretend money (optional—to buy the bait)
- Picnic baskets
- Pretend food
- Blankets
- Dishes
- Grill and blocks for campfire
- Trash can

Roles

- Fishermen and women
- Park ranger
- Children
- Bait shop clerk

Verbal Productions

Level of linguistic complexity varies with the role or competency of the child playing the role.

- "I caught a big fish" or "Big fish."
- "I like to go fishing with my dad. We go to the lake" or "Like fishing."
- "He has my pole. It is my turn" or "Mine."
- "We fished all day and caught 20 fish" or "Lots of fish."

Adult Facilitory Role

The adult's role is to facilitate role play and to help expand language use. Emphasis on different structures and/or vocabulary may be necessary depending on the child's needs and abilities. The adult(s) may model appropriate scripts, ask open questions, expand or recast a child's productions, redirect a child to request items from another child, use a modification of a cloze procedure to provide contrastive feedback, or provide confirmative feedback to a particular child.

DRAMATIC PLAY ACTIVITY PLAN

Dramatic Play: Fitness center _____ **Date:** _____

Type of Activity: (Central)   Sequential   Related

Objectives:
1. To learn new, and employ familiar, vocabulary
2. To learn new, and employ a variety of, syntactic constructions
3. To interact with peers
4. To sequence familiar routines
5. To expand conceptual knowledge of the world

General Description of Activity

A fitness center is a place where people exercise. There are many kinds of equipment, including stationary bikes and mini-trampolines. There are also areas to do aerobics and jog. Some centers have hot tubs, saunas, and swimming pools. The children can check in at the counter and then get on the equipment or do aerobic dancing. After exercising, they can go into the pool.

Settings

- Check-in counter
- Locker room
- Equipment area(s)
- Aerobic dancing area
- Pool
- Hot tub
- Sauna

Props

- Towels
- Stationary tricycles (mounted with front wheels off the floor so the front wheel is the only one to turn)
- Mini-trampoline
- Barbells (giant Tinker Toys or cardboard tubes)
- Other equipment, such as stepboards
- Wading pool or blue sheet (pool or hot tub)
- Check-in counter with pretend computer
- Music (for aerobic dancing)
- Mirror (for aerobic dancing)
- Costumes (sneakers, leotards, headbands, etc.)

Roles

- Fitness center attendants
- Customers
- Aerobics instructors
- Pool attendants
- Receptionist

Verbal Productions

Level of linguistic complexity varies with the role or competency of the child playing the role.

- "I jumped for 2 minutes" or "Jump."
- "He is riding the bike" or "He rides the bike."
- "She lifted the barbells high" or "Lift it."
- "My mommy does aerobics, and I go with her" or "My mommy go."
- "You have had a long turn. I want to ride the bike" or "My turn."

Adult Facilitory Role

The adult's role is to facilitate role play and to help expand language use. Emphasis on different structures and/or vocabulary may be necessary depending on the child's needs and abilities. The adult(s) may model appropriate scripts, ask open questions, expand or recast a child's productions, redirect a child to request items from another child, use a modification of a cloze procedure to provide contrastive feedback, or provide confirmative feedback to a particular child.

DRAMATIC PLAY ACTIVITY PLAN

Dramatic Play: Gardening   **Date:** _____

Type of Activity: Central   (Sequential)   Related

Objectives: 1.   To learn new, and employ familiar, vocabulary
2.   To learn new, and employ a variety of, syntactic constructions
3.   To interact with peers
4.   To sequence familiar routines
5.   To expand conceptual knowledge of the world

General Description of Activity

In a garden, the children can dig, plant seeds, and grow flowers or vegetables. Two or three large boxes (e.g., a refrigerator box) cut about 4–6 inches deep and filled with sand or soil makes a good garden. The children can use child-size gardening tools to prepare the sand or soil. Lima beans or other small objects (e.g., Lego blocks) make good "seeds." A seed and gardening store or a market for selling garden produce can be added to the play activity. (The adults need to be aware that the activity will need to be restarted after the plants have "grown" and have been "harvested.")

Settings

- Two or three garden areas
- Seed and gardening store (optional)
- Market (optional)

Props

- Two or three large boxes cut about 4–6 inches deep
- Sand or soil
- Child-size garden tools
- Gardening clothes (e.g., hats, gloves)
- Seeds or other small objects (e.g., lima beans, Lego blocks)
- Plants (e.g., pretend flowers and vegetables)
- Pails
- Watering can
- Counter (optional)
- Pretend cash register (optional)
- Pretend money (optional)

Roles

- Gardeners
- Store clerks (optional)
- Garden produce sellers (optional)
- Customers (optional)

Verbal Productions

Level of linguistic complexity varies with the role or competency of the child playing the role.

- "Do you have any flower seeds?" or "Seeds, please."
- "Do you have any shovels or pails?" or "Diggers?"
- "He is digging a big hole" or "Dig hole."
- "I want a large, round, orange pumpkin" or "Big pumpkin, please."

Adult Facilitory Role

The adult's role is to facilitate role play and to help expand language use. Emphasis on different structures and/or vocabulary may be necessary depending on the child's needs and abilities. The adult(s) may model appropriate scripts, ask open questions, expand or recast a child's productions, redirect a child to request items from another child, use a modification of a cloze procedure to provide contrastive feedback, or provide confirmative feedback to a particular child.

DRAMATIC PLAY ACTIVITY PLAN

Dramatic Play: Gas station/garage (mechanic)   **Date:** _____

Type of Activity: (Central)   Sequential   Related

Objectives:
1. To learn new, and employ familiar, vocabulary
2. To learn new, and employ a variety of, syntactic constructions
3. To interact with peers
4. To sequence familiar routines
5. To expand conceptual knowledge of the world

General Description of Activity

A gas station or garage is a place where vehicles can be repaired, gassed up, or tuned up. The oil in the car may need to be changed or the battery recharged. People can call ahead and make appointments. In one area, a receptionist/cashier desk is arranged. Another area can have a wooden or cardboard facsimile of a car with a hood that opens so that the mechanics can work under the hood if needed. Also, blocks or a vehicle erector set may be placed in one area to build cars. An optional activity is to have a parts counter or store.

Settings

- Garage/repair shop
- Desk
- Cashier's station
- Gas pumps
- Car lift (cardboard blocks holding a plastic truck high enough for a child to slide under)
- Parts counter or store (optional)

Props

- Appointment book and pencil or crayon
- Toy cash register
- Pretend money
- Hoses for pumps
- Car with hood, which can be made out of cardboard
- Dashboard
- Tools
- Pretend battery
- Pretend computer
- Pretend cans for oil change
- Play telephones
- Pretend parts to sell (optional)

Roles

- Mechanics
- Customers
- Receptionist
- Sales clerk
- Cashier

Verbal Productions

Level of linguistic complexity varies with the role or competency of the child playing the role.

- "May I please have the wrench?" or "Wrench, please."
- "Please start the car now" or "Start."
- "My car needs a new battery" or "Battery."

Adult Facilitory Role

The adult's role is to facilitate role play and to help expand language use. Emphasis on different sounds, structures, and/or vocabulary may be necessary depending on the child's needs and abilities. The adult(s) may model appropriate scripts, ask open questions, expand or recast a child's productions, redirect a child to request items from another child, use a modification of a cloze procedure to provide contrastive feedback, or provide confirmative feedback to a particular child.

DRAMATIC PLAY ACTIVITY PLAN

Dramatic Play: Grocery store   **Date:** _____

Type of Activity: Central   (Sequential)   Related

Objectives: 1. To learn new, and employ familiar, vocabulary
              2. To learn new, and employ a variety of, syntactic constructions
              3. To interact with peers
              4. To sequence familiar routines
              5. To expand conceptual knowledge of the world

General Description of Activity

The children pretend to be grocery shopping. They can make lists, take their "children" with them, choose the items on the list to put in their carts, pay, sack, and go home. Other children can be the grocery store workers. Some keep the shelves stocked, and others are checkers and baggers.

Settings

- Grocery store
- Shelves and aisles
- Check-out stand
- Customers' homes

Props

- Shelves
- Canned goods and other food items
- Fruit and vegetable area
- Pretend cash register
- Pretend money
- Pretend credit cards
- Pretend coupons
- Shopping carts
- Grocery bags
- Pencil and paper for making lists
- Table for checkout area

Roles

- Shoppers
- Cashiers
- Stockers
- Baggers

Verbal Productions

Level of linguistic complexity varies with the role or competency of the child playing the role.

- "Will that be all? Your total is $5" or "All? Five!"
- "Milk, please" or "Milk."
- "Do you have any cereal?" or "Want cereal."

Adult Facilitory Role

The adult's role is to facilitate role play and to help expand language use. Emphasis on different sounds, structures, and/or vocabulary may be necessary depending on the child's needs and abilities. The adult(s) may model appropriate scripts, ask open questions, expand or recast a child's productions, redirect a child to request items from another child, use a modification of a cloze procedure to provide contrastive feedback, or provide confirmative feedback to a particular child.

DRAMATIC PLAY ACTIVITY PLAN

Dramatic Play: Harvest (farm or garden)　　　　**Date:** _____

Type of Activity:　　Central　　Sequential　　(Related)

Objectives: 1.　To learn new, and employ familiar, vocabulary
2.　To learn new, and employ a variety of, syntactic constructions
3.　To interact with peers
4.　To sequence familiar routines
5.　To expand conceptual knowledge of the world

General Description of Activity

Different crops may be grown on a farm or in a garden. In the fall, these crops need to be harvested. A number of pretend crops should be available for the children to harvest. There may be a pumpkin patch (with paper or real miniature pumpkins for the children to pick) and/or a fruit tree with fruit (painted Ping-Pong balls attached to the "tree" with Velcro) to be picked. If possible, real corn stalks can be used so the children can harvest corn. An alternative is to let the children shell Indian corn into bowls. Small tractors and attachments (e.g., plow, combine) can be used in a large refrigerator box cut to 4–6 inches deep and filled with sand or soil so that the "fields" can be plowed. Another activity could include setting up a farmer's market where the produce could be sold.

Settings

- Farm house (Playskool house or dismantled cardboard boxes)
- Barn (Playskool house or dismantled cardboard boxes)
- Pumpkin patch (marked by masking tape or pretend fencing) with paper or real miniature pumpkins
- Fruit trees (cardboard "tree" shapes with painted Ping-Pong balls attached with Velcro)
- Planting area (sand or soil in a refrigerator box cut to 4–6 inches deep)
- Corn field area
- Farmer's market (optional)

Props

- Blocks for "fencing"
- Play farm machinery
- Scarecrow (optional)
- Cardboard tree (with removable painted "Ping-Pong" ball fruit)
- Paper or real, miniature pumpkins
- Indian corn and bowls to hold shelled corn or corn on stalks
- Other fall produce (real or pretend)
- Counters or stalls for the farmer's market (optional)

Roles

- Farmers
- Machinery operators
- People to pick pumpkins and other fruit
- Corn shellers or pickers
- Farmer's market vendors (optional)
- Customers (optional)

Verbal Productions

Level of linguistic complexity varies with the role or competency of the child playing the role.

- "It's my turn to drive the tractor" or "Drive tractor."
- "I plowed the field and then planted the corn," "I picked the apples," or "Apples."
- "He is picking the big pumpkin" or "Big pumpkin."

Adult Facilitory Role

The adult's role is to facilitate role play and to help expand language use. Emphasis on different structures and/or vocabulary may be necessary depending on the child's needs and abilities. The adult(s) may model appropriate scripts, ask open questions, expand or recast a child's productions, redirect a child to request items from another child, use a modification of a cloze procedure to provide contrastive feedback, or provide confirmative feedback to a particular child.

DRAMATIC PLAY ACTIVITY PLAN

Dramatic Play: Health clinic _____ **Date:** _____

Type of Activity: (Central)   Sequential   Related

Objectives: 1. To learn new, and employ familiar, vocabulary
2. To learn new, and employ a variety of, syntactic constructions
3. To interact with peers
4. To sequence familiar routines
5. To expand conceptual knowledge of the world

General Description of Activity

A health clinic consists of a waiting room and several examination rooms where a variety of health professionals see patients (e.g., doctors, nurses, ophthalmologists, audiologists). People call the receptionist and make appointments to be examined. The doctor or nurse examines the patient (a doll or another child) by looking into the mouth, ears, and eyes, checking reflexes and muscle tone, listening with the stethoscope, and so forth. Eyesight is tested by the reading of an eye chart. Pretend hearing tests can be done. A patient might have a broken bone that needs to be X-rayed, set in a cast, or wrapped with a bandage.

Settings

- Waiting room
- Examination rooms
- Patients' "homes"

Props

- Waiting room chairs
- Magazines for waiting room
- Toys for the waiting room
- Table with a play telephone, appointment book, and pencil or crayon
- Several tables or mats to represent examination rooms
- Doctor kit collage (see p. 311)
- Eye chart
- Pretend audiometer (box with knobs and earphones attached)
- X-ray machine and chalk pictures (X-rays) (see p. 290)
- Patients' "homes," including play telephones

Roles

- Doctors
- Nurses
- Ophthalmologist
- Audiologist
- X-ray technician
- Receptionist
- Patients
- Parents

Verbal Productions

Level of linguistic complexity varies with the role or competency of the child playing the role.

- "Open your mouth, please" or "Open mouth."
- "Where does it hurt?" or "Hurt."
- "I can see all of the letters" or "See letters."
- "I don't feel good. My tummy hurts" or "I sick."
- "Raise your hand when you hear the beep" or "Raise hand."

Adult Facilitory Role

The adult's role is to facilitate role play and to help expand language use. Emphasis on different structures and/or vocabulary may be necessary depending on the child's needs and abilities. The adult(s) may model appropriate scripts, ask open questions, expand or recast a child's productions, redirect a child to request items from another child, use a modification of a cloze procedure to provide contrastive feedback, or provide confirmative feedback to a particular child.

DRAMATIC PLAY ACTIVITY PLAN

Dramatic Play: House/apartment   **Date:** _____

Type of Activity: (Central)   Sequential   Related

Objectives:
1. To learn new, and employ familiar, vocabulary
2. To learn new, and employ a variety of, syntactic constructions
3. To interact with peers
4. To sequence familiar routines
5. To expand conceptual knowledge of the world

General Description of Activity

The housekeeping center is where the children can set up a pretend house or apartment, including a kitchen. Here the children can clean the house, take care of babies, cook food, set the table, make table decorations, and prepare for a party.

Settings

- Kitchen area
- Bedrooms
- Dining rooms
- Family rooms
- House (Playskool house or dismantled cardboard box—optional)

Props

- Play refrigerator
- Cupboards
- Play stove
- Play sink
- Dishes
- Pots and pans
- Beds
- Dolls
- Pretend food
- Baby bottles
- Mops and brooms
- Pretend vacuum
- Tablecloths (optional)
- Party decorations (optional)

Roles

- Mothers
- Fathers
- Babies and other children
- Party guests (optional)

Verbal Productions

Level of linguistic complexity varies with the role or competency of the child playing the role.

- "Clean the table" or "Clean."
- "Use the broom to sweep the floor" or "Sweep here."
- "I'll do it later" or "Okay."
- "The baby is hungry. Please get the bottle" or "Baby crying."
- "Do you want some more food?" or "Food?"
- "I'm glad you came" or "Hi, come in."

Adult Facilitory Role

The adult's role is to facilitate role play and to help expand language use. Emphasis on different structures and/or vocabulary may be necessary depending on the child's needs and abilities. The adult(s) may model appropriate scripts, ask open questions, expand or recast a child's productions, redirect a child to request items from another child, use a modification of a cloze procedure to provide contrastive feedback, or provide confirmative feedback to a particular child.

DRAMATIC PLAY ACTIVITY PLAN

Dramatic Play: Jungleland/safari _____ **Date:** _____

Type of Activity: (Central)   Sequential   Related

Objectives:
1. To learn new, and employ familiar, vocabulary
2. To learn new, and employ a variety of, syntactic constructions
3. To interact with peers
4. To sequence familiar routines
5. To expand conceptual knowledge of the world

General Description of Activity

A mock jungle is set up in the classroom with palm trees, vines, and a river. Various stuffed animals are available. A safari van can be used so that the children can pretend to take a tour. They can take pictures of the animals, pretend to be the animals, or be the tour guides and tell all about the animals they see. An extension of this activity is to make the jungle part of an amusement park scenario. Some of the children can be the workers at Jungleland and take tickets or feed the animals.

Settings

- Jungle (pretend palm trees and paper chain vines are hung around the dramatic play area)
- Safari van (a cardboard box in front of the Playskool house to make a cab area for the driver)
- River or pond (marked with tape or a blue sheet)
- Amusement park (optional)

Props

- Pretend palm trees (made from two pieces of tagboard stapled together over a pretend sign)
- Paper chains
- Variety of stuffed jungle animals
- Safari van (a cardboard box in front of the Playskool house)
- Play cameras
- Jungle pictures
- Food for animals
- Tickets for the safari van ride
- Pretend microphone for the tour guide
- Tour guide hat
- Pretend money
- Bridge over the river
- Concession stand (optional)
- Pretend rides for the amusement park (optional)

Roles

- Van driver
- Tour guide
- Passengers
- Animals
- Amusement park workers

Verbal Productions

Level of linguistic complexity varies with the role or competency of the child playing the role.

- "On the left, you see the big elephant, and on the right, the tiger" or "See tiger."
- "I want a ticket to ride on the van," "I want a ride," or "Ticket."
- "There is a baby elephant and a Mommy one" or "Baby."
- "I am the driver" or "It's my turn to drive."

Adult Facilitory Role

The adult's role is to facilitate role play and to help expand language use. Emphasis on different structures and/or vocabulary may be necessary depending on the child's needs and abilities. The adult(s) may model appropriate scripts, ask open questions, expand or recast a child's productions, redirect a child to request items from another child, use a modification of a cloze procedure to provide contrastive feedback, or provide confirmative feedback to a particular child.

DRAMATIC PLAY ACTIVITY PLAN

Dramatic Play: Laundromat **Date:** _____

Type of Activity: (Central) Sequential Related

Objectives:
1. To learn new, and employ familiar, vocabulary
2. To learn new, and employ a variety of, syntactic constructions
3. To interact with peers
4. To sequence familiar routines
5. To expand conceptual knowledge of the world

General Description of Activity

A laundromat is where people can use a variety of washing machines and dryers to do their laundry. Usually, quarters are inserted in slots to run the machines. Several large cardboard boxes can be cut so that they resemble washing machines and dryers. Important features of the machines include doors to open and close and a container, such as a bucket or tub inside the box, to hold the clothes. Plastic cups with a slit cut in the bottom of each could be mounted upside down on the boxes; the children could put quarters through the slits to make the machines "work." A waiting area could be set up with a soda pop machine. The dramatic play could be expanded to include a dry cleaner, where clothes can be dropped off, cleaned and pressed, and then picked up.

Settings

- Laundromat
- Waiting area
- Dry cleaner (optional)
- Homes (optional)

Props

- Washing machines (made from cardboard boxes with buckets or tubs inside to hold the clothes and plastic cups with slits cut in the bottoms mounted on top for coin collection)
- Dryers (made from cardboard boxes with buckets or tubs inside to hold the clothes and plastic cups with slits cut in the bottoms mounted on top for coin collection)
- Clothes
- Quarters or tokens (poker chips)
- Sink
- Laundry baskets
- Empty soap boxes
- Pretend dryer sheets
- Folding tables
- Irons and ironing boards
- Hangers

- Pretend money
- Play cash register
- Receipts (to pick up dry cleaning)
- Soda pop machine
- Magazines in waiting area

Roles

- Customers
- Cashiers
- Owner of laundromat
- Dry cleaners (optional)
- Janitor

Verbal Productions

Level of linguistic complexity varies with the role or competency of the child playing the role.

- "I need some soap for my dirty clothes" or "Need soap."
- "He is folding all of the shirts first" or "Fold shirts."
- "It's my turn to put the money in" or "My turn."
- "She ironed all of the dresses" or "My turn to iron."
- "Please, dry clean these clothes by tomorrow" or "Tomorrow."

Adult Facilitory Role

The adult's role is to facilitate role play and to help expand language use. Emphasis on different structures and/or vocabulary may be necessary depending on the child's needs and abilities. The adult(s) may model appropriate scripts, ask open questions, expand or recast a child's productions, redirect a child to request items from another child, use a modification of a cloze procedure to provide contrastive feedback, or provide confirmative feedback to a particular child.

DRAMATIC PLAY ACTIVITY PLAN

Dramatic Play: Library   **Date:** _____

Type of Activity: Central   (Sequential)   Related

Objectives:
1. To learn new, and employ familiar, vocabulary
2. To learn new, and employ a variety of, syntactic constructions
3. To interact with peers
4. To sequence familiar routines
5. To expand conceptual knowledge of the world

General Description of Activity

A library is a place where people can read books and magazines, look up items in a card catalog, and borrow books, magazines, and videotapes. The children can choose books, go to the counter, and check them out by having another child stamp a card with the picture of the book cover on it. Another child can put the card back in the book when it is returned. Children can sit in the reading room and look at books and magazines. Other children can put name cards in alphabetical order or pretend to. (Adults need to be aware that the books will need to be stacked back on the shelves in order to have the play activity continue.)

Settings

- Library with shelves for books, magazines, and videotapes
- Counter for checking out books
- Box for checked-in materials
- Reading room
- Office

Props

- Books
- Magazines
- Videotapes
- Rubber stamps and inkpads
- Card catalog (index card file)
- Index cards with pictures of the book covers
- Pretend computer
- Alphabet cards and other alphabet games

Roles

- Librarian
- Mothers
- Fathers
- Children (dolls or other children)
- Stacker (who puts returned materials back on the shelves)
- Sorter (who sorts card catalog entries)

Verbal Productions

Level of linguistic complexity varies with the role or competency of the child playing the role.

- "Do you want this book?" or "Book?"
- "Please find this book for me" or "That one."
- "This is a book on elephants" or "Elephants."
- "Stamp my card, please" or "Stamp, please."
- "He checked out a book about cars" or "My book."
- "This is the letter C" or "C."

Adult Facilitory Role

The adult's role is to facilitate role play and to help expand language use. Emphasis on different structures and/or vocabulary may be necessary depending on the child's needs and abilities. The adult(s) may model appropriate scripts, ask open questions, expand or recast a child's productions, redirect a child to request items from another child, use a modification of a cloze procedure to provide contrastive feedback, or provide confirmative feedback to a particular child.

DRAMATIC PLAY ACTIVITY PLAN

Dramatic Play: Motel _____ **Date:** _____

Type of Activity: (Central)   Sequential   Related

Objectives:
1. To learn new, and employ familiar, vocabulary
2. To learn new, and employ a variety of, syntactic constructions
3. To interact with peers
4. To sequence familiar routines
5. To expand conceptual knowledge of the world

General Description of Activity

A motel is a place people stay while they are on trips. People receive keys to rooms where there are beds, television sets, and telephones. Often there is a pool available. Sometimes there is a restaurant attached to the motel. Sometimes it is possible to order room service. Children can check in, go to their rooms, unpack their clothes, go out to eat, come back to their rooms, go swimming in the pool, make telephone calls, and then sleep. They can then awake, check out, and continue their trips. Sometimes people stay for several days in one motel.

Settings

- Check-in desk
- Different rooms with mats for beds
- Bathroom areas
- Pool
- Restaurant (optional)

Props

- Beds and pillows
- Play telephones
- Television sets (shoeboxes with a side cut out and a picture pasted over the cut-out area)
- Registration book
- Pretend cash register
- Pretend money
- Pretend credit cards
- Keys
- Dolls (for babies)
- Towels
- Toothbrushes
- Brooms and mops
- Restaurant tables
- Play dishes
- Pretend food

- Suitcases
- Clothes
- Blue sheet or wading pool (the "pool")

Roles

- Clerks
- Customers
- Maids
- Room service attendants
- Lifeguard
- Waiters and waitresses (optional)
- Cooks (optional)

Verbal Productions

Level of linguistic complexity varies with the role or competency of the child playing the role.

- "May I have a room, please?" or "Room?"
- "I'm going to call for tickets" or "I calling."
- "She cleaned this room yesterday" or "Clean room."
- "Do you want your room cleaned now?" or "Clean now."
- "No, I'm sleeping" or "No, sleep."

Adult Facilitory Role

The adult's role is to facilitate role play and to help expand language use. Emphasis on different structures and/or vocabulary may be necessary depending on the child's needs and abilities. The adult(s) may model appropriate scripts, ask open questions, expand or recast a child's productions, redirect a child to request items from another child, use a modification of a cloze procedure to provide contrastive feedback, or provide confirmative feedback to a particular child.

DRAMATIC PLAY ACTIVITY PLAN

Dramatic Play: Newspaper carrier   **Date:** _____

Type of Activity: (Central)   Sequential   Related

Objectives: 1. To learn new, and employ familiar, vocabulary
2. To learn new, and employ a variety of, syntactic constructions
3. To interact with peers
4. To sequence familiar routines
5. To expand conceptual knowledge of the world

General Description of Activity

A newspaper carrier is a person who delivers newspapers to various homes each day. The carrier folds the newspapers, puts them in his or her bag, and starts off to deliver to each address. It is important that the newspapers be delivered on the porch or placed in front of the door at each house or apartment. Each month, the carrier goes to the addresses to collect money to pay for the newspapers. The carrier also goes to the newspaper office each month to pay the bill for the number of papers delivered. The children pretend to be newspaper carriers by counting newspapers, folding them, securing them with rubber bands, and then delivering them to homes. They may have to call the newspaper office to have more papers delivered and collect money from the subscribers.

Settings

- Newspaper office
- Homes (Each home could be represented by a chair with a doll or another child. A mat placed in front of the chair could represent the porch.)
- Streets (marked with masking tape)

Props

- Bags (made by cutting two grocery bags in half, attaching straps so that there is a bag in front and a bag in back)
- Newspapers
- Rubber bands
- Homes (chairs with dolls or children seated in them and mats placed as the porches)
- Play money
- Route lists
- Play telephones
- Desk (for newspaper office)
- Paper and pencils

Roles

- Carriers
- Customers
- Office workers

Verbal Productions

Level of linguistic complexity varies with the role or competency of the child playing the role.

- "Here's your paper" or "Paper."
- "I need five more papers at 124 Lawrence Street" or "More paper."
- "He is collecting money for the newspaper. You owe $10" or "Money, please."

Adult Facilitory Role

The adult's role is to facilitate role play and to help expand language use. Emphasis on different structures and/or vocabulary may be necessary depending on the child's needs and abilities. The adult(s) may model appropriate scripts, ask open questions, expand or recast a child's productions, redirect a child to request items from another child, use a modification of a cloze procedure to provide contrastive feedback, or provide confirmative feedback to a particular child.

DRAMATIC PLAY ACTIVITY PLAN

Dramatic Play: Office worker   **Date:** _____

Type of Activity: Central   Sequential   (Related)

Objectives:
1. To learn new, and employ familiar, vocabulary
2. To learn new, and employ a variety of, syntactic constructions
3. To interact with peers
4. To sequence familiar routines
5. To expand conceptual knowledge of the world

General Description of Activity

People who work in an office often use computers or typewriters to write letters and reports. They sit at desks and answer telephones, have meetings, make notes, address and weigh envelopes, staple papers together, and so forth. They also put papers in file folders or notebooks. Some people dictate notes to others. There is often a receptionist who answers telephones and makes appointments.

Settings

- Offices
- Reception area
- Breakroom area
- Conference room
- Elevator

Props

- Desks and chairs
- Play telephones
- Papers
- Rubber bands
- Pretend stapler
- Lists
- Folders
- Pretend computers or typewriters
- Envelopes
- Stamps
- Scale
- Pencils or crayons
- Conference table
- Wastebaskets
- Mop and broom
- Pretend coffeemaker
- Pretend water cooler

Roles

- Receptionist
- Office workers
- Boss
- Janitor

Verbal Productions

Level of linguistic complexity varies with the role or competency of the child playing the role.

- "Here's your file" or "Need file."
- "I want a turn on the computer now" or "My turn."
- "He typed a 'J' for my name" or "J."
- "She stapled all of the papers" or "Staple papers."
- "That letter needs a stamp" or "Need stamp."

Adult Facilitory Role

The adult's role is to facilitate role play and to help expand language use. Emphasis on different structures and/or vocabulary may be necessary depending on the child's needs and abilities. The adult(s) may model appropriate scripts, ask open questions, expand or recast a child's productions, redirect a child to request items from another child, use a modification of a cloze procedure to provide contrastive feedback, or provide confirmative feedback to a particular child.

DRAMATIC PLAY ACTIVITY PLAN

Dramatic Play: Paramedic _____ **Date:** _____

Type of Activity: (Central)   Sequential   Related

Objectives:
1. To learn new, and employ familiar, vocabulary
2. To learn new, and employ a variety of, syntactic constructions
3. To interact with peers
4. To sequence familiar routines
5. To expand conceptual knowledge of the world

General Description of Activity

A paramedic often rides in an ambulance and is the first person to help after an accident or medical emergency. A pretend ambulance can be made from boxes or by using the Playskool house as the back of the ambulance and a box for the cab. Children can pretend to help others after an accident using doctor kits to treat the injured. A hospital can be set up so that the injured people can be taken to the hospital where doctors can treat them.

Settings

- Ambulance (a large box covered in white paper with a dashboard and a smaller box to form the cab or house)
- Hospital emergency room
- Roads (marked with masking tape)

Props

- Ambulance
- Play telephones
- Doctor kit collage (see p. 311)
- White coats
- Bandages
- Gurney
- Beds (mats)

Roles

- Dispatcher
- Paramedics
- Injured patients
- Ambulance driver
- Doctors
- Nurses
- Families of the patients

Verbal Productions

Level of linguistic complexity varies with the role or competency of the child playing the role.

- "I hurt my elbow. I think my arm is broken" or "I'm hurt."
- "I'm a paramedic. We'll take you to the hospital in the ambulance" or "Take to hospital."

Adult Facilitory Role

The adult's role is to facilitate role play and to help expand language use. Emphasis on different structures and/or vocabulary may be necessary depending on the child's needs and abilities. The adult(s) may model appropriate scripts, ask open questions, expand or recast a child's productions, redirect a child to request items from another child, use a modification of a cloze procedure to provide contrastive feedback, or provide confirmative feedback to a particular child.

DRAMATIC PLAY ACTIVITY PLAN

Dramatic Play: Pet store _____ **Date:** _____

Type of Activity: (Central) Sequential Related

Objectives: 1. To learn new, and employ familiar, vocabulary
2. To learn new, and employ a variety of, syntactic constructions
3. To interact with peers
4. To sequence familiar routines
5. To expand conceptual knowledge of the world

General Description of Activity

Children and adults buy pets at the pet store. There are a variety of pets (e.g., dogs, cats, birds, hamsters, turtles, fish) available on shelves and in cages. A clerk rings up sales on a cash register and is given money for the purchases. Children can then take the pets to their houses. Some of the workers in the store must care for the pets by feeding them and grooming them. Pretend pet food, leashes, collars, and pet toys can also be sold at the pet store. Different stuffed animals can be the pets or some of the children can pretend to be the animals.

Settings

- Pet store
- Counter
- Children's houses (Playskool houses or dismantled cardboard boxes)

Props

- Stuffed animals
- Pretend cash register
- Play money
- Pretend credit cards
- Shelves of pretend pet products (e.g., food, leashes, collars, toys)
- Cages
- Aquariums
- Bowls for food and water
- Brushes for grooming
- Pet carriers
- Pretend cleaning supplies
- Owners' cars (optional)

Roles

- Clerks
- Cashier
- Customers
- Animals

Verbal Productions

Level of linguistic complexity varies with the role or competency of the child playing the role.

- "How much is this doggy?" or "Buy doggy."
- "I need 5 pounds of cat food for Fuzzy" or "Cat food, please."
- "He is cleaning the dog's cage" or "Clean."
- "My turn to use the cash register" or "Mine."

Adult Facilitory Role

The adult's role is to facilitate role play and to help expand language use. Emphasis on different structures and/or vocabulary may be necessary depending on the child's needs and abilities. The adult(s) may model appropriate scripts, ask open questions, expand or recast a child's productions, redirect a child to request items from another child, use a modification of a cloze procedure to provide contrastive feedback, or provide confirmative feedback to a particular child.

DRAMATIC PLAY ACTIVITY PLAN

Dramatic Play: Pioneers   **Date:** _____

Type of Activity: (Central)   Sequential   Related

Objectives:
1. To learn new, and employ familiar, vocabulary
2. To learn new, and employ a variety of, syntactic constructions
3. To interact with peers
4. To sequence familiar routines
5. To expand conceptual knowledge of the world

General Description of Activity

Pioneers traveled by wagons or on horseback. They moved westward, settling new lands. All of their supplies, including farm animals, had to be taken with them. They camped each night and cooked over campfires until they reached their destination. Children can ride in pretend wagons or on stick horses. They can pretend to be the horses pulling the wagon. They can wear cowboy hats and boots or bonnets and long dresses. They can catch fish and then cook it over their campfires. They can play guitars and sing around their campfires or in the wagons.

Settings

- Wagons (made from cardboard boxes)
- Fishing area
- Camps

Props

- Wagons (made from cardboard boxes)
- Stick horses
- Cows and other farm animals (made out of brown paper bags)
- Wild animals (stuffed animals)
- Reins
- Dishes
- Pretend food
- Blue sheet (for lake or river)
- Fishing poles (with magnets attached to catch fish)
- Fish (with paper clips attached)
- Pots and pans
- Cowboy hats and boots
- Bonnets and long dresses
- Sleeping bags
- Guitars

Roles

- Mothers
- Fathers
- Children
- Animals
- Wagon train leader

Verbal Productions

Level of linguistic complexity varies with the role or competency of the child playing the role.

- "How far is it to the next camp?" or "How far?"
- "I need five fish for supper. Go catch some" or "Catch fish, please."
- "He is driving the wagon" or "Drive wagon."
- "My turn to play the guitar" or "My turn, now."

Adult Facilitory Role

The adult's role is to facilitate role play and to help expand language use. Emphasis on different structures and/or vocabulary may be necessary depending on the child's needs and abilities. The adult(s) may model appropriate scripts, ask open questions, expand or recast a child's productions, redirect a child to request items from another child, use a modification of a cloze procedure to provide contrastive feedback, or provide confirmative feedback to a particular child.

DRAMATIC PLAY ACTIVITY PLAN

Dramatic Play: Pizza parlor   **Date:** _____

Type of Activity: (Central)   Sequential   Related

Objectives:
1. To learn new, and employ familiar, vocabulary
2. To learn new, and employ a variety of, syntactic constructions
3. To interact with peers
4. To sequence familiar routines
5. To expand conceptual knowledge of the world

General Description of Activity

A pizza parlor is a restaurant where pizza is the main item on the menu. People are usually seated by a waiter or waitress and given menus. They then order pizzas with various toppings. Sometimes other items, such as spaghetti or bread sticks, are ordered. Children who are the cooks must construct the pizzas, which are then taken to the customers by the waiter or waitress. A pizza delivery van can also be used to deliver pizzas to homes.

Note

Real "pizzas" can be made at the snack table using English muffins as the crust. The children can add different toppings and the pizzas can be cooked in a microwave oven and eaten at snacktime.

Settings

- Restaurant kitchen
- Dining area
- Counter
- Carry-out window
- Salad bar (optional)

Props

- Tables and chairs
- Menus
- Pretend pizzas (plastic facsimiles or cardboard circles can be used for pizza crusts. A variety of cut-outs can be used to represent toppings, such as pepperoni, green peppers, and mushrooms. Pieces of yellow yarn can represent cheese. See p. 314.)
- Dishes and cups
- Trays
- Pretend soda pop dispenser
- Pretend cash register
- Pretend money

- Order form and pencils
- Delivery van (optional)
- Roads (marked with masking tape—optional)
- English muffins, real pizza toppings, and microwave oven (optional)

Roles

- Customers
- Waiters and waitresses
- Cashier
- Cooks
- Delivery van driver (optional)

Verbal Productions

Level of linguistic complexity varies with the role or competency of the child playing the role.

- "We have two kinds of pizza, pepperoni and cheese. Which do you want?" or "Which one?"
- "Cheese?" or "More pizza."
- "You ate my pizza" or "My pizza!"
- "You bought two pizzas and I bought one" or "One pizza."

Adult Facilitory Role

The adult's role is to facilitate role play and to help expand language use. Emphasis on different structures and/or vocabulary may be necessary depending on the child's needs and abilities. The adult(s) may model appropriate scripts, ask open questions, expand or recast a child's productions, redirect a child to request items from another child, use a modification of a cloze procedure to provide contrastive feedback, or provide confirmative feedback to a particular child.

DRAMATIC PLAY ACTIVITY PLAN

Dramatic Play: Police officer _____ **Date:** _____

Type of Activity: (Central) Sequential Related

Objectives: 1. To learn new, and employ familiar, vocabulary
2. To learn new, and employ a variety of, syntactic constructions
3. To interact with peers
4. To sequence familiar routines
5. To expand conceptual knowledge of the world

General Description of Activity

A police officer helps keep people safe. The police may be called to help find a lost child or help with a broken-down car on a road. By giving tickets, the police can make people drive at safe limits. The children can enact different scenarios. For example, police officers on motorcycles can stop those who speed or do not wear their seatbelts. Children can get separated from parents in the shopping area and need help. The police station can be set up as a place to bring the "lost" children and a place to pay the "tickets."

Settings

- Dispatcher's office
- Roads (marked by masking tape)
- Shopping areas
- Police station

Props

- Motorcycles (two paper plates together and affixed on each end of a yardstick)
- Tickets
- Pretend driver's licenses
- Pencils
- Traffic signs
- Play telephones
- Steering wheels (paper plates)
- Seatbelts (men's ties or string loosely tied around chairs)
- Microphones (for dispatcher's office)
- Walkie-talkies

Roles

- Police officers
- Police chief
- Parents
- Children
- Motorcycle riders
- Store clerks

Verbal Productions

Level of linguistic complexity varies with the role or competency of the child playing the role.

- "Where is your mommy?" or "Where Mommy?"
- "I don't know. I'm lost" or "I lost."
- "I've lost my child. Please help me" or "Help me."
- "You ran the stop sign, and I must give you a ticket" or "You went too fast."
- "I did not see the sign" or "Not see!"

Adult Facilitory Role

The adult's role is to facilitate role play and to help expand language use. Emphasis on different structures and/or vocabulary may be necessary depending on the child's needs and abilities. The adult(s) may model appropriate scripts, ask open questions, expand or recast a child's productions, redirect a child to request items from another child, use a modification of a cloze procedure to provide contrastive feedback, or provide confirmative feedback to a particular child.

DRAMATIC PLAY ACTIVITY PLAN

Dramatic Play: Post office _____ **Date:** _____

Type of Activity: Central   Sequential   (Related)

Objectives: 1. To learn new, and employ familiar, vocabulary
2. To learn new, and employ a variety of, syntactic constructions
3. To interact with peers
4. To sequence familiar routines
5. To expand conceptual knowledge of the world

General Description of Activity

A post office is a place where letters and packages are sorted and mailed and where stamps can be purchased. Mail carriers deliver the mail to various places—homes and business, for example. Children can bring envelopes and packages to mail, or they can buy stamps. Others can weigh the packages, cancel the stamps, sort the mail, or deliver the mail.

Settings

- Counter
- Houses (with mailboxes)
- Mailbox(es) at post office
- Sort area

Props

- Paper and pencils
- Envelopes
- Pretend computer or typewriter
- Stamps
- Inkpad and stamp
- Weighing machine
- Boxes
- Delivery bags
- Pretend cash register
- Pretend money
- Houses with mailboxes
- Mail truck

Roles

- Post office workers
- Mail carriers
- Customers
- Mail recipients

Verbal Productions

Level of linguistic complexity varies with the role or competency of the child playing the role.

- "I need a stamp, please" or "Stamp, please."
- "That weighs 2 pounds so you need to pay me $5" or "That will be $5."
- "Do you want to mail this letter?" or "Here's your mail."

Adult Facilitory Role

The adult's role is to facilitate role play and to help expand language use. Emphasis on different structures and/or vocabulary may be necessary depending on the child's needs and abilities. The adult(s) may model appropriate scripts, ask open questions, expand or recast a child's productions, redirect a child to request items from another child, use a modification of a cloze procedure to provide contrastive feedback, or provide confirmative feedback to a particular child.

DRAMATIC PLAY ACTIVITY PLAN

Dramatic Play: Rodeo   **Date:** _____

Type of Activity: Central   Sequential   (Related)

Objectives: 1. To learn new, and employ familiar, vocabulary
2. To learn new, and employ a variety of, syntactic constructions
3. To interact with peers
4. To sequence familiar routines
5. To expand conceptual knowledge of the world

General Description of Activity

A rodeo includes an arena where different types of cowboy activities take place. There is usually an opening ceremony in which the participants ride around the ring on their horses. Then different events occur, such as a barrel race, riding bucking broncos, and bull riding. A rodeo clown helps keep the bull or horses away from fallen riders. A judge decides whether a rider stayed on long enough to win. A barrel race could be set up using upside-down wastebaskets and stick horses. Children pretend to be horses or bulls, and dolls are used as riders. A separate area may feature a stationary horse set up for children to ride. Cowboy boots, hats, and vests should be available and a concession stand could also be set up.

Settings

- Arena
- Chute with gate that opens
- Barrel race area
- Judges' stand
- Spectator area
- Concession stand area (optional)

Props

- Stick horses (stuffed paper bag horse stapled onto a yardstick)
- Reins
- Clown costume
- Barrels (upside-down wastebaskets)
- Dolls (representing riders)
- Stationary horse with saddle
- Cowboy boots, hats, and vests
- Timer
- Judges' stand
- Awards for winners
- Soda pop dispenser

- Pretend cash register
- Pretend money
- Pretend food

Roles

- Announcer
- Rodeo clown
- Barrel race riders
- Rodeo participants
- Horses
- Bulls
- Audience members
- Judges
- Concession stand workers

Verbal Productions

Level of linguistic complexity varies with the role or competency of the child playing the role.

- "He stayed on the whole time. He gets 10 points" or "Ride long time."
- "I can go fast around the barrels" or "Fast."
- "He has had a long turn. It is my turn now" or "My turn."

Adult Facilitory Role

The adult's role is to facilitate role play and to help expand language use. Emphasis on different structures and/or vocabulary may be necessary depending on the child's needs and abilities. The adult(s) may model appropriate scripts, ask open questions, expand or recast a child's productions, redirect a child to request items from another child, use a modification of a cloze procedure to provide contrastive feedback, or provide confirmative feedback to a particular child.

DRAMATIC PLAY ACTIVITY PLAN

Dramatic Play: Sanitation worker   **Date:** _____

Type of Activity: Central   (Sequential)   Related

Objectives: 1. To learn new, and employ familiar, vocabulary
           2. To learn new, and employ a variety of, syntactic constructions
           3. To interact with peers
           4. To sequence familiar routines
           5. To expand conceptual knowledge of the world

General Description of Activity

Sanitation workers often ride a sanitation truck and pick up garbage around a town or area. Children can pretend to be sanitation workers who are picking up garbage from houses and from parks. The garbage is taken to a recycling (see p. 351) plant where it is sorted to be made into new things. A sanitation truck can be made out of a cart with wheels. Large bags can be attached so that the children can stop at a house, empty trash cans into the large bag, and then go on to the next house. If the cart is sturdy enough, some of the children can actually ride on it while others push it. When the large bag is full, the truck then goes to the plant to drop off the garbage. (The adults need to be aware that this activity will need someone to refill the wastebaskets so that the play activity can continue.)

Settings

- Sanitation truck (wheeled cart with large bags attached)
- Houses with wastebaskets
- Road (marked with masking tape)
- Recycling plant office
- Sorting area

Props

- Sanitation truck (wheeled cart with large bags attached)
- Wastebaskets
- Crunched-up "garbage" (newspaper)
- Plastic containers
- Aluminum cans
- Desks
- Telephones
- Boxes (for trash to be dumped into for sorting)

Roles

- Sanitation workers
- Home owners
- Truck drivers
- Workers at the recycling plant

Verbal Productions

Level of linguistic complexity varies with the role or competency of the child playing the role.

- "He picked up three trash cans, it's my turn" or "My turn."
- "I want to ride the cart, he has ridden it a long time" or "Ride long time."
- "We have three piles, one for cans, one for paper, and one for plastic" or "Three piles."

Adult Facilitory Role

The adult's role is to facilitate role play and to help expand language use. Emphasis on different structures and/or vocabulary may be necessary depending on the child's needs and abilities. The adult(s) may model appropriate scripts, ask open questions, expand or recast a child's productions, redirect a child to request items from another child, use a modification of a cloze procedure to provide contrastive feedback, or provide confirmative feedback to a particular child.

DRAMATIC PLAY ACTIVITY PLAN

Dramatic Play: School (bus)   **Date:** _____

Type of Activity: (Central)   Sequential   Related

Objectives:
1. To learn new, and employ familiar, vocabulary
2. To learn new, and employ a variety of, syntactic constructions
3. To interact with peers
4. To sequence familiar routines
5. To expand conceptual knowledge of the world

General Description of Activity

The school should be set up in imitation of the classroom. Various activities will be available, including name cards selection, alphabet cards, flannel board stories, books, writing materials, and so forth. A school bus is also set up. The children can board the bus, be driven to school, disembark, be checked in (the children playing the roles of staff check the "children's" throats to see if they are too sick to be in school), and then play the roles of teachers, staff, and children. When school is over, they can return home by riding on the bus again.

Settings

- School area (circle outlined on floor with masking tape)
- Bus (Playskool house with cardboard door that opens and closes and a box and dashboard in front to make the cab)
- Art area
- Quiet area (books and puzzles)

Props

- Name cards
- Alphabet cards
- Flannel board and flannel board stories
- Books
- Small blackboard
- Paper and pencils
- Art materials
- Flashlight (to use in check-in)

Roles

- Bus driver
- Children
- Teacher
- Staff members
- Principal

- School nurse
- Janitor
- Parents

Verbal Productions

Level of linguistic complexity varies with the role or competency of the child playing the role.

- "He wrote his name on the paper" or "Write name."
- "I am the bus driver. You need to sit down" or "Sit down."
- "I want to drive the bus. He has driven it for a long time" or "Drive bus."
- "What does this letter say?" or "What sound?"

Adult Facilitory Role

The adult's role is to facilitate role play and to help expand language use. Emphasis on different structures and/or vocabulary may be necessary depending on the child's needs and abilities. The adult(s) may model appropriate scripts, ask open questions, expand or recast a child's productions, redirect a child to request items from another child, use a modification of a cloze procedure to provide contrastive feedback, or provide confirmative feedback to a particular child.

DRAMATIC PLAY ACTIVITY PLAN

Dramatic Play: Scientist (bugs and birds)   **Date:** _____

Type of Activity: Central   Sequential   (Related)

Objectives:
1. To learn new, and employ familiar, vocabulary
2. To learn new, and employ a variety of, syntactic constructions
3. To interact with peers
4. To sequence familiar routines
5. To expand conceptual knowledge of the world

General Description of Activity

The children can pretend to be scientists, finding all kinds of insects, worms, and birds. The sand table or wading pool can be set up with pretend worms, ants, and other insects buried in the sand. Other children can look at the bugs under microscopes or through magnifying glasses. Binoculars can be used to locate birds throughout the classroom.

Settings

- Sand table or wading pool filled with sand
- Science laboratory

Props

- Sand table or wading pool filled with sand
- Plastic insects
- Shovels and pails
- Play microscope
- Slides
- Magnifying glasses
- Pretend binoculars (or two toilet-paper rolls taped together)
- Pictures of birds

Roles

- Laboratory scientists
- Field scientists
- Bird watchers

Verbal Productions

Level of linguistic complexity varies with the role or competency of the child playing the role.

- "He found a big bug" or "Big bug."
- "This is a microscope. I can see the bug" or "See bug."
- "She is digging in the sand" or "She found an ant."
- "The slide looks funny" or "Funny?"

Adult Facilitory Role

The adult's role is to facilitate role play and to help expand language use. Emphasis on different structures and/or vocabulary may be necessary depending on the child's needs and abilities. The adult(s) may model appropriate scripts, ask open questions, expand or recast a child's productions, redirect a child to request items from another child, use a modification of a cloze procedure to provide contrastive feedback, or provide confirmative feedback to a particular child.

DRAMATIC PLAY ACTIVITY PLAN

Dramatic Play: Scientist (water and air)   **Date:** _____

Type of Activity: Central   Sequential   (Related)

Objectives:
1. To learn new, and employ familiar, vocabulary
2. To learn new, and employ a variety of, syntactic constructions
3. To interact with peers
4. To sequence familiar routines
5. To expand conceptual knowledge of the world

General Description of Activity

The children can pretend to be scientists investigating water. A variety of experiments with water could be set up in the dramatic play area. The experiments could include mixing colored water and dripping water on various absorbent textures. The children can put drops of water on waxed paper, divide the droplets using a plastic chip, and then blow the droplets back together until they form a large droplet. The children can look at the droplets with a magnifying glass. Another activity could be transferring water from one container to another with sponges or using a microscope to look at slides.

Other science experiments might include those involving air. Balloons could be inflated, pinwheels made, fans used to blow things, paper airplanes made (see p. 274), and so forth.

Settings

- Colored water–mixing lab
- Droplet-cutting laboratory area
- Sponge area
- Microscope laboratory area
- Balloon area
- Fan area
- Paper airplane design area
- Other science laboratory areas

Props

- Bowls of colored water
- Mixing bowls
- Eye droppers
- Water
- Waxed paper
- Plastic chips
- Magnifying glasses
- Containers of water and sponges
- Microscope
- Slides

- Balloons
- Pinwheels
- Fans
- Paper airplanes

Roles

- Scientists at the microscope laboratory
- Scientists finding germs in slides
- Scientists conducting other experiments

Verbal Productions

Level of linguistic complexity varies with the role or competency of the child playing the role.

- "He mixed red and yellow and got orange" or "Orange."
- "This is a microscope. I can see the bug" or "See bug."
- "She is blowing the bubbles" or "See the big bubble."
- "I can blow the bubbles back together" or "Blow back."

Adult Facilitory Role

The adult's role is to facilitate role play and to help expand language use. Emphasis on different structures and/or vocabulary may be necessary depending on the child's needs and abilities. The adult(s) may model appropriate scripts, ask open questions, expand or recast a child's productions, redirect a child to request items from another child, use a modification of a cloze procedure to provide contrastive feedback, or provide confirmative feedback to a particular child.

DRAMATIC PLAY ACTIVITY PLAN

Dramatic Play: Space travel   **Date:** _____

Type of Activity: Central   Sequential   (Related)

Objectives:
1. To learn new, and employ familiar, vocabulary
2. To learn new, and employ a variety of, syntactic constructions
3. To interact with peers
4. To sequence familiar routines
5. To expand conceptual knowledge of the world

General Description of Activity

A rocket ship is used to travel in space. The children can pretend to be astronauts and go to the moon in a spacecraft. Once on the moon, they can find moon rocks, jump (on a mini-trampoline) to see how light they are, and so forth. Some of the children can remain on earth at the command center and talk to the astronauts. A brief videotape on the space program can be shown to the children so that they begin to understand about rocket ships, the need to wear special suits in space, and what the moon really looks like.

Settings

- Rocket ship (Playskool house with chairs placed sideways on the floor so the children lie in them and look upward)
- Command center (with pretend television sets and computers)
- Moon

Props

- Rocket ship (Playskool house with chairs placed sideways on the floor so the children lie in them and look upward)
- Helmets
- Backpacks
- Walking boards
- Moon rocks
- Mini-trampoline
- Television sets (shoe boxes with one side cut out and a picture pasted over the cut-out area)
- Microphones (toilet-paper rolls)
- Headsets
- Pretend computers
- Videotape about the space program
- Walkie-talkies
- Moon vehicle (optional)

Roles

- Astronauts
- Command center workers
- Technicians

Verbal Productions

Level of linguistic complexity varies with the role or competency of the child playing the role.

- "She found a big moon rock" or "Big."
- "I can jump high. Watch me!" or "Look!"
- "He is landing the rocket ship" or "He landed it."
- "You can see the earth. It is blue." "I see the moon."

Adult Facilitory Role

The adult's role is to facilitate role play and to help expand language use. Emphasis on different structures and/or vocabulary may be necessary depending on the child's needs and abilities. The adult(s) may model appropriate scripts, ask open questions, expand or recast a child's productions, redirect a child to request items from another child, use a modification of a cloze procedure to provide contrastive feedback, or provide confirmative feedback to a particular child.

DRAMATIC PLAY ACTIVITY PLAN

Dramatic Play: Sports   **Date:** _____

Type of Activity: Central   Sequential   (Related)

Objectives: 1. To learn new, and employ familiar, vocabulary
2. To learn new, and employ a variety of, syntactic constructions
3. To interact with peers
4. To sequence familiar routines
5. To expand conceptual knowledge of the world

General Description of Activity

Many people play a variety of sports as hobbies. This dramatic play focuses primarily on outdoor sports, such as baseball and soccer. (The older brothers and sisters of the preschoolers are often playing on summer teams.) A temporary baseball diamond is set up with only one base at first. A plastic ball and bat are used. A staff member pitches to a child, who attempts to hit the ball. Another staff member may have to help the child swing. If the child hits the ball, he or she runs to first base. Other children chase the ball and then throw it back to the pitcher.

Other children can play soccer by kicking the ball back and forth and trying to make a goal by kicking it into a large box.

Still other children can play hopscotch—hopping or jumping into and out of marked area. (A hopscotch diagram can be made on the sidewalk or it can be marked by laying yardsticks in the shape of rectangles on the grassy area.)

Settings

- Baseball diamond
- Soccer field
- Grassy area
- Sidewalk with hopscotch diagram

Props

- Plastic bat and ball
- Base at first on baseball diamond
- Mitts
- Rubber (soccer) ball
- Large box (for a soccer goal)
- Hopscotch diagram or chalk to make one on the sidewalk or playground

Roles

- Batters
- Catchers
- Fielders
- Umpire
- Referee
- Soccer players
- Hopscotch players

Verbal Productions

Level of linguistic complexity varies with the role or competency of the child playing the role.

- "She hit the ball hard" or "Hard."
- "I can hop. Watch me!" or "Look!"
- "He is kicking the soccer ball in the goal" or "He kicked it."
- "You hit a home run" or "I missed it."
- "Try again" or "Again."
- "This is fun" or "Fun."

Adult Facilitory Role

The adult's role is to facilitate role play and to help expand language use. Emphasis on different structures and/or vocabulary may be necessary depending on the child's needs and abilities. The adult(s) may model appropriate scripts, ask open questions, expand or recast a child's productions, redirect a child to request items from another child, use a modification of a cloze procedure to provide contrastive feedback, or provide confirmative feedback to a particular child.

DRAMATIC PLAY ACTIVITY PLAN

Dramatic Play: Television studio   **Date:** _____

Type of Activity: (Central)   Sequential   Related

Objectives:
1. To learn new, and employ familiar, vocabulary
2. To learn new, and employ a variety of, syntactic constructions
3. To interact with peers
4. To sequence familiar routines
5. To expand conceptual knowledge of the world

General Description of Activity

If possible, the children are shown a videotape featuring behind-the-scenes activities at a local television studio. The various roles of the director, producer, actors, and camera people are discussed. Stories that could be acted out are then suggested and described. Various props are available. The children then can go to the "studio," which has been arranged with "cameras," a stage, props, and an area for the technicians. A puppet show may also be performed. Children can pretend to videotape a show, act in a show, put on a puppet show, work with television equipment, and so forth.

Settings

- Stage
- Camera area
- Costume and prop area
- Dressing room
- Master booth (technician area)
- Puppet stage (optional)

Props

- Video cameras (plastic facsimiles or a video box with an attached paper towel roll, mounted on a tripod)
- Costumes
- Pretend make-up
- Scenery and props for story to be acted out
- Puppets
- Master board (a box with levers and buttons to represent a sound and videoboard)
- TV monitors (shoeboxes with a side cut out and a picture pasted over the cut-out area)

Roles

- Director
- Producer
- Actors
- Camera people
- Costume/prop director
- Make-up artist

Verbal Productions

Level of linguistic complexity varies with the role or competency of the child playing the role.

- "Stand there and pretend to be the wolf" or "You be wolf."
- "I'll huff and puff and blow your house in" or "Huff and puff."
- "Today we will have sunny weather" or "Sunny."
- "It's my turn to have the camera" or "My turn."

Adult Facilitory Role

The adult's role is to facilitate role play and to help expand language use. Emphasis on different structures and/or vocabulary may be necessary depending on the child's needs and abilities. The adult(s) may model appropriate scripts, ask open questions, expand or recast a child's productions, redirect a child to request items from another child, use a modification of a cloze procedure to provide contrastive feedback, or provide confirmative feedback to a particular child.

DRAMATIC PLAY ACTIVITY PLAN

Dramatic Play: (Delivery) Trucks _____ **Date:** _____

Type of Activity: (Central)   Sequential   Related

Objectives:
1. To learn new, and employ familiar, vocabulary
2. To learn new, and employ a variety of, syntactic constructions
3. To interact with peers
4. To sequence familiar routines
5. To expand conceptual knowledge of the world

General Description of Activity

Children learn that delivery trucks pick up goods and transport them to new locations and the goods are often stored in a warehouse. In this case, the children take turns being the trucks. As each child takes a turn being the truck, the trailer (a cardboard box) is tied around his or her waist. The children back up to the warehouse (Playskool house or other designated area). Other children load them up and then they drive around the room following the road (delineated by masking tape) until they reach the place where they are to unload (bookcases). An extension of this activity is to add a store area to receive the goods, police officers on motorcycles to make sure the drivers drive safely, or a gas station where they must gas up their trucks.

Settings

- Warehouse
- Loading areas
- Roads
- Various stores
- Gas station (optional)

Props

- Masking tape (to mark the road)
- Cardboard boxes
- Small lids or paper plates (steering wheels)
- Variety of goods (fruits and vegetables, toys, books, etc.)
- Motorcycles (optional—made from yardsticks with paper circles attached to both ends)
- Hose (optional—for gas)
- Pretend road signs
- Pad and pencil or crayon (to note shipments)
- Pretend money
- Cash register
- Police hat (optional)

Roles

- Drivers
- Warehouse workers
- Unloaders
- Store clerks
- Gas station/garage attendants (optional—see p. 196)
- Police officers (optional—see p. 226)

Verbal Productions

Level of linguistic complexity varies with the role or competency of the child playing the role.

- "I am ready to be loaded. Give me those boxes" or "Load up."
- "I want a table delivered tomorrow" or "Need a table."
- "You were going too fast. Here's your ticket" or "Too fast. Here's ticket."
- "Back your truck up . . . a little more . . . stop" or "Back up."

Adult Facilitory Role

The adult's role is to facilitate role play and to help expand language use. Emphasis on different structures and/or vocabulary may be necessary depending on the child's needs and abilities. The adult(s) may model appropriate scripts, ask open questions, expand or recast a child's productions, redirect a child to request items from another child, use a modification of a cloze procedure to provide contrastive feedback, or provide confirmative feedback to a particular child.

DRAMATIC PLAY ACTIVITY PLAN

Dramatic Play: Utility worker   **Date:** _____

Type of Activity: Central   Sequential   (Related)

Objectives: 1. To learn new, and employ familiar, vocabulary
2. To learn new, and employ a variety of, syntactic constructions
3. To interact with peers
4. To sequence familiar routines
5. To expand conceptual knowledge of the world

General Description of Activity

A utility worker maintains and repairs telephone lines, electric wires, or gas lines. (If possible, a utility worker might visit the classroom and describe his or her job.) One area of the classroom can be designated as a new subdivision. Gas lines (cardboard tubes) need to be laid, telephone and electric wires need to be strung, and so forth. The tubes can be laid under a throw rug so that they seem to be underground. The wires can be strung between poles made of the giant Tinker Toys. Another area can be set up for a pretend emergency; the utility workers come out to make repairs. Another aspect of the activity could be an office area where the receptionist answers the telephones and then calls the workers to tell them where they should go.

Settings

- New subdivision area
- Office area
- Roads (marked with masking tape)
- Truck

Props

- Cardboard tubes (gas pipes)
- Throw rug (to represent the ground)
- Yarn or string
- Giant Tinker Toys (to represent telephone poles)
- Tools (e.g., hammer, pliers)
- Tool belts
- Utility truck (made from dismantled cardboard boxes)
- Play telephone
- Desk

Roles

- Various utility workers
- Customers
- Drivers
- Receptionist

Verbal Productions

Level of linguistic complexity varies with the role or competency of the child playing the role.

- "You need a new gas line here. Let me call the office for a truck," "You need gas line," or "New line."
- "The phone doesn't work" or "Phone broken."
- "He laid the new pipe" or "New pipe."

Adult Facilitory Role

The adult's role is to facilitate role play and to help expand language use. Emphasis on different structures and/or vocabulary may be necessary depending on the child's needs and abilities. The adult(s) may model appropriate scripts, ask open questions, expand or recast a child's productions, redirect a child to request items from another child, use a modification of a cloze procedure to provide contrastive feedback, or provide confirmative feedback to a particular child.

DRAMATIC PLAY ACTIVITY PLAN

Dramatic Play: Veterinarian   **Date:** _____

Type of Activity: (Central)   Sequential   Related

Objectives:
1. To learn new, and employ familiar, vocabulary
2. To learn new, and employ a variety of, syntactic constructions
3. To interact with peers
4. To sequence familiar routines
5. To expand conceptual knowledge of the world

General Description of Activity

A veterinarian is a doctor for animals. People bring sick or injured animals to the veterinarian for treatment. There is often a waiting room with a receptionist. The veterinarian's office includes an examining table, a sink, a number of pet supplies, medicines, syringes, cotton balls, and other medical supplies. Often there are cages located in different areas of the office for animals that must stay overnight.

Settings

- Reception/waiting area
- Examining rooms
- Cages/kennels

Props

- Chairs in the reception area
- Reception desk
- Play telephone
- Doctor kit collage (see p. 311)
- White coats
- Stuffed animals
- Pet food
- X-ray machine
- Chalk pictures (X-rays) (see p. 290)
- Pretend cash register
- Pretend money

Roles

- Veterinarians
- Receptionist
- Customers
- Animals
- Kennel attendants

Verbal Productions

Level of linguistic complexity varies with the role or competency of the child playing the role.

- "What is wrong with your cat?" or "What matter?"
- "Cat sick" or "He needs a shot."
- "Your dog needs some stitches" or "Need stitches."
- "Your cat has fleas and needs a flea bath," "Fleas," or "Needs bath."
- "The doctor will see you now" or "You're next."

Adult Facilitory Role

The adult's role is to facilitate role play and to help expand language use. Emphasis on different structures and/or vocabulary may be necessary depending on the child's needs and abilities. The adult(s) may model appropriate scripts, ask open questions, expand or recast a child's productions, redirect a child to request items from another child, use a modification of a cloze procedure to provide contrastive feedback, or provide confirmative feedback to a particular child.

DRAMATIC PLAY ACTIVITY PLAN

Dramatic Play: Water play   **Date:** _____

Type of Activity: Central   Sequential   (Related)

Objectives:
1. To learn new, and employ familiar, vocabulary
2. To learn new, and employ a variety of, syntactic constructions
3. To interact with peers
4. To sequence familiar routines
5. To expand conceptual knowledge of the world

General Description of Activity

Water is put in the water table and in a wading pool. The children can experiment with various textures of objects as they play in the water. Some of the water toys are rough (e.g., play swordfish, walrus), some of them are smooth (e.g., various toy boats), some are sticky (e.g., play worms, small fish used as pretend bait), some are soft (e.g., blow-up toys), and some are hard (e.g., water pump). Another area can be set up with tubs and sponges for children to see how a sponge feels with and without water in it.

Settings

- Water table
- Wading pool

Props

- Smocks
- Toy boats
- Toy people
- Water pump
- Rubber and plastic water toys (e.g., fish, seal, walrus, worms)
- Sponges
- Cups
- Drainers

Roles

- Scientists
- Laboratory technicians

Verbal Productions

Level of linguistic complexity varies with the role or competency of the child playing the role.

- "This fish feels squishy" or "Fish soft."
- "Look, if you take the air out, the boat sinks," "Look, sink," or "Boat sink."
- "You splashed me" or "Splash."
- "I did not mean to—sorry" or "Sorry."

Adult Facilitory Role

The adult's role is to facilitate role play and to help expand language use. Emphasis on different structures and/or vocabulary may be necessary depending on the child's needs and abilities. The adult(s) may model appropriate scripts, ask open questions, expand or recast a child's productions, redirect a child to request items from another child, use a modification of a cloze procedure to provide contrastive feedback, or provide confirmative feedback to a particular child.

DRAMATIC PLAY ACTIVITY PLAN

Dramatic Play: Winter fun   **Date:** _____

Type of Activity: Central   Sequential   (Related)

Objectives: 1. To learn new, and employ familiar, vocabulary
2. To learn new, and employ a variety of, syntactic constructions
3. To interact with peers
4. To sequence familiar routines
5. To expand conceptual knowledge of the world

General Description of Activity

Fun winter activities include skating, skiing, building snow forts, and so forth. Children can make an igloo out of cardboard bricks that have been wrapped in white paper. Children can also make "snowballs" out of crushed newspapers. Newspaper confetti can be shaped into "snow banks" in which to jump. White pillow cases can be stuffed with newspaper "snow" to make snowmen. The children can pretend to ice skate by taking off their shoes and sliding on a large piece of plastic. They can build campfires to get warm and to make hot chocolate. They could also go pretend ice fishing.

Settings

- Igloo
- Ice pond
- Snowy field
- Ice fishing area
- Campfire

Props

- Cardboard bricks wrapped in white paper
- Newspaper (crumpled for "snowballs" and confetti for "snow")
- White bricks or blocks covered with white paper (pillows)
- Ice pond (large piece of plastic)
- Fishing poles (with magnets attached to catch fish)
- Fish (with paper clips attached)
- Ice fishing area (box covered with foil—the children break the foil to begin fishing)
- Campfire (sticks or blocks and red cellophane paper)
- Pillow case (to stuff to make a snowman)
- Cups
- Thermos of hot chocolate

Roles

- Children
- Mothers
- Fathers
- Ice skaters
- Ice fishermen and women
- Skiiers

Verbal Productions

Level of linguistic complexity varies with the role or competency of the child playing the role.

- "How many times did you fall?" or "How many?"
- "I need to have new skates" or "Two."
- "This is the biggest snowman" or "Big snowman."
- "Here's your hot chocolate" or "Hot."

Adult Facilitory Role

The adult's role is to facilitate role play and to help expand language use. Emphasis on different structures and/or vocabulary may be necessary depending on the child's needs and abilities. The adult(s) may model appropriate scripts, ask open questions, expand or recast a child's productions, redirect a child to request items from another child, use a modification of a cloze procedure to provide contrastive feedback, or provide confirmative feedback to a particular child.

DRAMATIC PLAY ACTIVITY PLAN

Dramatic Play: Zoo/zookeeper _____ **Date:** _____

Type of Activity: (Central) Sequential   Related

Objectives: 1. To learn new, and employ familiar, vocabulary
2. To learn new, and employ a variety of, syntactic constructions
3. To interact with peers
4. To sequence familiar routines
5. To expand conceptual knowledge of the world

General Description of Activity

A zoo can be set up with a variety of animals in cages or defined spaces (e.g., field areas for large animals, pond for ducks, pool areas for bears or penguins) in the dramatic play area. In general, a visit to the zoo involves buying a ticket, looking at the animals, and occasionally being allowed to feed them. In some zoos, visitors may take train rides through the zoo. Workers at the zoo take care of the animals by feeding them and cleaning their cages. Children at the zoo often buy balloons or other mementos. Food is either purchased at the zoo or visitors may bring a picnic basket.

Settings

- Cages
- Defined spaces for animals
- Pond (blue sheet)
- Pool area (blue sheet)
- Ticket office
- Concession stand area
- Train (optional)

Props

- Cages
- Fencing
- Stuffed animals
- Tickets
- Pretend cash register
- Pretend money
- Pretend food for animals
- Dishes for animal food
- Pretend food for visitors
- Tickets
- Balloons
- Soda pop dispensers
- Broom and mop
- Doctor kit collage (optional) (see p. 311)

Roles

- Zookeeper
- Animals
- Ticket vendor
- Visitors
- Concession stand vendors
- Veterinarian (optional)

Verbal Productions

Level of linguistic complexity varies with the role or competency of the child playing the role.

- "How many tickets do you want?" or "How many?"
- "I need to have six tickets" or "Six."
- "This is an African elephant. He is bigger than the Indian elephant" or "Big elephant."
- "I'm feeding the tigers now" or "Feed tigers."

Adult Facilitory Role

The adult's role is to facilitate role play and to help expand language use. Emphasis on different structures and/or vocabulary may be necessary depending on the child's needs and abilities. The adult(s) may model appropriate scripts, ask open questions, expand or recast a child's productions, redirect a child to request items from another child, use a modification of a cloze procedure to provide contrastive feedback, or provide confirmative feedback to a particular child.

ART ACTIVITIES

ART ACTIVITIES:
CONSTRUCTION

ART ACTIVITY PLAN

Art: __**Aquariums__   **Date:** _____

Objectives: 1. To foster creativity
2. To foster small motor development (drawing, painting, cutting, *pasting*, etc.)
3. To increase vocabulary knowledge
4. To practice turn-taking skills
5. To converse with peers and adults

General Plan

White glue is smeared on the bottom half of a paper plate using a Popsicle stick or a cotton swab. Sand is sprinkled into the glue to represent the bottom of the ocean. The children then glue different items that could be under the sea, such as fish cut-outs, shark cut-outs, seashells, and green construction paper or yarn to represent seaweed on the top half of the plate above the sand. The plate is then wrapped in blue plastic wrap, which is taped to the plate, to represent the water and to create an aquarium effect.

Supplies Needed

- White glue
- Paper plates
- Popsicle sticks or cotton swabs
- Sand
- Fish and shark cut-outs
- Seashells
- Green construction paper or yarn
- Blue plastic wrap

ART ACTIVITY PLAN

Art: *Badges _____ **Date:** _____

Objectives: 1. To foster creativity
2. To foster small motor development (drawing, painting, *cutting*, *pasting*, etc.)
3. To increase vocabulary knowledge
4. To practice turn-taking skills
5. To converse with peers and adults

General Plan

The children glue pieces of paper and bits of string onto cardboard previously cut in the shape of a badge. The "badge" is then covered with foil. The child can wear the badge by attaching it to the child's clothes with masking tape. The paper and string give the badges texture. An alternative is to have the children color predesigned badges, cut them out, and then paste them onto the cardboard already cut in the shape of badges.

Supplies Needed

- Cardboard cut in the shape of badges
- Glue (or paste)
- Scrap pieces of paper
- Pieces of string
- Foil (enough to cover the badges)
- Masking tape
- Predrawn badges to color (optional)
- Scissors (optional)
- Crayons or markers (optional)

ART ACTIVITY PLAN

Art: *Binoculars   **Date:** _____

Objectives: 1. To foster creativity
2. To foster small motor development (drawing, painting, cutting, pasting, etc.)
3. To increase vocabulary knowledge
4. To practice turn-taking skills
5. To converse with peers and adults

General Plan

The children can make pretend binoculars by taping two toilet paper rolls together. Strings can be attached by punching a hole in the roll and threading string or yarn through the holes. The children can then wear them around their necks. The children can decorate the binoculars using markers and stickers.

Supplies Needed

- Toilet paper rolls (at least two per child)
- Hole punch or scissors
- Scotch tape
- String or yarn
- Markers (optional)
- Stickers (optional)

ART ACTIVITY PLAN

Art: *Bird feeders _____   **Date:** _____

Objectives: 1. To foster creativity
2. To foster small motor development (drawing, painting, cutting, pasting, etc.)
3. To increase vocabulary knowledge
4. To practice turn-taking skills
5. To converse with peers and adults

General Plan

String or colored yarn is tied to a pine cone. Bird seed is placed in a shoebox lid. The children smear their pine cones with peanut butter using plastic knives and then roll the pine cones in the bird seed. For easy and neat transport home, the "bird feeders" can be placed in small plastic bags. Some of the extra "bird feeders" can be attached to trees on the playyard.

Supplies Needed

- String or colored yarn
- Pine cones (at least one per child)
- Bird seed
- Shoebox lids
- Peanut butter
- Plastic knives
- Small plastic bags

ART ACTIVITY PLAN

Art: Boats   **Date:** _____

Objectives: 1. To foster creativity
2. To foster small motor development (drawing, painting, cutting, *pasting*, etc.)
3. To increase vocabulary knowledge
4. To practice turn-taking skills
5. To converse with peers and adults

General Plan

Styrofoam meat trays are placed on the art table along with Popsicle sticks, stickers, or other decorations, construction paper, and glue. The children can decorate the trays. The precut triangle-shape construction paper is glued to the stick to make a sail. The stick is then pushed into the middle of the styrofoam tray. The boat can be sailed in the lake (water table or tub filled with water).

Supplies Needed

- Styrofoam meat trays
- Popsicle sticks
- Stickers or other decorations
- Precut construction paper triangles
- Glue (or paste)
- Water table or tub filled with water (optional—the "lake")

ART ACTIVITY PLAN

Art: Cornstarch-and-water sculpture   **Date:** _____

Objectives: 1. To foster creativity
2. To foster small motor development (drawing, painting, cutting, pasting, *sculpting*, etc.)
3. To increase vocabulary knowledge
4. To practice turn-taking skills
5. To converse with peers and adults

General Plan

The children put on their smocks. Water and corn starch are mixed together (by staff or children) in several containers or tubs to form soft "dough." Spoons may be used, but the children may wish to use their hands. The containers need to be big enough for at least two hands, but it is more fun and better facilitates language if the containers will hold at least four hands. This "dough" is very interesting for children because it feels stiff and figures can be made with it. Then, after a figure is formed, it begins to "melt." The children can make a variety of figures and then watch them slowly disintegrate. (The mixture washes off hands quite easily.)

Supplies Needed

- Smocks
- Water (2–2¼ cups per box of cornstarch)
- Cornstarch (one to two 1-pound boxes per container)
- Containers or tubs
- Spoons (optional)

ART ACTIVITY PLAN

Art: Craft dough   **Date:** _____

Objectives:
1. To foster creativity
2. To foster small motor development (drawing, painting, *cutting, rolling,* etc.)
3. To increase vocabulary knowledge
4. To practice turn-taking skills
5. To converse with peers and adults

General Plan

Craft dough (see recipe below) or Play-Doh is placed on the art table along with various presses, cutters, rolling pins, and wooden Popsicle sticks. The children can make objects out of the dough by rolling, cutting, or pressing. If craft dough is used, the children can use a cookie cutter to cut out hearts, pumpkins, or other shapes. A hole can be pressed out using a pencil and the shape allowed to dry on waxed paper. When dry, a piece of yarn can be threaded through the hole so the child can wear the shape as a necklace. The shape can also be painted with tempera paint. When the children are finished, they can roll the extra dough into a ball for others to use.

Supplies Needed

- Smocks
- Craft dough (see recipe below) or Play-Doh
- Presses
- Cutters of various shapes
- Rolling pins
- Wooden Popsicle sticks
- Boards for rolling
- Pencil
- Waxed paper
- Yarn
- Tempera paint
- Paintbrushes
- Airtight containers

Recipe for Craft Dough

1 cup cornstarch
2 cups salt
1½ cups boiling water

Mix cornstarch and salt together. Bring water to a boil in a saucepan and then remove from heat. Slowly add cornstarch-and-salt mixture to the water, while stirring. Continue to stir as mixture is cooked over low heat until the dough is hard to stir. Pour the dough into a bowl and, when cool, knead until a smooth dough is formed. Store in an airtight container until used. Cut in shapes and let dry on waxed paper. Dough will dry in approximately 24 hours and can be painted when dry.

ART ACTIVITY PLAN

Art: *Egg carton caterpillars   **Date:**

Objectives: 1. To foster creativity
     2. To foster small motor development (drawing, painting, cutting, pasting, *constructing*, etc.)
     3. To increase vocabulary knowledge
     4. To practice turn-taking skills
     5. To converse with peers and adults

General Plan

The children make caterpillars out of colored styrofoam (or cardboard) egg cartons by decorating them with crayons and markers, glueing on eyes, and making antennae and legs out of pipe cleaners. The egg cartons should be cut into two strips lengthwise before the children begin the activity. If the children have trouble poking the pipe cleaners through the styrofoam, a single-hole punch can be used first. Then, the pipe cleaner can be pushed through, bent, and twisted around itself to hold it on. The cut-out circles from the hole punching can be glued on as eyes.

Supplies Needed

- Various colors of styrofoam or cardboard egg cartons (precut into two strips lengthwise)
- Crayons
- Markers
- Glue (or paste)
- Paper scraps
- Various colors of pipe cleaners cut to lengths of 2–3 inches
- Single-hole punch

ART ACTIVITY PLAN

Art: **Kites   **Date:** _____

Objectives: 1.   To foster creativity
2.   To foster small motor development (drawing, cutting, *pasting, constructing*, etc.)
3.   To increase vocabulary knowledge
4.   To practice turn-taking skills
5.   To converse with peers and adults

General Plan

The children glue two Popsicle sticks together in an "X" to make the kite frame. Then yarn or string is tied to the kite frame where the Popsicle sticks cross to be the string for the kite. (Staff may need to do this.) The children decorate diamond-shape pieces of paper (using markers, crayons, and/or stickers) and then glue them to the kite frames. A hole is punched in the bottom of the diamond-shape paper, and yarn is added to make a tail for the kite. The children can glue small bits of paper to the tail for decoration.

Supplies Needed

- Popsicle sticks (two per kite)
- Glue (or paste)
- Yarn or string
- Diamond-shape pieces of construction paper (approximately 4 inches square) (one per kite)
- Markers or crayons
- Stickers (optional—for decoration)
- Single-hole punch
- Small scraps of paper

ART ACTIVITY PLAN

Art: *Lacing_____   **Date:** _____

Objectives: 1. To foster creativity
            2. To foster small motor development (drawing, painting, cutting, pasting, *lacing*, etc.)
            3. To increase vocabulary knowledge
            4. To practice turn-taking skills
            5. To converse with peers and adults

General Plan

The children can practice lacing (and tying) by lacing a paper boot (made from card stock for stability). The children can take turns lacing up the paper boot with a piece of yarn by starting at the bottom holes and criss-crossing the yarn through the other holes until they reach the top of the boot. The ends of the yarn are wrapped with tape to make it easier to thread the yarn through the holes. The children can then color the boot or draw designs on it.

Variation

Lacing formboards could be used instead of paper boots.

Supplies Needed

- Boots (made from card stock) with holes punched for lacing
- Yarn
- Tape
- Markers or crayons
- Lacing formboards (optional)

ART ACTIVITY PLAN

Art: *Macaroni necklace _____   **Date:** _____

Objectives: 1. To foster creativity
2. To foster small motor development (drawing, painting, cutting, pasting, *beading*, etc.)
3. To increase vocabulary knowledge
4. To practice turn-taking skills
5. To converse with peers and adults

General Plan

Different kinds of macaroni can be used, and/or macaroni can be dyed different colors prior to the activity. A staff member should tie one piece of macaroni to one end of an 18- to 24-inch piece of string so that the other macaroni pieces will not fall off the string after they are strung. One end of the string is taped to make stringing of the macaroni easier. The children then string several pieces of macaroni to make a necklace. Small pieces of construction paper or straws precut to different lengths can be strung between the macaroni pieces to make the necklaces colorful and interesting.

Supplies Needed

- Different kinds of macaroni (with holes big enough for string or yarn to be laced through them
- Small bowls or containers to hold the macaroni
- Dye (optional)
- String or yarn (precut in 18- to 24-inch lengths)
- Tape
- Pieces of construction paper
- Straws (precut in different lengths)

ART ACTIVITY PLAN

Art: *Mickey Mouse ears   **Date:** _____

Objectives: 1. To foster creativity
2. To foster small motor development (*drawing*, painting, cutting, pasting, etc.)
3. To increase vocabulary knowledge
4. To practice turn-taking skills
5. To converse with peers and adults

General Plan

The children decorate a head band made from sentence strips or construction-paper strips using markers, crayons, stickers, or construction-paper cut-outs. Two black construction-paper circles are stapled onto the strips for ears. (For safety, staff should do the stapling or closely supervise the children.) The headband is placed around a child's head and the ends are stapled together to fit the child's head. The ears and headband should be stapled with the rough edges on the outside, or tape should be placed on top of the staples so that the staples do not scratch the children when they wear the headbands.

Supplies Needed

- Sentence strips or construction-paper strips long enough for headbands (one per child)
- Markers or crayons
- Stickers or construction paper cut-outs (optional)
- Black construction paper circles approximately 2 inches in diameter (two per headband)
- Stapler
- Tape

ART ACTIVITY PLAN

Art: Paper airplanes   **Date:** _____

Objectives:
1. To foster creativity
2. To foster small motor development (drawing, painting, cutting, *folding*, etc.)
3. To increase vocabulary knowledge
4. To practice turn-taking skills
5. To converse with peers and adults

General Plan

A paper airplane is begun by decorating the paper. Drawings or different colors and stickers can be used. The 8½-inch × 11-inch sheet of paper (different dimensions can be used) is then folded to make an airplane.

To make the airplane, follow these instructions:

1. Fold the paper in half lengthwise.
2. Fold a top edge down until it is even with the folded bottom to form a triangle shape.
3. Turn the paper over and fold the other side the same way so that one third of the paper is slanted and ending in a point.
4. Clip a paper clip to the point of the triangle. (A paper clip is used on the "nose" of the airplane to hold the plane together and to provide appropriate weight so the airplane will fly.)
5. Fold the rest of the top edge even with the bottom fold and make a crease.
6. Let go of the paper so it sticks out to make a wing.
7. Turn the paper over and fold the other side in the same way.

The paper airplane is then ready to fly. (Other paper folding can be done to form other styles of airplanes.)

Supplies Needed

- 8½-inch × 11-inch paper
- Markers or crayons
- Paper clips
- Stickers (optional)

ART ACTIVITY PLAN

Art: Paperbag puppets   **Date:** _____

Objectives: 1. To foster creativity
2. To foster small motor development (*drawing*, painting, cutting, *pasting*, etc.)
3. To increase vocabulary knowledge
4. To practice turn-taking skills
5. To converse with peers and adults

General Plan

The children make paperbag puppets by decorating small brown paperbags. The fold that creates the base of the bag is the "face" so that when the child's hand is placed inside the bag, the fold can be used to open and close the "mouth." Red construction paper may be glued or pasted inside the fold to represent the tongue. Other construction paper cut-outs can be used for facial features, such as ears, noses, and mouths. Markers or crayons can also be used to draw the facial features. Yarn can be used for fur. When finished the children can stick their hands into their bags and make their puppets "talk."

Supplies Needed

- Paperbags (one or two per child)
- Construction-paper (red and other colors) cut-outs such as circles, triangles, and so forth
- Glue (or paste)
- Markers or crayons
- Yarn
- Scissors

ART ACTIVITY PLAN

Art: Playdough _____ **Date:** _____

Objectives: 1. To foster creativity
2. To foster small motor development (drawing, painting, *cutting*, pasting, *rolling*, etc.)
3. To increase vocabulary knowledge
4. To practice turn-taking skills
5. To converse with peers and adults

General Plan

Playdough (see recipe below) is placed on the art table along with various presses, cutters, rolling pins, and wooden Popsicle sticks. The children can make pretend food or any other objects out of the dough using rolling, cutting, or pressing motions. They can form animals or people by rolling a main body and then adding heads, arms, and legs. Yarn can be used for hair (if the children want to take their objects home). When the children are finished, they can roll the dough into a ball and put it back in the middle of the table for others to use. The playdough should be stored in airtight containers for future use.

Note

Children should wash their hands before and after using playdough. Having the children wear smocks is also advisable so that any dye from the playdough does not get on their clothes.

Supplies Needed

- Playdough (see recipe below or use commercially sold Play-Doh)
- Presses
- Cutters
- Rolling pins
- Flat Popsicle sticks
- Smocks
- Airtight containers
- Boards to roll play dough on (optional)
- Yarn (optional)

Recipe for Playdough

3 cups flour
1½ cups salt
1 tablespoon cream of tartar
1 tablespoon alum

1 tablespoon oil
Food coloring or tempera paint
1 cup of hot water (additional hot water as needed)

Mix first five ingredients together. Add food coloring or tempera paint to the hot water and pour into flour mixture. Knead until a dough-like consistency is reached, adding hot water as needed.

ART ACTIVITY PLAN

Art: *Popsicle cages _____ **Date:** _____

Objectives: 1. To foster creativity
2. To foster small motor development (drawing, painting, cutting, *pasting*, etc.)
3. To increase vocabulary knowledge
4. To practice turn-taking skills
5. To converse with peers and adults

General Plan

Large and small Popsicle sticks are arranged on the art tables. The children glue (or paste) the sticks together to form a square (the cage). The children then glue or paste pictures of zoo animals inside the cage. Yarn, string, construction paper strips, and/or additional Popsicle sticks can be glued or pasted to the "cage" to make "bars," food bowls, and so forth.

Variation

The Popsicle sticks can be used to make fences, instead of cages, for the animals.

Supplies Needed

- Large and small Popsicle sticks
- White glue (or paste)
- Zoo animal pictures (some precut and some available for the children to cut themselves)
- Scissors
- Markers
- Yarn
- String
- Strips of construction paper
- Small pieces of paper of various sizes and colors

ART ACTIVITY PLAN

Art: Popsicle constructions   **Date:** _____

Objectives: 1. To foster creativity
2. To foster small motor development (drawing, painting, cutting, *pasting*, etc.)
3. To increase vocabulary knowledge
4. To practice turn-taking skills
5. To converse with peers and adults

General Plan

Large and small Popsicle sticks are arranged on the art tables. The children glue or paste the sticks together to form a variety of constructions. They can make triangle shapes or "log" cabins, or they can form people or animals (or anything else). Items such as yarn, markers and crayons, and scissors and construction paper should be available for the children to use in their constructions.

Supplies Needed

- Large and small Popsicle sticks
- White glue (or paste)
- Yarn
- Markers and crayons
- Scissors
- Construction paper of various sizes and colors (small pieces and 9-inch × 12-inch pieces in case the children want to paste sticks on the paper)

ART ACTIVITY PLAN

Art: __**Wind socks__   **Date:** _____

Objectives: 1. To foster creativity
2. To foster small motor development (*drawing*, painting, *cutting*, *pasting*, etc.)
3. To increase vocabulary knowledge
4. To practice turn-taking skills
5. To converse with peers and adults

General Plan

Wind socks are made by using sentence strips to make a sturdy circle and glueing or stapling strips of tissue paper or crêpe paper to the circle. String or yarn can be stapled to the circle so that it can be hung or used as a kite. The children can decorate their wind socks by drawing pictures or pasting various stickers or pieces of construction paper to the circle.

Variation

Another way to make wind socks is to decorate the children's old socks and use wire inserts to form the circles. (Straightened paper clips could be used for the wire inserts.) For each, the top of the sock would be wrapped around the wire and taped or stapled to it. The children could then decorate the wind socks as described above.

Supplies Needed

- 18- to 24-inch sentence strips (smaller lengths could also be used) (one per child)
- Glue or paste
- Stapler
- Tissue paper or crêpe paper strips
- String or yarn
- Markers or crayons
- Stickers
- Construction paper
- Scissors
- Children's old socks (one per child) (optional)
- Wire inserts (Straightened paper clips may be used.) (optional)
- Scotch tape (optional)

ART ACTIVITIES: CUTTING

ART ACTIVITY PLAN

Art: *Cut-out cars   **Date:** _____

Objectives:
1. To foster creativity
2. To foster small motor development (drawing, painting, *cutting*, pasting, etc.)
3. To increase vocabulary knowledge
4. To practice turn-taking skills
5. To converse with peers and adults

General Plan

The children cut out simple car shapes and two separate wheels. The cars and wheels can be decorated with crayons or markers. Then, the wheels are attached to the car with brads (i.e., round-head paper fasteners) so that the wheels can turn.

Variation

For an added challenge, the children can first trace the car and wheels from cardboard templates and then cut them out, decorate them, and fasten the wheels on with brads.

Supplies Needed

- Outlines of cars on various colors of construction paper (Outlines should be drawn with heavy lines to make cutting easy.)
- Predrawn outlines of wheels on construction paper
- Scissors
- Crayons or markers
- Brads (i.e., round-head paper fasteners)
- Car and wheel templates (optional)

ART ACTIVITY PLAN

Art: Magazine collage   **Date:** _____

Objectives: 1. To foster creativity
2. To foster small motor development (drawing, painting, *cutting*, *pasting*, etc.)
3. To increase vocabulary knowledge
4. To practice turn-taking skills
5. To converse with peers and adults

General Plan

The children cut out various pictures from different magazines and glue them on construction paper or paper plates to make a collage. The collage can have a theme, such as foods, animals, plants, houses, and so forth. Or the collage can be general, with an emphasis on color and design. The main purpose is to give the children practice in cutting and in making their own creations. The children may wish to write or draw on their collages and write their names on them.

Supplies Needed

- A variety of magazines
- Scissors
- Glue or glue stick
- Construction paper (or paper plates)
- Pencils or markers

ART ACTIVITY PLAN

Art: *Newspaper collage _____   **Date:** _____

Objectives: 1. To foster creativity
2. To foster small motor development (drawing, painting, *cutting, pasting,* etc.)
3. To increase vocabulary knowledge
4. To practice turn-taking skills
5. To converse with peers and adults

General Plan

The children are given white or newsprint paper on which columns have been blocked off with dark lines. Various newspapers, articles, pictures are available for them to cut out and glue or paste to make a "newspaper." Some children may notice letters and words that they recognize. Pencils, pens, and markers should be available for the children to write their own "words" and sign their "articles" (their own "bylines"). They could draw their own cartoons, too.

Supplies Needed

- White or newsprint paper with columns blocked off as described above
- A variety of newspapers, articles, and pictures
- Scissors
- Pencils
- Pens
- Markers
- Glue (or paste)

ART ACTIVITY PLAN

Art: __**Snowflakes__   **Date:** _____

Objectives: 1. To foster creativity
2. To foster small motor development (drawing, painting, *cutting*, pasting, etc.)
3. To increase vocabulary knowledge
4. To practice turn-taking skills
5. To converse with peers and adults

General Plan

Each child cuts pieces out of a folded square sheet of white paper (see the instructions below for preparing the paper) and then unfolds it to make a "snowflake." Each snowflake will be different because each child will cut different shapes and sizes from the original squares of paper. If desired, the children may color or decorate the finished "snowflakes" using crayons, markers, or glitter. Snowflakes may also be pasted onto colored construction paper. Different sizes of paper should be used for snowflakes of different sizes.

Preparing the Paper to Make Snowflakes

1. Fold a square sheet of white paper in half and then in half again so a square results.
2. Fold the resulting square in half diagonally so a triangle results.
3. Have the children use a zigzag pattern to cut off the top of the triangle.
4. The children can cut any shapes they want into the sides of the triangle. However, they should be cautioned not to cut the whole way across the triangle.
5. The children can unfold the triangles to see their snowflakes.

Supplies Needed

- Folded square sheets of white paper in a variety of sizes
- Scissors
- Markers or crayons
- Glitter (optional)
- Glue, glue sticks, or paste (optional)

ART ACTIVITIES: DRAWING

ART ACTIVITY PLAN

Art: Chalk pictures (rubbings)   **Date:** _____

Objectives:
1. To foster creativity
2. To foster small motor development (*drawing*, painting, cutting, pasting, etc.)
3. To increase vocabulary knowledge
4. To practice turn-taking skills
5. To converse with peers and adults

General Plan

The children don smocks and are given construction paper and colored chalk to draw pictures. They can draw people, animals, houses, trees, rainbows, or anything else they might like. Some of the children may want to make chalk rubbings by placing cardboard cut-outs (e.g., animals, shapes, vehicles) underneath the paper and, holding the chalk at both ends, rubbing the chalk on the paper until the outline of the object shows through. Staff members can then spray chalk fixative on the pictures or rubbings to keep them from smudging. (This should be done outside or in a well-ventilated area away from the children.)

Supplies Needed

- Smocks
- Construction paper
- Colored chalk
- Cardboard cut-outs (optional)
- Chalk fixative

ART ACTIVITY PLAN

Art: Chalk pictures (with liquid starch)   **Date:** _____

Objectives: 1. To foster creativity
2. To foster small motor development (*drawing*, painting, cutting, pasting, etc.)
3. To increase vocabulary knowledge
4. To practice turn-taking skills
5. To converse with peers and adults

General Plan

The children don smocks and are given colored construction paper and colored chalk. Liquid starch is poured onto flat dishes. The children dip one end of the chalk into the liquid starch and then draw on the paper. The liquid starch makes the colors become more vibrant and the need for chalk fixative is eliminated. The children can draw designs or pictures that follow the daily theme, or they can draw pictures that have nothing to do with the theme.

Supplies Needed

- Smocks
- Colored construction paper
- Colored chalk
- Liquid starch
- Flat dishes to hold the starch

ART ACTIVITY PLAN

Art: Chalk pictures (X-rays)   **Date:** _____

Objectives: 1. To foster creativity
2. To foster small motor development (*drawing*, painting, cutting, pasting, etc.)
3. To increase vocabulary knowledge
4. To practice turn-taking skills
5. To converse with peers and adults

General Plan

The children are given black construction paper and white chalk. They can draw X-ray pictures by making line drawings of skeleton-like people. Some of the X-ray pictures could be of "broken" arms, which then could be incorporated into the doctor's office dramatic play (see pp. 182–183). (The artists could be the "radiologists.") Other children might want to draw pictures that have nothing to do with X-rays. When the children are finished with their pictures, staff members can spray chalk fixative on the pictures to keep them from smudging. (This should be done outside or in a well-ventilated area away from the children.)

Supplies Needed

- Black construction paper
- White chalk
- Chalk fixative

ART ACTIVITY PLAN

Art: Drawings   **Date:** _____

Objectives:
1. To foster creativity
2. To foster small motor development (*drawing*, painting, cutting, pasting, etc.)
3. To increase vocabulary knowledge
4. To practice turn-taking skills
5. To converse with peers and adults

General Plan

The children don smocks and are given paper and a selection of crayons and/or markers. The children draw anything they want. Staff may suggest that the children draw themselves, their families, their pets, different scenes, designs, rainbows, and so forth.

Variation

Crayon drawings can become "crayon washes" when the children paint over their pictures with light coats of watered-down tempera paint. The paint does not stick to the crayon but "fills" in where there are no crayon marks to create a colored background.

Supplies Needed

- Smocks
- Paper (white or colored)
- Crayons and/or markers
- Watered-down tempera paint (The amount of water added depends on how vibrant staff want the colors to be.) (optional)
- Paintbrushes

ART ACTIVITY PLAN

Art: Leaf rubbings   **Date:** _____

Objectives: 1. To foster creativity
2. To foster small motor development (drawing, painting, cutting, pasting, *rubbing*, etc.)
3. To increase vocabulary knowledge
4. To practice turn-taking skills
5. To converse with peers and adults

General Plan

The children select a variety of leaves. Then, they place a leaf or a group of leaves under a piece of newsprint or tracing paper. Holding the chalk at both ends, the children rub a crayon (with paper covering removed) over the paper, back and forth until the shapes of the leaves appear. The children can use different colored crayons and different arrangements of leaves under the paper to make a variety of pictures.

Variation

Instead of actual leaves, cardboard cut-outs in the shapes of leaves could be used.

Supplies Needed

- A variety of freshly fallen leaves
- Newsprint or tracing paper
- Crayons (paper covering removed)
- Container to hold crayons
- Cardboard cut-outs in the shape of leaves (optional)

ART ACTIVITY PLAN

Art: Rubbings   **Date:** _____

Objectives:
1. To foster creativity
2. To foster small motor development (drawing, painting, cutting, pasting, *rubbing*, etc.)
3. To increase vocabulary knowledge
4. To practice turn-taking skills
5. To converse with peers and adults

General Plan

Each child selects a variety of cardboard cut-outs and then places one or more under a piece of newsprint or tracing paper. Then, holding the chalk at both ends, they rub a crayon (with paper covering removed) over the paper, back and forth until the shapes of the objects below appear. The children can use different colored crayons and different arrangements of shapes under the paper to make a variety of pictures.

Variation

For an outside activity, a large piece of paper can be taped on a brick wall. The children can rub their crayons on the paper to make a "wall" rubbing. Similarly, paper can be placed on a sidewalk, manhole cover, and so forth, to make other interesting "rubbings."

Supplies Needed

- A variety of cut-outs
- Newsprint or tracing paper
- Crayons (paper covering removed)
- Container to hold crayons
- Brick wall, sidewalk, and so forth (optional—for outside rubbings)
- Tape (optional)

ART ACTIVITY PLAN

Art: Vehicle rubbings   **Date:** _____

Objectives: 1. To foster creativity
2. To foster small motor development (drawing, painting, cutting, pasting, *rubbing*, etc.)
3. To increase vocabulary knowledge
4. To practice turn-taking skills
5. To converse with peers and adults

General Plan

Various outlines of vehicles are cut out of cardboard. The children place these cut-outs under newsprint or tracing paper. Holding the chalk at both ends, children rub a crayon (with paper covering removed) over the paper, back and forth until the shape is slowly revealed. A variety of other cut-outs can be used to add to the picture.

Supplies Needed

- Precut cardboard vehicle cut-outs
- Newsprint or tracing paper
- Crayons (paper removed)
- Container to hold crayons
- Other cut-outs

ART ACTIVITIES: PAINTING

ART ACTIVITY PLAN

Art: Coffee-filter painting   **Date:** _____

Objectives:
1. To foster creativity
2. To foster small motor development (drawing, *painting*, cutting, pasting, etc.)
3. To increase vocabulary knowledge
4. To practice turn-taking skills
5. To converse with peers and adults

General Plan

The children don smocks and paint pictures on flattened clean coffee filters using water colors. Because the filters are porous, the paint runs, making interesting designs.

Variation 1

An alternative method is to fold the coffee filters and have the children paint on one side. When the filters are opened, the colors will form a design throughout the filter.

Variation 2

The coffee-filter paintings can be glued to paper stems created from green construction paper to make flowers. The children's flowers can be displayed on a large bulletin board, resulting in a "flower garden."

Supplies Needed

- Coffee filters (at least one per child)
- Water-color paint
- Paintbrushes
- Small bowls of water for rinsing paintbrushes
- Green construction paper (optional)
- Scissors
- Glue sticks (optional)
- Bulletin board (optional)

ART ACTIVITY PLAN

Art: __**Crayon wash__   **Date:** _____

Objectives: 1. To foster creativity
2. To foster small motor development (*drawing*, *painting*, cutting, pasting, etc.)
3. To increase vocabulary knowledge
4. To practice turn-taking skills
5. To converse with peers and adults

General Plan

The children draw on Manila paper or white construction paper with vivid-colored crayons, pressing hard so that the lines can be seen easily. They may want to make pictures of their families, pets, or houses, or of flowers, shapes, or something related to the daily or weekly theme. After the drawings are completed, the children paint over their pictures with watered-down tempera paint. The paint does not stick to the crayon but fills in a background color. Frames can be painted around the pictures using full-strength tempera paint of the same, or a contrasting, color from that used in the "wash."

Variation

For holidays such as Halloween, pictures of pumpkins, cats, bats, and so forth can be drawn and then watered-down orange tempera paint can be used to make the "wash."

Supplies Needed

- Manila paper or white construction paper
- Crayons (vivid colors)
- Container to hold crayons
- Watered down tempera paint (The amount of water added depends on how vibrant staff want the colors to be.)
- Tempera paint (Regular strength—for border)
- Paintbrushes
- Small bowls of water for rinsing paintbrushes

ART ACTIVITY PLAN

Art: *Doghouse and paw prints   **Date:** _____

Objectives: 1. To foster creativity
2. To foster small motor development (drawing, *painting*, cutting, *pasting*, etc.)
3. To increase vocabulary knowledge
4. To practice turn-taking skills
5. To converse with peers and adults

General Plan

Children can make doghouses out of square and triangular pieces of paper, which are glued or pasted on pieces of white construction paper. The square pieces of paper are used to form the sides of the doghouse, and the triangular pieces form the roof. The children don smocks and make paw prints by dipping the tips of their fingers and thumbs into tempera paint and then pressing them onto the paper. The children can also make drawings of dogs or other animals.

Variation

Ink pads, instead of paint, could be used to make the "paw prints."

Supplies Needed

- Large precut pieces of paper
- Precut triangular pieces of paper
- Glue (or paste)
- Smocks
- White construction paper (at least one piece per child)
- Tempera paint
- Markers
- Shallow dishes to hold the paint
- Towels to wipe off paint or ink
- Ink pads (optional)

ART ACTIVITY PLAN

Art: Easel painting   **Date:** _____

Objectives:
1. To foster creativity
2. To foster small motor development (drawing, *painting*, cutting, pasting, etc.)
3. To increase vocabulary knowledge
4. To practice turn-taking skills
5. To converse with peers and adults

General Plan

Easel boards are set up with two to four different colors of tempera paint in the painting cups. Each cup has its own paintbrush. (It is helpful to have cup covers with holes in them for the brushes. As the brushes are dipped into the paint and then pulled through the holes, some of the excess paint is removed.) Large sheets of paper are clipped to the easelboards.

The children put on their smocks and then paint shapes, objects, or anything else they want on large sheets of paper. Sometimes children will paint pictures and then experiment by painting other colors on top. Staff might have the children tell about their paintings. The painting can later be labeled for display. (The children should decide whether they want their paintings displayed.) An area should be designated for drying the pictures. A wooden clothes rack can be used to dry the pictures.

Notes

- It is helpful to place the easels over plastic or newspaper so that the drips won't stain the floor.
- This is a large muscle activity, particularly appropriate for children 3 years and older.

Supplies Needed

- Easels
- Easel boards
- Tempera paint (two to four colors per easel)
- Cups to hold the paint (one per color of paint)
- Large paintbrushes (one per color of paint)
- Large sheets of paper
- Smocks
- 12-inch × 18-inch or 18-inch × 24-inch paper
- Wooden rack or other area for drying
- Plastic or newsprint to place under the easels

ART ACTIVITY PLAN

Art: Fingerpainting   **Date:** _____

Objectives:
1. To foster creativity
2. To foster small motor development (drawing, *painting*, cutting, pasting, etc.)
3. To increase vocabulary knowledge
4. To practice turn-taking skills
5. To converse with peers and adults

General Plan

A dab of fingerpaint should be placed on each child's paper. The children put on their smocks and then can use their hands and fingers to smear the paint all over the paper. They can then use fingers to draw or write in the paint. They make abstract designs or full hand prints, or they use their fingers to draw pictures or practice writing letters or numbers. Fingerpaint can be used to decorate Halloween or Valentine's Day bags.

Variation

For additional effect, glitter can be mixed into the fingerpaint before the children create their designs.

Supplies Needed

- Fingerpaint
- Fingerpaint paper (one sheet per child)
- Smocks (one per child)
- Bags for Halloween or Valentine's Day (optional)
- Glitter (optional)

ART ACTIVITY PLAN

Art: Mural painting   **Date:**

Objectives: 1. To foster creativity
2. To foster small motor development (drawing, *painting*, cutting, pasting, etc.)
3. To increase vocabulary knowledge
4. To practice turn-taking skills
5. To converse with peers and adults

General Plan

A large piece of paper (e.g., 3 feet × 8 feet) is taped to a wall or laid on the floor (on top of plastic or newsprint). The children don smocks and paint pictures or designs on the paper using tempera paint. The children may choose to draw with crayons or markers instead of using tempera paint.

Variation

If painting scenery for a dramatic play, the children can paint in the objects previously outlined by the staff. For example, the teacher might outline a house or tree, and the children can add the colors in the outlines.

Supplies Needed

- Large sheet of paper (e.g., 3 feet × 8 feet)
- Masking tape (optional)
- Plastic or newsprint to place on the floor
- Smocks
- Tempera paint
- Paint cups
- Paintbrushes
- Crayons or markers (optional)
- Small bowls of water for cleaning paintbrushes at the end of the activity

ART ACTIVITY PLAN

Art: Shaving-cream fingerpainting   **Date:** _____

Objectives: 1. To foster creativity
2. To foster small motor development (drawing, *painting*, cutting, pasting, etc.)
3. To increase vocabulary knowledge
4. To practice turn-taking skills
5. To converse with peers and adults

General Plan

A dab of shaving cream is placed on each child's formboard. The children use their hands and fingers to smear the shaving cream all over the board and then use their fingers to draw and write in the shaving cream. They can make designs, draw pictures, or write letters and numbers. They can also use Popsicle sticks, paintbrushes, or other tools to draw in the shaving cream.

Supplies Needed

- Shaving cream
- Formboards (one per child)
- Popsicle sticks
- Paintbrushes (one per child)
- Other tools for drawing in the shaving cream

ART ACTIVITY PLAN

Art: *String painting _____ **Date:** _____

Objectives: 1. To foster creativity
2. To foster small motor development (drawing, *painting*, cutting, pasting, etc.)
3. To increase vocabulary knowledge
4. To practice turn-taking skills
5. To converse with peers and adults

General Plan

Each child is given a piece of construction paper that has been folded in half and then unfolded. The children put on their smocks. Each child then dips a piece of string into tempera paint and arranges it on half of the sheet of construction paper. The strings can be arranged in "S" patterns, in circles, or any other patterns the children create. The paper is then refolded so that the end of string extends from the paper. The children pull the protruding end of the string while keeping the paper folded. After the string has been removed from the folded paper, the paper is unfolded, and there will be mirror-image designs on both sides of the fold. Two-color designs can be made by dipping a second piece of string in different paint and repeating the procedure. The paper can then be unfolded and allowed to dry.

Supplies Needed

- Construction paper folded in half (one per child)
- Smocks (one per child)
- Strings to dip (each approximately 20 inches long)
- Tempera paint
- Cups or shallow plates to hold the paint
- Drying racks or drying area

ART ACTIVITY PLAN

Art: Veggie prints   **Date:** _____

Objectives: 1. To foster creativity
2. To foster small motor development (drawing, *painting*, cutting, pasting, etc.)
3. To increase vocabulary knowledge
4. To practice turn-taking skills
5. To converse with peers and adults

General Plan

Different vegetables are sliced or chopped before the children arrive. Small amounts of tempera paint are poured into shallow containers, such as Styrofoam meat trays. The children then don smocks and dip the vegetables into the paint and press them on construction paper to make prints of the vegetables' shapes. The greater the selection of vegetables and colors of paint, the more creative and colorful the prints.

Variation

Before the children arrive, staff can cut potatoes in half and carve different shapes into each half. The children can then dip the potatoes into the paint, and the shapes can be printed on construction paper to make designs.

Supplies Needed

- Assortment of sliced or chopped vegetables (e.g., peppers, carrots, broccoli, cauliflower, celery, potatoes)
- Tempera paint
- Shallow containers for paint (e.g., Styrofoam meat trays)
- Construction paper
- Smocks

ART ACTIVITY PLAN

Art: Water-color painting   **Date:** _____

Objectives: 1. To foster creativity
2. To foster small motor development (drawing, *painting*, cutting, pasting, etc.)
3. To increase vocabulary knowledge
4. To practice turn-taking skills
5. To converse with peers and adults

General Plan

White construction paper, water-color paintboxes, and paintbrushes are laid out on the art tables. Tubs of water to clean the brushes are placed above the paper. The children put on smocks and sit down at the art tables. Each child selects a brush, wets it, and chooses a paint color. The children then paint on the paper, rinsing the brush before selecting new colors. The children can paint collages of colors or animals, people, houses, flowers, and so forth.

Supplies Needed

- White construction paper
- Water-color paintboxes
- Paintbrushes
- Tubs of water
- Smocks
- Drying racks or counter space

ART ACTIVITIES: PASTING

ART ACTIVITY PLAN

Art: Cheerio art   **Date:** _____

Objectives: 1. To foster creativity
2. To foster small motor development (drawing, painting, cutting, *pasting*, etc.)
3. To increase vocabulary knowledge
4. To practice turn-taking skills
5. To converse with peers and adults

General Plan

Before the children arrive, staff draw different shapes with markers on pieces of paper. The children outline the shapes by glueing or pasting Cheerios on the lines. Children may make other pictures with the Cheerios, either following lines or pasting the Cheerios in a free-form design.

Variation

The children could draw shapes themselves and then proceed to glue or paste the Cheerios on the lines.

Supplies Needed

- Paper with a variety of shapes or objects drawn on it
- Cheerios
- White glue (or paste)

ART ACTIVITY PLAN

Art: Cottonball chickens   **Date:** _____

Objectives: 1. To foster creativity
2. To foster small motor development (drawing, painting, cutting, *pasting*, etc.)
3. To increase vocabulary knowledge
4. To practice turn-taking skills
5. To converse with peers and adults

General Plan

Children are given a paper with an outline of a chicken on it. The children then glue (or paste) yellow cottonballs inside the chicken outline to make "feathers." They may draw a beak onto the chicken outline and may draw grass or make fences or anything else on their paper.

Supplies Needed

- Paper (predrawn with the outlines of chickens—at least one or two per child)
- Yellow cottonballs (If yellow cottonballs are not available, they can be made from white cottonballs by putting dry yellow tempera paint in a paper bag with the cottonballs and shaking the bag.)
- Glue (or paste)
- Crayons

ART ACTIVITY PLAN

Art: *Crowns _____   **Date:** _____

Objectives: 1. To foster creativity
2. To foster small motor development (*drawing*, painting, cutting, *pasting*, etc.)
3. To increase vocabulary knowledge
4. To practice turn-taking skills
5. To converse with peers and adults

General Plan

The children are each given a strip of construction paper to decorate a crown. The children then use white glue to outline the points on the top edge of the crowns. They sprinkle glitter over the glue. To do this, the crowns are laid in a shallow box lid and the glitter is sprinkled over the glue. The crowns are then lifted and shaken slightly so that the excess glitter falls back into the box lid. After drying, the ends of the crown are stapled together by staff so that the crown fits the children's heads. Tape is placed over the staples so that they do not scratch the children's heads.

Variation

The children can also decorate the crowns with drawings using markers.

Supplies Needed

- 2- to 3-inch strips of construction paper (approximately 28–30 inches long) with the top edge cut in a zigzag manner
- White glue
- Glitter
- Shallow box lids
- Staplers
- Tape
- Markers (optional)

ART ACTIVITY PLAN

Art: Doctor kit collage   **Date:** _____

Objectives:
1. To foster creativity
2. To foster small motor development (drawing, painting, cutting, *pasting*, etc.)
3. To increase vocabulary knowledge
4. To practice turn-taking skills
5. To converse with peers and adults

General Plan

The children paste medical items, such as cotton swabs, tongue depressors, cottonballs, and construction-paper cut-outs in the shapes of pill bottles, syringes, and so forth, on half of a piece of black construction paper. The black paper is then folded in half (with the collage on the inside), to make the doctor's kit. Staff can then staple strips of black construction paper onto the bag for handles.

Variation

The black construction-paper cut-outs could be cut with the handles included so that they resemble bags.

Supplies Needed

- Glue (or paste)
- Cotton swabs
- Tongue depressors
- Cottonballs
- Construction-paper cut-outs in the shapes of medical equipment (e.g., pill bottles, syringes)
- Black construction paper (one piece per child)
- Strips of black construction paper
- Yarn (which can be used to make "stethoscopes")
- Black construction paper cut in the shape of a bag (at least one per child—optional)
- Stapler

ART ACTIVITY PLAN

Art: Faces   **Date:** _____

Objectives:
1. To foster creativity
2. To foster small motor development (*drawing*, painting, cutting, *pasting*, etc.)
3. To increase vocabulary knowledge
4. To practice turn-taking skills
5. To converse with peers and adults

General Plan

Each child makes a face using a paper plate or a construction-paper circle as a base. The children then glue or paste a variety of shapes onto the plate to make facial features such as eyes, noses, mouths, and so forth. The shapes should be placed in separate containers so the children can easily choose the shapes they want. Other items, such as yarn for hair, extra paper, scissors, and markers, can also be available. Children can make whatever "face" they want by drawing and glueing or pasting various items on the plate or circle. Staff can verbally label the different shapes and colors as the children paste them on the faces they are creating.

Variation

Instead of separating the various cut-out shapes, staff may place all the cut-outs in one shallow container so the children must communicate to get the pieces they want.

Supplies Needed

- Paper plates or large construction-paper circles
- Construction-paper cut-outs in various colors and shapes (e.g., circles, triangles, squares, crescents)
- Containers for the cut-outs
- Glue (or paste)
- Yarn
- Sheets of construction paper
- Scissors
- Markers or crayons
- Shallow container (optional)

ART ACTIVITY PLAN

Art: Gingerbread characters   **Date:** _____

Objectives:
1. To foster creativity
2. To foster small motor development (*drawing*, painting, cutting, *pasting*, etc.)
3. To increase vocabulary knowledge
4. To practice turn-taking skills
5. To converse with peers and adults

General Plan

The children decorate gingerbread characters (previously cut by staff from brown construction paper) by glueing or pasting small pieces of construction paper cut in various shapes onto the figures. The shapes should be placed in separate containers so that the children can easily choose the shapes they want. Other items, such as yarn, extra paper, scissors, and markers, are also available. Children can decorate their gingerbread characters in any way they want by glueing various items on them or by drawing on them.

Variation

Instead of separating the various cut-out shapes, staff may place all the cut-outs in one shallow container so the children must communicate to get the pieces they want.

Supplies Needed

- Gingerbread characters cut out of brown construction paper
- Glue (or paste)
- Construction-paper cut-outs in various colors and shapes (e.g., circles, triangles, squares, crescents)
- Containers for the cut-outs
- Yarn
- Sheets of construction paper
- Scissors
- Crayons or markers
- Shallow container (optional)

ART ACTIVITY PLAN

Art: *Pizzas _____ **Date:** _____

Objectives: 1. To foster creativity
2. To foster small motor development (drawing, painting, *cutting*, *pasting*, etc.)
3. To increase vocabulary knowledge
4. To practice turn-taking skills
5. To converse with peers and adults

General Plan

The children glue or paste construction-paper cut-outs in the shapes of pizza ingredients (previously cut by staff from construction paper) on a paper plate "crust" to make their own pizza art. Each different "ingredient" should be placed in a separate container so the children can easily choose the "toppings" they want. Children can first paste red circles for tomato sauce and then glue mushrooms, green peppers, pepperoni, onions, and cheese (yellow yarn) on top of their paper plates to make their pizzas. They can also cut out their own ingredients. Following this activity, the "pizzas" can be used in a pizza parlor dramatic play activity (see pp. 224–225).

Variation

Instead of separating the various cut-out shapes, staff may place all the cut-outs in one shallow container so the children must communicate to get the pieces they want.

Supplies Needed

- Glue (or paste)
- Construction-paper cut-outs in the shapes of pizza ingredients: large red circles for tomato sauce, grey mushrooms, green peppers, white onions, and small red circles for pepperonis
- Paper plates (at least one per child)
- Containers for the cut-outs (one per "ingredient")
- Yellow yarn
- Scissors
- Shallow container (optional)

ART ACTIVITY PLAN

Art: *Popcorn letters   **Date:** _____

Objectives: 1. To foster creativity
2. To foster small motor development (drawing, painting, cutting, *pasting*, etc.)
3. To increase vocabulary knowledge
4. To practice turn-taking skills
5. To converse with peers and adults

General Plan

The children choose letters of the alphabet (previously outlined by staff on various colors of construction paper), often their initials. Glue is drizzled onto the marker lines. The children then place popped popcorn one kernel at a time on the lines of glue.

Variation

The children outline all of the letters of the alphabet to display around the room.

Supplies Needed

- Popped popcorn
- Containers to hold the popcorn
- Markers
- White glue
- Tape (optional)

ART ACTIVITY PLAN

Art: Postcard art   **Date:**

Objectives:
1. To foster creativity
2. To foster small motor development (drawing, painting, *cutting*, *pasting*, etc.)
3. To increase vocabulary knowledge
4. To practice turn-taking skills
5. To converse with peers and adults

General Plan

Each child cuts out different pictures from magazines and glues them on one side of an index card. They then write messages to their family and friends on the other side of their cards. It is helpful to have messages such as, "Dear Mom and Dad," "I am having fun," and "Love," written on the chalkboard (or a chart) for the children to copy.

Supplies Needed

- Scissors
- A variety of magazines
- Glue or paste
- Index cards (3-inch × 5-inch or 4-inch × 6-inch)
- Markers or crayons
- Chalkboard and chalk or a chart

316

ART ACTIVITY PLAN

Art: Pumpkins (jack o'lanterns)   **Date:** _____

Objectives: 1. To foster creativity
2. To foster small motor development (drawing, painting, cutting, *pasting*, etc.)
3. To increase vocabulary knowledge
4. To practice turn-taking skills
5. To converse with peers and adults

General Plan

Each child makes a jack o'lantern out of a construction-paper cut-out in the shape of a pumpkin by pasting on eyes, a nose, and a mouth. The shapes should be placed in separate containers so that the children can easily choose the shapes they want. The children can add other decorations as they see fit by cutting out extra shapes. The pumpkins may be big or little.

Variation

Instead of separating the various cut-out shapes, staff may place all the cut-outs in one shallow container so the children must communicate to get the pieces they want. Another option is for each child to decorate a real miniature pumpkin using a black marker to indicate the eyes, a nose, a mouth, teeth, and so forth.

Supplies Needed

- Construction-paper cut-outs in the shape of pumpkins but of various sizes (at least one per child)
- Construction-paper cut-outs in various sizes and shapes (e.g., circles, triangles, rectangles, crescents)
- Containers for the cut-outs (one per shape)
- Glue sticks
- Sheets of black construction paper
- Scissors
- Miniature pumpkins (optional—at least one per child)
- Black markers (optional)
- Shallow container (optional)

ART ACTIVITY PLAN

Art: **Sand pictures _____   **Date:** _____

Objectives: 1. To foster creativity
2. To foster small motor development (drawing, painting, cutting, pasting, etc.)
3. To increase vocabulary knowledge
4. To practice turn-taking skills
5. To converse with peers and adults

General Plan

Each child places a piece of construction paper in a shallow box lid. The children then drip white or colored glue in a pattern on their paper. The pattern may be an abstract design or an outline of an object. Then, the children sprinkle sand on top of the glue to form a textured picture. The box lid can be tipped in various directions so that the sand sticks to the glue. The paper is then lifted and the excess sand is left in the box lid. The sand can then be poured back into a container.

Variation

Glitter could be used instead of sand.

Supplies Needed

- Construction paper (at least one piece per child)
- Shallow box lids (large enough to hold the construction paper)
- White or colored glue (To make colored glue, mix a small amount of tempera paint with white glue.)
- Sand
- Containers to hold the sand
- Glitter (optional)

ART ACTIVITY PLAN

Art: School bus   **Date:**

Objectives: 1. To foster creativity
2. To foster small motor development (drawing, painting, *cutting*, *pasting*, etc.)
3. To increase vocabulary knowledge
4. To practice turn-taking skills
5. To converse with peers and adults

General Plan

Each child is given a yellow construction-paper cut-out of a school bus. The children glue or paste their school buses on white pieces of paper. They then paste black circle cut-outs on the bus for wheels. Using extra paper or crayons, the children can make windows, children riding the bus, or a road. Some children may be able to cut out the bus and/or wheel shapes themselves.

Supplies Needed

- Yellow construction-paper cut-outs in the shape of school buses (one per child)
- White construction paper
- Black construction-paper cut-outs of circles (four per child)
- Glue (or paste)
- Extra construction-paper of various colors
- Scissors
- Crayons

ART ACTIVITY PLAN

Art: Shape pictures   **Date:** _____

Objectives: 1. To foster creativity
               2. To foster small motor development (drawing, painting, cutting, *pasting*, etc.)
               3. To increase vocabulary knowledge
               4. To practice turn-taking skills
               5. To converse with peers and adults

General Plan

The children can make a variety of pictures or designs by pasting construction-paper cut-outs of different shapes on paper. The shapes may be pasted on paper to form people, animals, houses, toys, designs, and so forth. Extra paper and scissors can be provided so the children can cut their own shapes.

Variation

Instead of separating the various cut-out shapes, staff may place all the cut-outs in one shallow container so the children must communicate to get the pieces they want.

Supplies Needed

- Construction-paper cut-outs in a variety shapes, colors, and sizes
- Containers for the cut-outs
- White construction paper
- Paste or glue
- Extra construction paper
- Scissors
- Markers (optional)
- Crayons (optional)
- Shallow container (optional)

ART ACTIVITY PLAN

Art: Snowmen   **Date:** _____

Objectives:
1. To foster creativity
2. To foster small motor development (*drawing*, painting, cutting, *pasting*, etc.)
3. To increase vocabulary knowledge
4. To practice turn-taking skills
5. To converse with peers and adults

General Plan

The children make snowmen by glueing three circles of different sizes on blue construction paper. The largest circle goes on the bottom, the medium-size circle is glued on top of it, and finally, the smallest circle is placed on top to make the head. The children can add details by pasting on pieces of paper or cloth for scarves, hats, and mittens. Black markers can be used to add facial features and arms. The children can use white chalk to make snowflakes and/or snow on the ground.

Supplies Needed

- White construction-paper cut-outs of circles (three sizes—small, medium, and large)
- Glue sticks
- Blue construction paper (one piece per child)
- Scraps of construction paper
- Scraps of cloth
- Black markers
- White chalk

ART ACTIVITY PLAN

Art: Teddy bears   **Date:** _____

Objectives:
1. To foster creativity
2. To foster small motor development (*drawing*, painting, cutting, *pasting*, etc.)
3. To increase vocabulary knowledge
4. To practice turn-taking skills
5. To converse with peers and adults

General Plan

Each child is given a piece of paper with a teddy bear outlined on it. The children can draw different faces on their bears with markers. The teddy bears can be filled in by glueing on different kinds of cloth or paper or by coloring. The children may also outline the bears with Cheerios. Brown construction-paper teddy bear cut-outs may be used instead of paper with outlines of teddy bears. The children can then draw the bears' faces or glue on cloth or paper to make the face and clothes for the bears.

Supplies Needed

- Paper with teddy bear outlines (at least one per child)
- Markers or crayons
- Glue or paste
- Scraps of cloth
- Scraps of paper
- Scissors
- Cheerios
- Teddy bear cut-outs (optional)

ART ACTIVITY PLAN

Art: **Tissue-paper art   **Date:** _____

Objectives: 1. To foster creativity
2. To foster small motor development (drawing, painting, cutting, *pasting*, etc.)
3. To increase vocabulary knowledge
4. To practice turn-taking skills
5. To converse with peers and adults

General Plan

Multicolored tissue paper that has been cut into small pieces is given to the children, who crush them and then paste them onto a pre-cut construction-paper form (e.g., fish, flower). The forms can be of various sizes. The tissue paper may be crushed by wrapping it around the eraser end of a pencil and then pushing it off onto the glue or paste that is already on the form. A crayon could be used instead of a pencil. Or the children can just crumple the squares and then paste them on the paper. When the forms are completely covered, the results are three-dimensional pictures or pictures with "texture."

Supplies Needed

- Multicolored tissue paper pieces (1-inch pieces)
- Paste or glue
- Pre-cut construction-paper forms (e.g., fish, flower) (one per child)
- Pencils or crayons
- Containers to hold the pencils, crayons, and tissue paper

ART ACTIVITY PLAN

Art: Trucks   **Date:**

Objectives:
1. To foster creativity
2. To foster small motor development (*drawing*, painting, cutting, *pasting*, etc.)
3. To increase vocabulary knowledge
4. To practice turn-taking skills
5. To converse with peers and adults

General Plan

Each child glues or pastes a large rectangular cut-out onto a piece of construction paper to make a truck trailer. Then, each child pastes a smaller square or triangle in front of the rectangle to make the cab of the truck. The children can use circles to make the wheels. Additional details (e.g., windows, lettering on the truck) can be drawn on the truck using markers or crayons.

Variations

Instead of separating the various cut-out shapes, staff may place all the cut-outs in one shallow container so the children must communicate to get the pieces they want. Other types of vehicles can be made using a variety of cut-outs made from different shapes.

Supplies Needed

- Construction-paper cut-outs in a variety of colors, sizes, and shapes (e.g., rectangles, circles, squares, triangles)
- Containers to hold the cut-outs (one per shape)
- Glue (or paste)
- White construction paper (one sheet per child)
- Markers or crayons

ART ACTIVITY PLAN

Art: *Valentine's Day cards   **Date:** _____

Objectives: 1. To foster creativity
2. To foster small motor development (drawing, painting, cutting, *pasting*, etc.)
3. To increase vocabulary knowledge
4. To practice turn-taking skills
5. To converse with peers and adults

General Plan

The children can make Valentine's Day cards by glueing or pasting different sizes of precut red, pink, and white construction paper hearts on a pink piece of construction paper folded in half to make a card. They can decorate their cards with glitter, paper doilies, and drawings. The children can also cut out their own heart shapes. To do this, paper is folded and half of a heart shape is outlined on the paper. The children cut out the heart by following the outline. They then unfold the paper to see the full heart shape.

Variation

A white piece of paper can be stapled inside the card for messages. A variety of messages can be available for the children to copy (e.g., "To Mom," "I love you," "Be my valentine")

Supplies Needed

- Precut heart shapes of all sizes in red, pink, and white colors
- Pink construction paper folded in half (at least one per child)
- Glue (or paste)
- Glitter
- Paper doilies
- Crayons or markers
- Scissors
- Extra red, pink, and white paper
- Stapler (optional)
- White paper (one sheet per card)
- Chalkboard and chalk (optional)

GROUP ACTIVITIES

GROUP ACTIVITIES:
LABELING AND MATCHING

GROUP ACTIVITY PLAN

Group: *Bones in a skeleton   **Date:**

Objectives:
1. To foster listening skills
2. To increase conceptual knowledge
3. To teach appropriate group interaction skills
4. To practice turn taking

Introduction

The children look at Smiley, the skeleton. The teacher tells the children that Smiley has a lot of bones and that they are going to take turns finding some of the bones. One child is asked to point to one of Smiley's toes; another child locates one of Smiley's fingers.

Group Participation

One by one, the children find bones on their own bodies and then locate them on Smiley (e.g., rib, hand, arm, leg, shoulder, backbone, head, jaw).

Summary/Transition Activity

The various bones are reviewed by the teacher, who locates them on Smiley.

Materials Needed

- Skeleton

GROUP ACTIVITY PLAN

Group: Care of a pet   **Date:** _____

Objectives:
1. To foster listening skills
2. To increase conceptual knowledge
3. To teach appropriate group interaction skills
4. To practice turn taking

Introduction

Water dishes, food dishes, collars, leashes, and cages are placed in front of the children. The teacher asks them, "Who uses these?" After they have responded (e.g., dogs, cats, pets), the teacher tells the children that the day's activity is about taking care of a pet.

Group Participation

The teacher holds up a food dish and has one child come to the front of the class to put some cat or dog food in it. The children are reminded that animals need food. The teacher might ask, "Why do animals need food?" or, "What do you feed your pet?" The teacher then asks, "What else do pets need?" and has another child fill a water dish. The class discusses different places that pets sleep and pets' need for some kind of shelter. The class also discusses what to do if a pet gets sick or needs shots and how a pet gets exercise. The teacher should continue to ask the children about their pets' needs (e.g., love, attention) until each child has had a chance to speak.

Variation

Care of other kinds of pets (e.g., fish, hamsters, birds) could also be discussed. For example, a fish would need an aquarium, a hamster a maze, a bird a cage, and so forth.

Summary/Transition Activity

Items pets need are reviewed with the children. The appropriate items are pointed out as each is mentioned.

Materials Needed

- Water dishes
- Food dishes
- Leashes
- Collars
- Cages (or dog houses)
- Pet food (both cat and dog food)
- Water
- Bird cages (optional)
- Aquariums (optional)
- Fish food (optional)

GROUP ACTIVITY PLAN

Group: Colors—yellow   **Date:** _____

Objectives: 1. To foster listening skills
2. To increase conceptual knowledge
3. To teach appropriate group interaction skills
4. To practice turn taking

Introduction

A yellow tub and a blue tub are placed in the front of the classroom. The teacher holds up a piece of yellow construction paper and names the color as "Yellow." The children are asked to look around the room to find other yellow items. One child is asked to choose an object that is yellow and place it in the yellow tub.

Group Participation

Other children are asked to choose objects that are yellow from a selection of red, yellow, and blue objects. The children place the yellow items in the yellow tub. Occasionally, a child is asked to choose a blue item and place it in the blue tub.

Summary/Transition Activity

The children are dismissed one by one after they point to something yellow on their clothes. (This activity should be done on "yellow" day so all of the children should be wearing something yellow.)

Variation

Similar activities can be done for other colors and should be organized according to the color assigned for the day. (At LAP, the children wear a particular color on Thursdays of every month [e.g., September is *blue* month, October is *yellow* month, November is *red* month].)

Materials Needed

- Yellow construction paper
- Yellow tub
- Blue tub
- A variety of yellow objects
- A few blue objects (for contrast with yellow)
- A few red objects (for contrast with yellow)

GROUP ACTIVITY PLAN

Group: "Feely" bag _____ **Date:** _____

Objectives: 1. To foster listening skills
2. To increase conceptual knowledge
3. To teach appropriate group interaction skills
4. To practice turn taking

Introduction

The children are told that they will be learning about the different senses. The teacher holds up the "feely" bag, which has a draw string top and contains several objects. The teacher then tells the children that they are going to try to guess what an object is by using their sense of *touch*. To demonstrate, a staff member then puts his or her hand into the bag and, without looking, tries to identify the object. He or she problem-solves out loud by saying things like, "It feels sort of round. It is soft. I know—it's a Nerf ball!"

Group Participation

One child is invited to come to the front of the class and try to identify an object. After the child makes a guess, he or she holds up the object so all can see. Other children come down one at a time and try to identify the objects by touch. After identifying an object, the child can either put it back in the bag or set it to one side.

Note

In order to facilitate turn taking, the group of children could be divided into two or three smaller groups, each with its own "feely" bag.

Summary/Transition Activity

The children are asked, "What was easy and what was hard about guessing the objects?" or, "What sense were we using to name the objects?" The children are reminded that the sense of touch is only one of the senses we have.

Materials Needed

- Drawstring bags (or boxes) (one per small group of children)
- Ten to 20 toy objects contained in the bags (e.g., Nerf ball, spool, car, cup, boat, bead, different kinds of plastic fruit, sandpaper)

GROUP ACTIVITY PLAN

Group: Seasons—spring _____   **Date:** _____

Objectives: 1. To foster listening skills
2. To increase conceptual knowledge
3. To teach appropriate group interaction skills
4. To practice turn taking

Introduction

One child is asked to come to the front of the class and move the arrow on the seasons dial to *spring.* The teacher tells the children that a new season has begun and soon the flowers will be blooming.

Group Participation

The children are shown some pictures and asked to find spring things in them. They list things that happen during spring. All of their suggestions are written on the chalkboard.

Summary/Transition Activity

All of the seasons are reviewed using the seasons dial. The spring items listed on the chalkboard are quickly reviewed and the children prepare for music time.

Variation

A similar activity can be done at the beginning of the other seasons (e.g., summer, fall, winter).

Materials Needed

- Seasons dial (a handmade object similar to a clock that is divided into four labeled sections [fall, winter, spring, and summer] and includes an arrow or "hand" that can be moved to point to a particular section)
- Pictures of spring
- Chalkboard
- Chalk
- Pictures of summer, fall, or winter (optional)

GROUP ACTIVITY PLAN

Group: Shapes—Circles I   **Date:** _____

Objectives: 1. To foster listening skills
               2. To increase conceptual knowledge
               3. To teach appropriate group interaction skills
               4. To practice turn taking

Introduction

Using colored tape, a large circle and a small circle are made on the floor in front of the children. Tracing around each shape with an index finger, the teacher names each circle as large or small. The teacher then holds up a cardboard circle (many are available) and says, "This is a circle—a large circle. I'm going to put it in the large circle area."

Group Participation

One at a time the children are then asked to place a cardboard circle in either the large or small circle area. Some of the children are asked to make circles in the air.

Note

Having two circle areas (large and small) allows the teacher to make different types of requests. One child can be asked to label the shape as a circle and helped to place it in the appropriate outline. Another child can be asked to identify the large circle and focus on both the shape and size of a cut-out. The activity, then, can be used to review the concept of large and small while the new concept of shapes is introduced.

Summary/Transition Activity

A circle cut-out and a square cut-out are held up and the children are asked to choose the circle. Then a circle cut-out and a triangle cut-out are held up and again the children are asked to identify the circle.

Variation

Similar activities can be done to introduce squares and then triangles.

Materials Needed

- Colored tape
- Circle cut-outs in a variety of sizes
- Square cut-out
- Triangle cut-out

GROUP ACTIVITY PLAN

Group: Circles II   **Date:** _____

Objectives: 1. To foster listening skills
2. To increase conceptual knowledge
3. To teach appropriate group interaction skills
4. To practice turn taking

Introduction

Using colored tape, a large circle and a small circle are made on the floor in front of the children. Using a finger, the teacher traces around each shape, labeling each circle as "large" or "small." The teacher then holds up a construction paper circle and says, "This is a circle. I'm going to put it in the big circle."

Group Participation

One at a time different children place a circle cut-out in either the large or small circle areas. Many different sizes of circles are available. Some children make circles in the air to show the shape of a circle.

Variation

An alternate activity is to have a child place a foot in one taped circle area and a hand in another circle area. Another child could put a knee in one circle area and his or her head in another, and so forth.

Summary/Transition Activity

The teacher holds up a circle and a square and asks the children to label or identify the circle. The teacher then holds up a circle and a triangle. Again, the children identify and/or label the circle. The children are then instructed to put away their chairs and prepare for music time by sitting in a circle.

Materials Needed

- Colored tape (to make large and small taped outlines on the floor)
- Ten large circle cut-outs (of various colors)
- Ten small circle cut-outs (of various colors)
- One square cut-out
- One triangle cut-out

GROUP ACTIVITY PLAN

Group: *Shapes—rectangle _____ **Date:** _____

Objectives: 1. To foster listening skills
2. To increase conceptual knowledge
3. To teach appropriate group interaction skills
4. To practice turn taking

Note

Prior to this activity, lessons following the format below should be presented to teach the children about circles (see p. 336), squares, and triangles.

Introduction

Using colored tape, a large rectangle and a small rectangle are made on the floor in front of the children. (From previous activities, circle, square, and triangle outlines may already be taped on the floor.) Tracing around the rectangles with an index finger, the teacher notes for the children that each rectangle has four sides and four corners. The teacher then tells the children, "It is kind of like a square, but it is different because all the sides are not the same size. Two of the sides are short, and two of the sides are long." The teacher holds up a cardboard rectangle and asks, "How do I know that this is a rectangle?" Responding together, the teacher and the children say, "Because it has four corners and long and short sides." A square cut-out is then shown to remind the children that the square has four equal sides and four corners. One child is asked to put the large rectangle into the large rectangle area on the floor.

Group Participation

One at a time the children are asked to place a cardboard rectangle in either the large or small rectangle area. To review earlier lessons, some of the children are asked to put squares, circles, or triangles in the appropriate shape areas.

Summary/Transition Activity

The teacher alternately presents three rectangles, three triangles, three squares, and three circles, having the children, in chorus, quickly label the shapes. A rectangle is presented last.

Materials Needed

- Colored tape (to make large and small taped outlines on the floor)
- Rectangle cut-outs in a variety of sizes
- Circle cut-outs in a variety of sizes
- Square cut-outs in a variety of sizes
- Triangle cut-outs in a variety of sizes

GROUP ACTIVITY PLAN

Group: *Shapes—diamond   **Date:** _____

Objectives: 1. To foster listening skills
                2. To increase conceptual knowledge
                3. To teach appropriate group interaction skills
                4. To practice turn taking

Note

Prior to this activity, lessons should have been presented to teach the children about circles (see p. 336), squares, triangles, and rectangles (see p. 337).

Introduction

From previous activities, circle, square, triangle, and rectangle outlines may already be taped on the floor. The teacher points to the various shape outlines and has the children, in chorus, label them. Using colored tape, the teacher then adds large and small diamond shapes and labels them for the children.

Group Participation

Diamond-shaped cut-outs in a variety of colors are available. Each child is given a diamond-shaped cut-out. Based on the color of the cut-out each child is holding, actions are assigned (e.g., those with yellow diamond cut-outs stand up and put their diamonds in a box, those with orange diamond cut-outs place their cut-outs in the big diamond outline, those with red diamond cut-outs put their cut-outs in the small diamond outline).

Summary/Transition Activity

The labels of the shapes are reviewed by having some of the children locate and stand in the appropriate outlined shape area. The diamond shape is featured last.

Materials Needed

- Colored tape (to make large and small taped outlines on the floor)
- Diamond-shaped construction-paper cut-outs in a variety of colors and sizes

GROUP ACTIVITY PLAN

Group: Shapes—review   **Date:** _____

Objectives: 1. To foster listening skills
2. To increase conceptual knowledge
3. To teach appropriate group interaction skills
4. To practice turn taking

Note

Prior to this activity, lessons should have been presented to teach the children about circles (see p. 336), squares, triangles, rectangles (see p. 337), and diamonds (see p. 338).

Introduction

From previous activities, circle, square, triangle, rectangle, and diamond shapes should already be taped on the floor. The teacher points to the different outlines on the floor and labels each one (e.g., circle, square, triangle, rectangle, diamond). A child is asked to name his or her favorite shape. Based on the child's response, the teacher stands in the outlined area of that shape (e.g., if the child chooses the circle, the teacher stands in the circle area).

Group Participation

Different children are asked to stand in the various shape areas. The difficulty of the requests can be varied by asking some children to identify only the shape and others to select a size (large or small) in addition to identifying a shape. Color can be included in the requests as well (e.g., "Find the big red square") if different colored tape was used to make the different outlines. The task can be made more challenging by having children place a hand in one shape area and a foot in another. It may be necessary to divide the children into smaller groups.

Summary/Transition Activity

The teacher reviews the shape labels by pointing to or standing in the outlined area.

GROUP ACTIVITY PLAN

Group: Video—jungle   **Date:** _____

Objectives: 1. To foster listening skills
2. To increase conceptual knowledge
3. To teach appropriate group interaction skills
4. To practice turn taking

Introduction

The teacher tells the children that they are going to see a movie about a jungle and that they should notice what kinds of plants and animals live in the jungle. They should also look for plants and animals that are different from the ones they see in their neighborhoods.

Group Participation

The children sit so they can easily see the monitor and watch the videotape. Periodically, staff members point out plants and animals that appear in the videotape.

Summary/Transition Activity

After the videotape has ended, the children are asked to name some of the insects, plants, and animals they saw. The children might also tell what they liked about the videotape.

Variation

Other videotapes can be used to help the children identify animals of different environments, features of science, customs of different cultures, and so forth.

Materials Needed

- Videotape about a jungle (e.g., "The Jungle Book")
- VCR and monitor

GROUP ACTIVITY PLAN

Group: *What does ____ eat?_____   **Date:** _____

Objectives: 1. To foster listening skills
              2. To increase conceptual knowledge
              3. To teach appropriate group interaction skills
              4. To practice turn taking

Introduction

The teacher begins a discussion about the kinds of foods people eat. The children are told that they are going to look at a book called *My First Book of Nature* (Kuhn, 1993), which tells what different animals eat. The book is opened and the children are shown a picture of a bird. The teacher points out that the mama bird is feeding her babies worms.

Group Participation

Before each picture of an animal is shown, the teacher asks the children to guess what the animal eats. Then the teacher shows the picture of the animal. So, for example, the teacher might begin by asking the children, "What do kittens eat?" When the children guess milk, the teacher shows them the picture of the kittens drinking milk. The teacher then continues in the same manner, introducing the other animals in the book.

Summary/Transition Activity

The lesson is ended by reviewing that some animals eat grass, some milk, some fish, and so forth.

Materials Needed

- *My First Book of Nature* (Kuhn, 1993)

GROUP ACTIVITIES: CLASSIFICATION

GROUP ACTIVITY PLAN

Group: Big and little   **Date:** _____

Objectives: 1. To foster listening skills
             2. To increase conceptual knowledge
             3. To teach appropriate group interaction skills
             4. To practice turn taking

Introduction

A big tub and a little tub are placed in front of the children. The teacher holds up a big object and a little object (e.g., a big toy horse and a little toy horse). The teacher then puts the big object in the big tub and the little object in the little tub. He or she then tells the children they are going to help sort some objects into big and little items.

Group Participation

The teacher holds up other items that are the same except for size and has different children put the items in the two tubs. They tell why they put the items where they did. ("I put it there because it is a big ____ or a little ____.") The class proceeds through several item pairs. A variety of sizes are available so the children begin to understand that it is the comparison between the items that determines whether something is big or little. (For later lessons, the terms large and small may be used.)

Summary/Transition Activity

Two children come to the front of the classroom and the rest of the children say who is big and who is little. The child who is little then sits down. Another child who is taller than the "big" child comes up. Then, the children decide who is bigger. Finally, an adult stands by the last child and asks who is bigger? (Another way would be to have the big child sit down and place a doll by the little child and ask, "Now who is bigger?") The teacher should be careful not to choose the smallest child in the class or a child who is particularly sensitive about his or her size.

Materials Needed

- Big tub
- Little tub
- Ten pairs of items of different sizes
- Doll (optional)

GROUP ACTIVITY PLAN

Group: Empty and full   **Date:** _____

Objectives: 1. To foster listening skills
               2. To increase conceptual knowledge
               3. To teach appropriate group interaction skills
               4. To practice turn taking

Introduction

The teacher holds up two containers, one filled with small objects and one that is empty, and labels each (e.g., "This one is full of Lego blocks, and this one is empty—nothing there"). One child is asked to come to the front of the class and to identify the full container.

Group Participation

Two different containers are placed in front of the children. This time one is full of water and one is empty. In chorus, the class labels the containers as "full" or "empty" as the teacher points to each container. Then an empty cup and a full cup are placed in front of the children. One child is asked to come to the front of the class and to point to the empty cup. The activity is continued with two containers being presented and the child's task (e.g., to point to the full or empty one) varied.

Variation

Children may be asked to pour water (or objects) into empty containers to make them full containers.

Summary/Transition Activity

In chorus, the whole class again labels two containers—one as "empty" and one as "full." Then the children put their "empty" chairs where they belong and get ready for music time.

Materials Needed

- Several containers of varying shapes, sizes, and materials
- A variety of objects (e.g., toys, plastic food, blocks)
- Water

GROUP ACTIVITY PLAN

Group: Farm and zoo animals   **Date:** _____

Objectives:
1. To foster listening skills
2. To increase conceptual knowledge
3. To teach appropriate group interaction skills
4. To practice turn taking

Introduction

A farm area (a toy barn with a toy fence) and a zoo area (a plastic or cardboard mat with zoo scenes drawn on it) are created. The teacher tells the children that they are going to put the farm animals by the barn and the zoo animals in the zoo. One child is asked to put a toy cow in the farm area, and another child is asked to place a toy elephant in the zoo area.

Group Participation

Several different toy animals are distributed to the children. One at a time the children are called upon to come to the front of the class, label an animal, and decide where it goes. The children can then be asked to name animals not represented as toys and tell where they live.

Variation

If toy animals are not available, pictures of animals could be used instead.

Summary/Transition Activity

The classifications of farm and zoo are reviewed, renaming a few of the animals in each classification.

Materials Needed

- Toy barn
- Toy fence
- Zoo mat
- Toy farm animals
- Toy zoo animals
- Pictures of farm and zoo animals (optional)

GROUP ACTIVITY PLAN

Group: Float and sink   **Date:** _____

Objectives:
1. To foster listening skills
2. To increase conceptual knowledge
3. To teach appropriate group interaction skills
4. To practice turn taking

Introduction

A clear plastic container is filled with water, and a boat that will float is placed on top of the water. The teacher says, "The boat is floating." Next, a penny is placed in the water, and the children watch it sink. A child comes to the front of the class and identifies the object that floats.

Group Participation

One at a time, the children come to the front of the class and choose an object. Each child predicts whether the object will sink or float. Then the child puts the object in the water and the class judges whether the child was correct. The activity is repeated until all children have had a chance to put an object in the water. The children may pass around a plastic spoon and a metal spoon to feel the difference in their weights. Then one child can demonstrate which floats and which sinks.

Summary/Transition Activity

The children try to tell why an object will float or sink. The teacher demonstrates that some things that are big float and some things that are small sink. The children should note that why an object floats depends on the material the object is made out of, rather than the size.

Materials Needed

- A clear plastic container filled with water
- Objects that will float (e.g., boats, corks, plastic spoon)
- Objects that will sink (screw, metal spoon, penny)

GROUP ACTIVITY PLAN

Group: *Fruits and vegetables   **Date:**

Objectives:
1. To foster listening skills
2. To increase conceptual knowledge
3. To teach appropriate group interaction skills
4. To practice turn taking

Introduction

The teacher holds up a plastic apple and a plastic carrot and asks the children to tell which one is the fruit and which is the vegetable. If they do not respond, the teacher labels each item and puts each in a different tub.

Group Participation

Each child is given a plastic fruit or vegetable. One at a time, each child places his or her item into the appropriate tub. Each child also labels his or her item as a fruit or vegetable before placing it in the appropriate tub. If a child makes an error, the teacher removes the item from the wrong tub and has the child place it in the appropriate tub.

Variation

Rather than each child being given an item, the children could choose their own items from an assortment.

Summary/Transition Activity

As a group, the children are asked to label the items in the fruit category and then label the items in the vegetable category.

Materials Needed

- Plastic fruit (e.g., apple)
- Plastic vegetables (e.g., carrot)
- Two tubs

GROUP ACTIVITY PLAN

Group: Hot and cold   **Date:** _____

Objectives: 1. To foster listening skills
              2. To increase conceptual knowledge
              3. To teach appropriate group interaction skills
              4. To practice turn taking

Introduction

An ice cube is placed in a dish in front of the children, and a cup of water is heated in a microwave oven or on a stove so the children can see the steam. The steaming water is placed next to the ice cube. The ice cube is labeled as something cold and the hot water as something hot. Each child is permitted to touch the ice cube (but not the water). The children are told that the class is going to sort out things that are usually hot and things that are usually cold by putting them either on the play stove or in the play refrigerator (from the house area). The children are asked if soup is hot or cold. After the children answer "hot," one child should place a picture of a bowl of soup on the play stove. The teacher then asks whether ice cream is hot or cold. After a child answers "cold," another child places a picture of an ice cream cone in the play refrigerator.

Note

The concept of "hot" should be associated with *not* touching.

Group Participation

Half of the children are given pictures of hot foods and the other half are given pictures of cold foods. Each child comes to the front of the class and puts his or her picture on the stove or in the refrigerator, depending on which kind of food he or she has.

Variation

Plastic food items could be used instead of pictures of food.

Summary/Transition Activity

After everyone has participated, each item on the stove or in the refrigerator is reviewed by labeling it as hot or cold (e.g., "hot coffee," "cold milk").

Materials Needed

- Ice cube
- Dish
- Microwave oven or stove
- Hot water in a cup
- Play stove
- Play refrigerator
- Pictures of cold foods
- Pictures of hot foods
- Plastic cold foods (optional)
- Plastic hot foods (optional)

GROUP ACTIVITY PLAN

Group: Loud and soft   **Date:** _____

Objectives: 1. To foster listening skills
               2. To increase conceptual knowledge
               3. To teach appropriate group interaction skills
               4. To practice turn taking

Introduction

A drum is placed in the middle of the floor. The teacher hits it hard so the sound is *loud*. Then the teacher hits the drum softly so that the sound is soft. Each sound is labeled. The teacher then hits a triangle (the musical instrument) softly. It is then hit hard so the sound produced is loud. The sounds are labeled again.

Group Participation

Different children are invited to hit the drum (or triangle or other instruments) either hard or softly. The other children decide whether the sound is loud or soft. A child is then asked to speak softly (or loudly). The class decides if the child's voice was loud or soft. The class is asked to yell when the teacher's hand is raised high and whisper when the teacher's hand is lowered.

Summary/Transition Activity

The terms *loud* and *soft* are reviewed. A widely known song (e.g., ABC song) is sung loudly when the teacher raises her hand and softly when the hand is lowered.

Materials Needed

- Drum
- Triangle
- Other instruments (optional)

GROUP ACTIVITY PLAN

Group: *Recycling   **Date:** _____

Objectives: 1. To foster listening skills
             2. To increase conceptual knowledge
             3. To teach appropriate group interaction skills
             4. To practice turn taking

Introduction

The teacher begins the lesson by explaining what the word *recycle* means. He or she tells the children that some items that are often thrown away could be re-used but must be taken to special places to be specially processed. A pile of recyclable items is placed in front of the children. The teacher presents different items, showing the recycle symbol where possible (i.e., on the plastic or styrofoam item). Plastic, cardboard, aluminum, newspaper, and styrofoam bins are set up.

Group Participation

The children sort the "trash" into the recycling bins, checking the plastic and styrofoam items for symbols indicating they can be recycled. Each child is given an opportunity to sort some of the "trash" into the appropriate bins. Staff should help the children find the recycle symbol on bottles and other items.

Summary/Transition Activity

Each recycling bin set up in the front of the class is labeled. The children are reminded that many trash items can be recycled by sorting them into bins and taking them to a recycling center.

Materials Needed

- Plastic bottles
- Newspapers
- Sodapop cans
- Cardboard
- Styrofoam items
- Bins (one per type of item to be recycled)

GROUP ACTIVITY PLAN

Group: Same and different   **Date:** _____

Objectives:
1. To foster listening skills
2. To increase conceptual knowledge
3. To teach appropriate group interaction skills
4. To practice turn taking

Introduction

The teacher holds up two objects that are exactly the same and talks about what is the same about them. He or she then puts them into one "pile" or tub and holds up two new objects that are different from each other (e.g., a car and a boat). The teacher labels these as different and puts them in another "pile" or tub.

Group Participation

The teacher continues to present pairs of objects to the children and have each child decide whether a pair of objects is the same or different and place the objects in the appropriate pile or tub. The class should start out with objects that are exactly the same or are quite different from each other. Then, the class proceeds to objects that vary somewhat but that can still be labeled the same (e.g., different color cars). The teacher should focus on the fact that items can be the same even when they are alike in some ways, but are not necessarily alike in every way and explain that often things are the same if they can be labeled with the same word (e.g., cars).

Summary/Transition Activity

The teacher reviews the meaning of the words: *same* describes things that are alike in some way, and *different* describes things that are not alike.

Materials Needed

- Five exactly matched pairs of objects
- Ten other objects (e.g., cars, dolls, boats, balls)
- Two tubs (optional)

GROUP ACTIVITY PLAN

Group: *Things that hold paper together _____ **Date:** _____

Objectives: 1. To foster listening skills
2. To increase conceptual knowledge
3. To teach appropriate group interaction skills
4. To practice turn taking

Introduction

A stapler and a paper clip are placed in front of the children, who are asked what is alike about the two items. The teacher helps the children determine that both can be used to hold paper together. A child is asked to come to the front of the class to demonstrate how each item works to hold paper together.

Group Participation

A variety of other items (see list below) is added to the display. The children are asked to decide whether each new item can be used to hold paper together. The children should demonstrate how paper can be held together with each item. (This demonstration is particularly important if other children question whether an item really holds paper together.) After all of the items have been discussed and classified, note that the rejected items can all be used to write.

Variation

The teacher may note that items can be alike in function even though they look quite different. For example, a paper clip and a stapler do not look similar to each other, but they perform similar purposes.

Summary/Transition Activity

The items that hold paper together are listed.

Materials Needed

- Paper
- Things that hold paper together: stapler, paper clips, tape, folder, glue, rubber bands, binder clips, and so forth
- Things used to write: pen, marker, chalk, crayon, pencil, typewriter

GROUP ACTIVITY PLAN

Group: Things found in water   **Date:** _____

Objectives: 1. To foster listening skills
2. To increase conceptual knowledge
3. To teach appropriate group interaction skills
4. To practice turn taking

Introduction

A tub of water is placed on a mat on the floor. Beside the mat are a variety of objects, some that can go in water and some that should not be placed in water. A toy boat and a piece of paper are presented to the children. The teacher asks the children to choose which object can be found in or on water. Following the children's response, one child is then asked to place the boat in the water.

Group Participation

Individual children are asked to choose between two objects, one of which goes in water and one of which does not. After several children have had turns, the tub of water is removed and the children are asked to sort pictures of objects. Those that are found in water are placed in one pile and those objects not found in water in a different pile.

Variation

Rather than just sorting pictures of objects, an activity best suited for older children, the children could sort a variety of objects.

Summary/Transition Activity

The category of objects that go in water is reviewed as the teacher quickly holds up a few pictures from the water pile.

Materials Needed

- Tub filled with water
- Mat
- Objects that go in water (e.g., toy boats, toy fish, shells)
- Objects that do not go in water (e.g., paper, toy cars, a doll bed, a chair)
- Pictures of objects that go in water (e.g., seaweed, shells, fishing pole, boats)
- Pictures of objects that do not go in water (e.g., houses, radios)
- Towels

GROUP ACTIVITIES:
SEQUENCING

GROUP ACTIVITY PLAN

Group: Acting out stories   **Date:**

Objectives: 1. To foster listening skills
2. To increase sequencing ability
3. To increase knowledge of story telling
4. To teach appropriate group interaction skills
5. To practice turn taking

Introduction

The children are reminded of a familiar story as a staff member reads it or quickly summarizes it.

Group Participation

Children are assigned roles from the story. The children not chosen the first time are assured that everyone will have a turn and that they have the very important job of being a good listening audience. The teacher narrates the story as the children act it out. They should say as many of the lines as they can, with prompts given when needed. The story is repeated with new actors until all the children have had turns.

Variation

Several stories may be acted out instead of one being repeated.

Summary/Transition Activity

After everyone has had a turn, the children can talk about other stories that they would like to act out another day. The teacher should compliment the children's acting.

Materials Needed

- Book(s)
- Props for the stories

GROUP ACTIVITY PLAN

Group: Color patterns   **Date:** _____

Objectives:
1. To foster listening skills
2. To increase ability to recognize and sequence patterns on the basis of color
3. To teach appropriate group interaction skills
4. To practice turn taking

Introduction

A pattern of 1-inch colored cubes (e.g., red-yellow-red-yellow) is presented, and the teacher shows the children how to continue the pattern by adding the appropriate blocks.

Variation

Another strategy is to have the children repeat the pattern by creating new rows of blocks that match the teacher's pattern (i.e., a matching activity).

Group Participation

The children approach the displayed pattern one at a time (or two at a time for peer support and help). A block pattern appropriate for the child's level is placed on the floor. Some children repeat a simple pattern (e.g., red-blue-red-blue), while others do more complicated patterns (e.g., red-blue-blue-red-blue-blue, red-blue-green-green-red-blue-green-green). The activity continues until all the children have had turns.

Variation

For a greater challenge, the teacher could make a pattern, cover it with a piece of cardboard, and then have the child repeat the pattern from memory.

Summary/Transition Activity

Each child is given a small pile of blocks to create a pattern. The children might want to do this and then trade with a partner to see if they can copy each other's patterns. Staff then collect the blocks and review colors.

Materials Needed

- One-inch colored cubes
- Cardboard (optional)

GROUP ACTIVITY PLAN

Group: Flannel-board story   **Date:** _____

Objectives:
1. To foster listening skills
2. To increase conceptual knowledge
3. To teach appropriate group interaction skills
4. To practice turn taking

Introduction

The flannel board is set up, and the felt pieces are laid out. The teacher tells a story, placing the appropriate felt pieces on the flannel board.

Group Participation

Some of the children are given felt pieces. One child is invited to come up to the front of the class to retell the story. As the storyteller tells the story, the children with the appropriate felt pieces come to the flannel board and place them on it.

Variation

The story could be presented a third time while the children act it out.

Summary/Transition Activity

Some of the children help to take the felt pieces off the flannel board, placing the pieces in story order in the storage container.

Materials Needed

- Flannel board
- Felt pieces
- Storybook
- Props (optional)
- Container for the felt pieces

GROUP ACTIVITY PLAN

Group: Sound sequencing   **Date:** _____

Objectives: 1. To foster listening skills
2. To increase the ability to recognize and sequence patterns
3. To teach appropriate group interaction skills
4. To practice turn taking

Introduction

A drum is placed in front of the children. The teacher taps out a simple pattern while the children listen. The teacher then repeats the pattern while they listen again. One child is invited to come up to the front of the class and try to make the same pattern. (The child can be helped if necessary so that the sound pattern matches.)

Group Participation

A different pattern is played and another child tries to match it. This continues until all the children have had at least one turn. The patterns can vary from two short taps to complicated patterns involving a series of taps grouped in two or three sequences. For example, one pattern might be tap-tap-pause-tap. Another might be tap-tap-tap-pause-tap-tap. Still another might be tap-pause-tap-tap-tap. Other sample patterns include the following:

- Tap-tap-pause-tap-tap
- Tap-tap-tap-pause-tap
- Tap-pause-tap-tap
- Loud tap-pause-soft tap
- Loud tap-loud tap-pause-soft tap-soft tap

Variation

- A keyboard can be used to set a rhythm.
- The children may clap the rhythms.

Summary/Transition Activity

The teacher reviews that the day's activity involved matching patterns and then plays a rhythm from a song that is to be sung during music time.

Materials Needed

- Drum
- Keyboard (optional)

GROUP ACTIVITY PLAN

Group: *Writing a class newsletter   **Date:**

Objectives: 1. To foster listening skills
               2. To increase knowledge about newsletters
               3. To foster sequencing skills
               4. To teach appropriate group interaction skills
               5. To practice turn taking

Introduction

A large piece of poster paper with columns drawn on it to resemble a newspaper is taped to the blackboard. The teacher tells the children that they are going to write a class newsletter to tell their parents what has been happening in the class. The title of the newsletter (e.g., *LAPlines*; see Appendix A) and the date are written at the top. The children are asked for ideas about what to write.

Group Participation

The teacher writes down the children's ideas. Then, two or three at a time, the children come up to sign the articles or to draw pictures. Two or three news stories are written, and a couple of advertisements could be written or illustrated.

Summary/Transition Activity

The teacher rereads all of the stories, pointing out the headlines, bylines, illustrations, and so forth.

Materials Needed

- Poster paper with columns drawn on it
- Tape
- Blackboard
- Markers and crayons

GROUP ACTIVITY PLAN

Group: Writing an experience story   **Date:** _____

Objectives: 1. To foster listening skills
              2. To increase sequencing skills
              3. To foster the ability to tell a story
              4. To teach appropriate group interaction skills
              5. To practice turn taking

Introduction

A large piece of poster board is taped on the blackboard. The teacher tells the children that the class is going to write a story about what happened to something the class created earlier that week (e.g., their gingerbread cookies).

Group Participation

One child is asked to tell the first thing the class did (e.g., made cookies), and a staff member writes it on the poster board. Another child tells what happened next (e.g., went outside while the cookies were baking). The activity continues in this fashion, with the staff member writing down what the children say (e.g., "The cookies were missing when we got back. We asked people if they had seen our cookies. They said they saw them running down the hall. Finally, we found our cookies in the library, and we ate them."). The teacher rereads the story after it is completed.

Summary/Transition Activity

The story can be illustrated with pictures drawn by the children.

Variation

Instant pictures can be taken as the experience occurs. The pictures are then used to help the children in developing and sequencing the story. The pictures can be used as illustrations.

Materials Needed

- A large piece of poster board
- Tape
- Blackboard
- Markers
- Paper
- Crayons
- Instant camera and film (optional)

GROUP ACTIVITIES:
SAFETY AND LIFE SKILLS

GROUP ACTIVITY PLAN

Group: *Emergency information _____ **Date:** _____

Objectives: 1. To foster listening skills
2. To increase conceptual knowledge
3. To teach appropriate group interaction skills
4. To practice turn taking

Introduction

The teacher asks the children what they need to know in case of an emergency. If the children do not seem to understand the word *emergency,* the teacher should explain and give examples. After some brainstorming by the children, the teacher suggests that knowing their full names, addresses, and telephone numbers is important if they need to call for a police officer, an ambulance, or the help of an emergency agency. A staff member might pretend to be an ambulance dispatcher and ask one or two children to say their full names, addresses, and telephone numbers. (If some children do not know any of the information, the teacher should tell them and have them repeat it.)

Group Participation

The children divide into groups of 5–10 children per adult. Each child is asked to say his or her full name, a parent's name, and his or her address. If the child knows his telephone number, he or she should say that, too. The children practice looking at the number that is listed on the program's telephone so that if in an emergency they can "read" the numbers to the 911 operator. The children role play being 911 dispatchers and callers who are asking for information. The activity is extended by having a pretend emergency in which one child is to call 911 and tell what is happening and then try to follow the instructions given by the 911 operator (usually the adult).

Summary/Transition Activity

The children can end the activity by recombining into one group and doing a fingerplay:

> Five little monkeys jumping on the bed,
> one fell off and hurt his head.
> Mama called the doctor and the doctor said,
> "No more monkeys jumping on the bed."

Materials Needed

- Children's addresses and telephone numbers written on index cards
- Play telephones

GROUP ACTIVITY PLAN

Group: Fire safety rules   **Date:** _____

Objectives:
1. To foster listening skills
2. To increase conceptual knowledge
3. To teach appropriate group interaction skills
4. To practice turn taking

Introduction

The teacher asks the children what they should do if the fire alarm at the preschool sounds. They discuss what they should do if their house catches on fire. The teacher facilitates a conversation about crawling on the floor and touching doors to see if they are hot before opening them. The teacher might show pictures of children following this procedure. The class also discusses calling 911 and giving their names and addresses when the dispatcher asks them for them.

Group Participation

Some of the children practice crawling and touching the classroom door before opening it. Then the class problem-solves about what to do if the door is hot. In addition, the class should talk about having a place for family members to gather outside if their house does catch on fire. The teacher should explain that this helps everyone know where each person is. Some children practice calling 911 on play telephones. Finally, the class discusses what to do if their clothing catches on fire. Some children demonstrate the "stop, drop, and roll" technique (i.e., the children stop moving, drop to the ground, and roll over and over to put out the fire on their clothes). The teacher shows pictures of children doing the "stop, drop, and roll" technique.

Variation

A real fire drill can be planned and implemented.

Summary/Transition Activity

The teacher reviews what to do in case of a fire at school, at home, or when clothing catches on fire.

Materials Needed

- Pictures of children crawling and touching a door
- Pictures of children stopping, dropping, and rolling to put out a fire on their clothing
- Play telephones

GROUP ACTIVITY PLAN

Group: Seatbelt safety   **Date:** _____

Objectives: 1. To foster listening skills
2. To increase conceptual knowledge
3. To teach appropriate group interaction skills
4. To practice turn taking

Introduction

The teacher tells the children that when they ride in cars they should wear their seatbelts. The children put on pretend seatbelts (neckties wrapped around the children's chairs) and pretend to drive to the park.

Group Participation

Toy examples of a car, tractor, motorcycle, and boat are placed in front of the children. Different children come up and pretend to ride in the different vehicles. The teacher asks the children which vehicles have seatbelts and makes sure the children riding those vehicles have put on their seatbelts.

Summary/Transition Activity

The teacher leads a discussion of why seatbelts should be worn.

Materials Needed

- Neckties (pretend seatbelts)
- Toy car
- Toy tractor
- Toy motorcycle
- Toy boat

GROUP ACTIVITIES: PREACADEMICS

Many of the group activities previously provided involving matching, sequencing, and classification activities underlie the development of preacademic skills. However, in this section, particular emphasis is placed on beginning literacy activities, which leads to knowledge of the letters of the alphabet, associated sounds, and beginning number skills. Presenting a new letter each week meets the objective of introducing the concept of alphabet letters and representation of sounds. It is not expected that preschool children will learn to write each letter. Opportunities for writing are provided briefly as part of each lesson, particularly for children whose names begin with the target letter, but writing should not be the main focus of the activity. It is, however, important that children have many opportunities to write. Writing their names on art projects is one way to emphasize writing. Other ways include having chalkboards, paper, and pencils available for the children to use, or including writing as part of a dramatic play activity (e.g., registration book for the motel dramatic play [see p. 212], appointment books for a doctor's office dramatic play [see p. 182]). Perfect letter formation is not necessarily a goal, although many children learn to print legibly. The major goal of providing writing activities for preschool children is to give them experiences in holding a pencil and practice in drawing or writing, which aids in the development of fine motor skills.

Here, general alphabet lesson procedures are given; they can be used to introduce each alphabet letter and associated sound(s). In addition, several letters–sound activities involving rhyming and discrimination are described. Activities that are marked with an asterisk are more difficult than the introductory lessons and should be implemented later in the school year. Five sample activity plans (for letters A, B, E, N, and R) are used to illustrate how the general plan can be implemented.

Number recognition and numerical concepts can be addressed throughout the preschool activities (e.g., calendar time for number recognition, snacktime for counting). However, a few structured lessons designed to teach number recognition, writing of numbers, and numerical concepts may also be provided during group time. Three sample lessons of this nature are provided here following the five alphabet activity plans.

GENERAL ALPHABET LESSON PROCEDURES

Introduction

1. The children are seated in a semicircle around the teacher. The alphabet song may be sung.
2. The teacher writes both the upper- and lowercase letter targeted for learning on a special place on the blackboard (or on poster paper).
3. The teacher then introduces the target letter and emphasizes the target letter sound(s). Words the children have heard can be given as examples of the various sounds associated with the target letter. For vowels, the short and long sounds are usually the focus, although the teacher should mention that the letter has several sounds.
4. The children's attention is then directed to the alphabet picture displays around the classroom.

Group Participation

5. Children whose names begin with the target sound are invited to write the target letter on the blackboard (or poster paper). In the early phases of teaching the alphabet, the children write only the capital letters because the uppercase letters are generally motorically easier to write. Lowercase writing can be practiced on an individual basis, particularly when writing names on art projects. Help is provided as needed, and ongoing verbal guidance is given as the children write on the blackboard. The children may not understand all of the words used in describing the way to write the letters; however, they will see the writing as well as hear the description so they will understand what is meant. The verbal description may provide a focus on how to write letters, particularly for children just beginning to learn to write alphabet letters.
6. The children are asked to generate words that begin with the target letter. Help can be provided by giving children pictures of objects (or objects themselves) with names that begin with the target sound. A staff member writes the words on the blackboard (or on poster paper) as the children suggest them; if possible, quick sketches are drawn to accompany the words. It is difficult to draw some words, such as those representing general concepts (e.g., fun, some, want). If poster paper is used, rather than the blackboard, the drawings and writings can then be kept and made into an alphabet book for later review.
7. If a child suggests a word that does not begin with the target letter, he or she is told, "No, that begins with a ____" and the sound is compared to the sound(s) associated with the target letter.
8. If the class has difficulty arriving at words that begin with the target letter (e.g., "X"), a picture dictionary can also be used. Another option is to use a videotape that shows objects and words beginning with the target letter (e.g., *Sesame Street Learning About Letters* [Children's Television Workshop, 1986]).

Summary/Transition Activity

9. The activity is ended with a review of the words, emphasizing the target sound.
10. As an additional summary activity, staff could give the children cards with the target letters written on them to take home. Each child should be asked to repeat the target letter name and sound(s) as the card is handed to him or her.

VARIATIONS

Rhyming Activities

1. The children could practice rhyming activities—one sound at the beginning of a word is replaced by a different sound (e.g., *h*at, *c*at, *b*at).
2. Poems or books with rhyming lines could be read (e.g., *Is Your Mama a Llama?* [Guarino, 1989]; *Brown Bear, Brown Bear, What Do You See?* [Martin & Carle, 1967]).
3. Songs with rhyming words could be sung (e.g., Twinkle, Twinkle, Little Star; Teddy Bear, Teddy Bear, Touch the Ground).

Discrimination Activities

*1. After the children have been given words starting with a particular sound, the teacher might say the same letter combination but with a different beginning sound (e.g., "red . . . bed") and ask the children if they are the same words.
2. Songs that involve changing the sounds in words (e.g., "I like to eat "*a*pples and b*a*n*a*n*a*s," which changes to "*e*pples and b*e*n*e*n*e*s," then "*i*pples and b*i*n*i*n*i*s," and so forth through the vowels) could be sung.
*3. The children could discriminate between the long and short vowel sounds by separating pictures of objects beginning with those sounds or the objects themselves into two piles. For example, the children might put pictures (or objects) of words that begin with a long "A" sound in one pile and the short "A" sound in another (e.g., *ate* and *ace* versus *ant* and *apple*).
*4. The children could be asked to identify short and long vowel sounds within words by sorting pictures of objects (or objects themselves) into the two groups (see p. 372).

Materials Needed

- Blackboard or poster paper
- Chalk or markers
- Alphabet picture displays
- Pictures of objects (or objects themselves) with names that begin with the target letter
- Picture dictionary (optional)
- Alphabet videotape (optional)
- Poems or books with rhyming lines (optional)

GROUP ACTIVITY PLAN

Group: Letter "A"   **Date:** _____

Objectives:
1. To foster listening skills
2. To increase knowledge of the alphabet and sounds
3. To teach appropriate group interaction skills
4. To practice turn taking

Introduction

The class sings the alphabet song while the teacher points to the letters on an alphabet chart. The teacher then writes an upper- and lowercase letter "A" on the blackboard (or on poster paper) and tells the children, "The letter *A* has several sounds, but one of them is 'ă' (/æ/) like the beginning sound of 'apple' or 'ant.' The other sound is 'ā' (/eI/), which sounds like its name, as in a word like 'ate.'" The children's attention is then directed to the alphabet picture displays around the room.

Group Participation

The teacher asks if anyone's name starts with "A" (e.g., Angie, Andrew, April) and has those children write the letter "A" on the blackboard. Two or three children whose names do not begin with "A" are given the opportunity to write the letter "A" on the blackboard. If necessary, staff members help the children write the letter. As the children write the uppercase letter "A," The teacher provides verbal guidance: "Start at the top and go down at a slant. Now, start at the top and go down at a slant the other way. Draw a line across the middle to connect the two other lines." The children are then asked to think of words that begin with "A." the teacher writes the words on the blackboard and draws quick sketches (when possible) of the suggested words. If a child suggests a word that does not begin with "A," he or she is told, "No, that begins with a ____" and the sound is compared to "A." The teacher should focus on the short and long "A" sounds; however, words that begin with other "A" sounds (e.g., airplane) can be accepted. Pictures or objects representing "A" can be used as prompts for children who do not know any words so that they can participate. (Cards can be handed out at the beginning of the lesson or as the lesson proceeds). Additional words can be sought in a picture dictionary if the class has difficulty arriving at words beginning with "A."

Summary/Transition Activity

After about 10–15 words have been suggested, the teacher reviews the words, emphasizing the "A" sounds.

Materials Needed

- Alphabet chart
- Blackboard and chalk
- Alphabet picture displays
- Pictures of objects (or objects themselves) with names that begin with the letter "A"
- Picture dictionary (or an alphabet video dictionary)

GROUP ACTIVITY PLAN

Group: Letter "B"　　　　　　　　　　　　　　**Date:**

Objectives: 1. To foster listening skills
2. To increase knowledge of the alphabet and sounds
3. To teach appropriate group interaction skills
4. To practice turn taking

Introduction

The teacher writes an upper- and lowercase letter "B" on the blackboard (or on poster paper) and gives several examples of words that begin with "B," emphasizing the /b/ or "buh" sound at the beginning of the words. (The teacher may hold up pictures of objects (or objects themselves) with names that begin with "B.") The teacher then directs the children's attention to the alphabet picture displays around the room.

Group Participation

The teacher asks if anyone's name begins with "B" (e.g., Betty, Bob). Those children write the letter "B" on the blackboard (or poster paper). Two or three other children are given the opportunity to write the letter "B" on the blackboard. If necessary, staff help the children write the letter. As the children write the uppercase letter "B," the teacher provides verbal guidance: "Start at the top and draw a straight line down. Go back to the top and make a half circle to the middle of the line. Now, make another half circle from the middle to the bottom of the line." Some of the other children can practice writing a "B" in the air with their fingers (or use individual chalkboards). The teacher then asks the children to think of words that begin with "B" and writes the words on the blackboard, drawing quick sketches (when possible) of the suggested words. If a child suggests a word that does not begin with "B," he or she is told, "No, that begins with a _____" and the sound is compared to the "B" sound. Pictures or objects representing "B" words can be provided as prompts for children who do not know any words so that they can participate. (Cards can be handed out at the beginning of the lesson or as the lesson proceeds.) Additional words can be sought in a picture dictionary if the class has difficulty arriving at words that begin with "B."

Summary/Transition Activity

After about 10–15 words have been suggested, the teacher reviews the words, emphasizing the "B" sound.

Materials Needed

- Blackboard and chalk
- Pictures of objects (or objects themselves) with names that begin with "B"
- Alphabet picture displays
- Picture dictionary (or an alphabet video dictionary)
- Poster paper and markers (optional)
- Individual chalkboards (optional)

GROUP ACTIVITY PLAN

Group: Letter "E" _____ **Date:** _____

Objectives: 1. To foster listening skills
2. To increase knowledge of the alphabet and sounds
3. To teach appropriate group interaction skills
4. To practice turn taking

Introduction

The teacher writes an upper- and lowercase letter "E" on the blackboard (or on poster paper). He or she then tells the children, "*E* has several sounds. You hear one of them when the letter sounds like its name —- /i/ ('eeee') as in the word '*e*asy.' Another sound is like the name '*E*mily' or the word '*e*lephant.' Can you hear the /ε/ ('ehh') sound?" The children should practice saying the long and short "E" sounds.

Group Participation

Two children are invited to the front of the class. Each is given a picture of an object (or the object itself) with a name that begins with "E." One child's picture (or object) should begin with the long "E" sound and the other with the short "E" sound. The children should verbally label their pictures (or objects) for the class. The teacher can help them to elongate the long or short "E" sound, as appropriate. The children then place their pictures (or objects) in different places, beginning a pile for each of the "E" sounds. In twos, other children are invited to the front of the class to take a turn at naming "E" words and placing the pictures (or objects) in the correct piles.

Summary/Transition Activity

The teacher reviews the long and short vowel sounds of "E" by saying the sounds one last time and holding up representative pictures.

Materials Needed

- Blackboard and chalk
- Pairs of pictures of objects (or objects themselves) whose names begin with "E," such as *envelope* and *eat*, *elephant* and *eel*, *Eddie* and *Elaine*, and *Eskimo* and *eagle*
- Poster paper and markers (optional)

GROUP ACTIVITY PLAN

Group: Letter "N"   **Date:** _____

Objectives: 1. To foster listening skills
2. To increase knowledge of the alphabet and sounds
3. To teach appropriate group interaction skills
4. To practice turn taking

Introduction

Two or three children are invited to the front of the class to sing the alphabet song. The teacher points to the letters on the alphabet chart as the song is sung and then writes an upper- and lowercase "N" on the blackboard (or poster paper). The teacher then gives several examples of words that begin with "N", emphasizing the /n/ ("nnn") sound at the beginning of the words. (The teacher may hold up objects or pictures of objects whose names begin with "N.") The teacher then directs the children's attention to the alphabet picture displays around the room.

Group Participation

The teacher asks if anyone's name starts with "N" (e.g., Ned, Nancy). Those children write the letter "N" on the blackboard. Two or three other children are given the opportunity to write the letter "N" on the blackboard. If necessary, the teacher helps the children write the letter. As the children write the uppercase letter "N," the teacher provides verbal guidance: "Start at the top and draw a straight line down. Go back to the top and draw a slanted line from the first line to the bottom. Stay at the bottom and draw a straight line back up, even with the top." Some of the other children can practice writing an "N" in the air with their fingers (or use individual chalkboards). The teacher asks the children to think of words that begin with "N." He or she writes the words on the blackboard and draws quick sketches (when possible) of the suggested words. If a child suggests a word that does not begin with "N," he or she is told, "No, that begins with a ____" and the sound is compared to the "nnn" sound. Pictures or objects representing words that begin with "N" can be provided as prompts for children who do not know any words so that they can participate. (Cards can be handed out at the beginning of the lesson or as the lesson proceeds.) Additional words can be sought in a picture dictionary if the class has difficulty arriving at words that begin with "N."

Summary/Transition Activity

After about 10–15 words have been suggested, the teacher reviews the words, emphasizing the "N" sound. The children can also be given cards or adhesive notes with the upper- and lowercase letter "N" written on them as they identify the letter or the sound. The children can then take the cards or notes home.

Materials Needed

- Alphabet chart
- Blackboard and chalk
- Pictures of objects (or objects themselves) with names that begin with "N"
- Alphabet picture displays
- Picture dictionary (or an alphabet video dictionary)
- Poster paper and markers (optional)
- Individual chalkboards (optional)
- Cards or adhesive notes with "N" and "n" written on them (optional)

GROUP ACTIVITY PLAN

Group: Letter "R"   **Date:** _____

Objectives: 1. To foster listening skills
2. To increase knowledge of the alphabet and sounds
3. To teach appropriate group interaction skills
4. To practice turn taking

Introduction

The teacher writes an upper- and lowercase letter "R" on the blackboard (or on poster paper). He or she then gives several examples of words that begin with "R," emphasizing the /r/ ("ruh") sound at the beginning of the words. (The teacher may hold up objects or pictures of objects whose names begin with "R.") The teacher directs the children's attention to the alphabet picture displays around the room.

Group Participation

The teacher asks if anyone's name starts with "R" (e.g., Robert, Rhonda). Those children write the letter "R" on the blackboard. Two or three other children are given the opportunity to write the letter "R" on the blackboard. If necessary, staff help the children write the letter. As the children write the uppercase letter "R," the teacher provides verbal guidance: "Start at the top and draw a straight line down. Go back to the top and draw a half circle, ending at the middle of the straight line. Now, draw a slanting line from the half circle to the bottom." Some of the other children can practice writing an "R" in the air with their fingers (or use individual chalkboards). Ask the children to think of words that begin with "R." The teacher then writes the words on the blackboard and draws quick sketches (when possible) of the suggested words. If a child suggests a word that does not begin with "R," he or she is told, "No, that begins with a ____" and the sound is compared to "R." Pictures or objects representing "R" words can be provided as prompts for children who do not know any words so that they can participate. (Cards can be handed out at the beginning of the lesson or as the lesson proceeds.) Additional words can be sought in a picture dictionary if the class has difficulty arriving at words beginning with "R."

Variation

The teacher can lead an activity in which the children discriminate between words that begin with "R" and other words that rhyme (e.g., *r*ed, bed, led; *r*ope, soap; *r*attle, battle; *r*un, fun, sun, bun).

Summary/Transition Activity

After about 10–15 words have been suggested, the teacher reviews the words, emphasizing the "R" sound.

Materials Needed

- Blackboard and chalk
- Pictures of objects (or objects themselves) with names that begin with "R"
- Alphabet picture displays
- Picture dictionary (or an alphabet video dictionary)
- Poster paper and markers (optional)
- Individual chalkboards (optional)
- List of words to discriminate among initial sounds (optional)

GROUP ACTIVITY PLAN

Group: *How to write numbers 2–9 _____ **Date:** _____

Objectives: 1. To foster listening skills
2. To increase conceptual knowledge
3. To teach appropriate group interaction skills
4. To practice turn taking

Introduction

The teacher holds up a card with the targeted number written on it. The teacher then traces the number with a finger and invites several children to come to the front of the class to trace the number, too. As the children trace, the teacher recites the appropriate description from those below:

2: Around and back on the railroad track—2, 2, 2.
3: Around the tree, around the tree, that's the way to make a 3.
4: Down and over and down once more, that's the way to make a 4.
5: Down around, make a hat, and look what you've found.
6: Down and around until it sticks, that's the way to make a 6.
7: Over and down, it's not heaven, over and down makes a 7.
8: Make an "S" and go back straight, that's the way to make an 8.
9: A balloon and a line makes 9.

Group Participation

The teacher distributes individual chalkboards and chalk (or paper and pencils) to the children. The children then practice writing the target number(s).

Summary/Transition Activity

The children are asked to hold up their chalkboards and show each other their numbers.

Materials Needed

- Cards with the numbers 2–9 written on them
- Chalkboards and chalk
- Paper and pencils (optional)

GROUP ACTIVITY PLAN

Group: *Number recognition   **Date:** _____

Objectives: 1. To foster listening skills
2. To increase conceptual knowledge
3. To teach appropriate group interaction skills
4. To practice turn taking

Introduction

The teacher holds up a card with a number between 1 and 10 written on it. The children are asked to yell out the number as each card is displayed. As the children identify each number, the teacher places the number card on the floor to form a number line.

Group Participation

One child is asked to pick a number card out of a box. The child then places the chosen number card below the corresponding number on the number line. Other children repeat the activity until a second number line is created on the floor. This activity can be repeated with additional sets of number cards so more children can participate in recognizing and labeling the numbers.

Variation

For children who know the numbers from 1 to 10, higher numbers can be chosen and labeled on a 1–100 number line.

Summary/Transition Activity

The class counts as the teacher picks up the number cards.

Materials Needed

- At least two sets of cards with the numbers 1–9 written on them
- Box
- A set of cards with numbers 1–100 written on them (optional)

GROUP ACTIVITY PLAN

Group: *Introduction to Unifix blocks   **Date:**

Objectives: 1. To foster listening skills
            2. To increase conceptual knowledge
            3. To teach appropriate group interaction skills
            4. To practice turn taking

Introduction

The teacher holds up 10 interlocked Unifix blocks and shows the class how the blocks can come apart. The teacher separates them, counting them one by one. Each child is then given 10 blocks and mats or boards on which to lay them.

Group Participation

The children count their blocks while laying them, one at a time, on the mat. Next they are asked to arrange them in groups of two. The children should note how many groups of two there are. Staff then ask the children to do other groupings (e.g., "How many groups of three can you make? Of four?") The children should be encouraged to experiment with forming different groups. (Some of the children may just play with the blocks.)

Summary/Transition Activity

The children are asked to link their blocks until all 10 are interlocked. The class counts together, making sure everyone still has 10 blocks. Then the children put the blocks back into the box.

Materials

- Unifix blocks
- Small mats or boards (at least one per child)

References

Baker, N., & Nelson, K.E. (1984). Recasting and related conversational techniques for triggering syntactic advances by young children. *First Language, 5,* 3–22.

Blank, M., Rose, S., & Berlin, L. (1978). *The language of learning: The preschool years.* New York: Grune & Stratton.

Bunce, B.H., & Liebhaber, G. (1989). *Curriculum: Development and implementation* (Language Acquisition Preschool working papers). Lawrence: Department of Speech-Language-Hearing, University of Kansas.

Bunce, B.H., & Watkins, R.V. (1995). Language intervention in a preschool classroom: Implementing a language-focused curriculum. In M.L. Rice & K.A. Wilcox (Eds.), *Building a language-focused curriculum for the preschool classroom: Vol. I. A foundation for lifelong communication* (pp. 39–71). Baltimore: Paul H. Brookes Publishing Co.

Bunce, B.H., Watkins, R.V., Eyer, J., Torres, T., Ray, S., & Ellsworth, J. (1995). The language-focused curriculum in other settings. In M.L. Rice & K.A. Wilcox (Eds.), *Building a language-focused curriculum for the preschool classroom: Vol. I. A foundation for lifelong communication* (pp. 199–219). Baltimore: Paul H. Brookes Publishing Co.

Constable, C.M. (1986). The application of scripts in the organization of language intervention contexts. In K. Nelson (Ed.), *Event knowledge: Structure and function in development* (pp. 205–230). Hillsdale, NJ: Lawrence Erlbaum Associates.

Dunn, L.M., & Dunn, L.M. (1981). *Peabody Picture Vocabulary Test–Revised (PPVT–R).* Circle Pines, MN: American Guidance Service.

Fivush, R., & Slackman, E.A. (1986). The acquisition and development of scripts. In K. Nelson (Ed.), *Event knowledge: Structure and function in development* (pp. 71–96). Hillsdale, NJ: Lawrence Erlbaum Associates.

French, L.A., Lucariello, J., Seidman, S., & Nelson, K. (1985). The influence of discourse content and context on preschoolers' use of language. In L. Galda & A.D. Pellegrini (Eds.), *Play, language and stories* (pp. 1–27). Norwood, NJ: Ablex.

Goldman, R., & Fristoe, M. (1969). *Goldman-Fristoe Test of Articulation (GFTA).* Circle Pines, MN: American Guidance Service.

Heath, S.B. (1986). Separating "things of the imagination" from life: Learning to read and write. In W. Teale & E. Sulzby (Eds.), *Emergent literacy* (pp. 156–172). Norwood, NJ: Ablex.

Lucariello, J., Kyratzis, A., & Engel, S. (1986). Event representations, context, and language. In K. Nelson (Ed.), *Event knowledge: Structure and function in development* (pp. 137–159). Hillsdale, NJ: Lawrence Erlbaum Associates.

Nelson, K. (1981). Social cognition in a script framework. In J.H. Flavell & L. Ross (Eds.), *Social cognitive development* (pp. 97–118). Cambridge: Cambridge University Press.

Nelson, K. (Ed.). (1986). *Event knowledge: Structure and function in development.* Hillsdale, NJ: Lawrence Erlbaum Associates.

Nelson, K., & Seidman, S. (1984). Playing with scripts. In I. Bretherton (Ed.), *Symbolic play: The development of social understanding* (pp. 45–71). New York: Academic Press.

Pellegrini, A.D. (1984). The effect of classroom ecology on preschoolers' functional uses of language. In A.D. Pellegrini & T.D. Yawkey (Eds.), *The development of oral and written language in social contexts* (pp. 129–141). Norwood, NJ: Ablex.

Reynell, J.K., & Gruber, C.P. (1990). *Reynell Developmental Language Scales–U.S. Edition.* Los Angeles: Western Psychological Services.

Rice, M.L. (1993). "Don't talk to him; He's weird." A social consequences account of language and social interactions. In A.P. Kaiser & D.B. Gray (Eds.), *Communication and language intervention series: Vol. 2. Enhancing children's communication: Research foundations for intervention* (pp. 139–155). Baltimore: Paul H. Brookes Publishing Co.

Rice, M.L. (1995). The rationale and operating principles for a language-focused curriculum for preschool children. In M.L. Rice & K.A. Wilcox (Eds.), *Building a language-focused curriculum for the preschool classroom: Vol. I. A foundation for lifelong communication* (pp. 27–38). Baltimore: Paul H. Brookes Publishing Co.

Rice, M.L., Buhr, J., & Nemeth, M. (1990). Fast mapping word-learning abilities of language-delayed preschoolers. *Journal of Speech and Hearing Disorders, 55,* 33–42.

Rice, M.L., Sell, M.A., & Hadley, P.A. (1990). The Social Interactive Coding System (SICS): A clinically relevant, descriptive tool. *Language, Speech, and Hearing Services in the Schools, 21,* 2–14.

Rice, M.L., & Wilcox, K.A. (Eds.). (1995). *Building a language-focused curriculum for the preschool classroom: Vol. I. A foundation for lifelong communication.* Baltimore: Paul H. Brookes Publishing Co.

Silliman, E.R., & Wilkinson, L.C. (1991). *Communicating for learning: Classroom observation and collaboration.* Gaithersburg, MD: Aspen Publishers, Inc.

Watkins, R.V., Rice, M.L., & Moltz, C. (1993). Verb use by language-impaired and normally developing children. *First Language, 13,* 133–144.

Bibliography
of Children's Books

Accorsi, W. (1992). *Friendships first Thanksgiving*. New York: Scholastic.
Amery, H. (1988). *Cinderella*. London, England: Usborne Publishing, Ltd.
Amery, H., & Cartwright, S. (1984). *At the seaside*. Saffron Hill, London: Usborne Publishing, Ltd.
Arnosky, J. (1987). *Raccoons and ripe corn*. New York: Scholastic.
Asch, F. (1985). *Bear shadow*. New York: Scholastic.
Asch, F. (1992). *Little fish, big fish*. New York: Scholastic.
Barbaresi, N. (1984). *Jenny's in the hospital*. Racine, WI: Western Publishing.
Barchas, S.E. (1975). *I was walking down the road*. New York: Scholastic.
Barkan, J. (1991). *Whiskerville grocery*. New York: Grosset & Dunlap.
Berenstain, S., & Berenstain, J. (1991). *The Berenstain bears don't pollute*. New York: Random House.
Bond, F. (1983). *The Halloween performance*. New York: Scholastic.
Bottner, B. (1987). *Zoo song*. New York: Scholastic.
Bourgeois, P. (1989). *Big Sarah's little boots*. New York: Scholastic.
Branley, F.M. (1960). *Big tracks, little tracks*. New York: Scholastic.
Bridwell, N. (1966). *Clifford's Halloween*. New York: Scholastic.
Brown, M.W. (1947). *Goodnight, moon*. New York: Scholastic.
Brown, M.W. (1992). *Red light, green light*. New York: Scholastic.
Brown, R. (1994). *What rhymes with snake?* New York: Tambourine Books.
Burningham, J. (1970). *Mr. Gumpy's outing*. New York: Holt, Rinehart & Winston.
Burton, V.L. (1943). *Katy and the big snow*. New York: Scholastic.
Calhoun, M. (1979). *Cross-country cat*. New York: Mulberry Books.
Carne, E. (1987). *A house for hermit crab*. New York: Scholastic.
Children's Television Workshop. (1986). *Sesame Street learning about letters* [Videotape]. New York: Random House.
Civardi, A. (1992a). *Going on a plane*. Tulsa, OK: EDC Publishing.
Civardi, A. (1992b). *Going to the doctor*. London, England: Usborne Publishing Ltd.
Cohen, M. (1967). *Will I have a friend?* New York: Scholastic.
Day, A. (1985). *Good dog, Carl*. New York: Scholastic.
DePaola, T. (1983). *The legend of Bluebonnet*. New York: Scholastic.
Eastman, P.D. (1960). *Are you my mother?* New York: Random House.
Eastman, P.D. (1961). *Go dog go*. New York: Random House.
Ehlet, L. (1991). *Red leaf, yellow leaf*. New York: Scholastic.
Elliott, D. (1982). *Grover goes to school*. New York: Random House/Children's Television Workshop.
Evans, J. (1979). *The three bears*. Allen, TX: Developmental Learning Materials.
Evans, J. (1982). *The gingerbread man*. Allen, TX: Developmental Learning Materials.
Fleming, D. (1992). *Count*. New York: Scholastic.
Freeman, D. (1968). *Corduroy*. New York: Scholastic.
Gretz, S. (1984). *Teddy bear cures a cold*. New York: Scholastic.
Guarino, D. (1989). *Is your mama a llama?* New York: Scholastic.
Henderson, K. (1988). *Don't interrupt*. London, England: Frances Lincoln, Ltd.
Herman, G. (1988). *The fire engine*. New York: Random House.
Herriot, J. (1984). *Moses, the kitten*. New York: St. Martin's Press.

Hoberman, M.A. (1986). *A house is a house for me*. Richmond Hill, Ontario, Canada: Scholastic-TAB Publications, Ltd.

Holland, M. (1988). *Monsters don't scare me*. Worthington, OH: Willowisp Press.

Huston, W. (1991). *Jamal's busy day*. New York: Scholastic.

Hutchins, H., & Ohi, R. (1992). *And you can be the cat*. North York, Ontario: Annick Press, Ltd.

Hutchins, P. (1987). *Rosie's walk*. New York: Scholastic.

Johnson, A. (1990). *Do you like Kayla?* New York: Scholastic.

Keats, E.J. (1968). *A letter to Amy*. New York: Harper & Row.

Korman, J. (1993). *Working hard with the mighty loader*. New York: Scholastic.

Kovalcik, T. (1993). *What's under your hood, Orson?* New York: Scholastic.

Kuhn, D. (1993). *My first book of nature*. New York: Cartwheel Books.

Maestro, B. (1989). *Snow day*. New York: Scholastic.

Martin, B., Jr. (1985). *Here are my hands*. New York: Scholastic.

Martin, B., Jr., & Carle, E. (1967). *Brown bear, brown bear, what do you see?* New York: Holt, Rinehart & Winston.

Mayer, G., & Mayer, M. (1993). *Trick or treat little critter*. Racine, WI: Western Publishing.

Mayer, M. (1986). *Just me and my little sister*. Racine, WI: Western Publishing.

Mayer, M. (1987). *Just a mess*. Racine, WI: Western Publishing.

McNaught, H. (1978). *The truck book*. New York: Random House.

McQueen, L. (1985). *The little red hen*. New York: Scholastic.

Moché, D.L. (1982a). *My first book about space*. Racine, WI: Western Publishing.

Moché, D.L. (1982b). *We're taking an airplane trip*. Racine, WI: Western Publishing.

Moncure, J.B. (1973). *Try on a shoe*. Elgin, IL: The Child's World.

Morris, A. (1989). *Bread, bread, bread*. New York: Scholastic.

Most, B. (1990). *The cow that went oink*. New York: Scholastic.

Nister, E. (1991). *Our farmyard*. New York: Penguin Books.

Numeroff, L.J. (1985). *If you give a mouse a cookie*. New York: Scholastic.

Pfister, M. (1993). *Rainbow fish*. New York: North-South Books, Scholastic, Inc.

Rey, H.A. (1952). *Curious George rides a bike*. New York: Scholastic.

Robbins, K. (1989). *Boats*. New York: Scholastic.

Rockwell, A. (1989). *Apples and pumpkins*. New York: Scholastic.

Rosen, M. (1989). *We're going on a bear hunt*. New York: Margaret K. McElderry Books.

Rowe, J. (1990). *Scallywag*. New York: Ashton Scholastic.

Ryder, J. (1987). *Chipmunk song*. New York: Dutton.

Sendak, M. (1963). *Where the wild things are*. New York: Scholastic.

Serfozo, M. (1988). *Who said red?* New York: Scholastic.

Sharmat, M. (1980). *Gregory, the terrible eater*. New York: Four Winds Press.

Shaw, C.G. (1947). *It looked like spilt milk*. New York: Harper & Row.

Shone, V. (1990). *Wheels*. New York: Scholastic.

Silverstein, S. (1964). *The giving tree*. New York: Harper & Row.

Tafuri, N. (1986). *Who's counting?* New York: Scholastic.

Waber, B. (1972). *Ira sleeps over*. New York: Scholastic.

Webb, J. (1986). *Play it safe*. Racine, WI: Western Publishing.

Yoshi, A.C. (1988). *Big Al*. New York: Scholastic.

~A~

LAPlines

LAPlines is a weekly newsletter distributed on the first day of class each week to the families of children enrolled in LAP. *LAPlines* contains information about the week's planned activities and special events (e.g., a picnic, a classroom visitor, children's birthdays). Ideas for activities to do at home are also usually included in the newsletter.

Newsletters can be very helpful in communicating with the children's families. They provide a means for parents to continue the classroom experience in the home and to generate topics of conversation with their child. For example, a newsletter can inform parents that pudding making is a planned class activity for Tuesday. Then, when a parent picks up the child, rather than asking, "What did you do today in school?" (a question that can be overwhelming to a young child), the parent can ask, "Did you have fun making pudding today?" This gives parents an opportunity to build on vocabulary items that were introduced in the classroom while the children get a chance to tell their parents about the things they have learned or experienced. The at-home activity suggestions provide ways for parents to stimulate their children's language and learning. Distributing the newsletter at the beginning of the week allows parents time to prepare for upcoming activities. Children often bring in props for a particular dramatic play activity or items for sharing that are particularly relevant to the weekly theme. In summary, newsletters keep parents informed about classroom activities and help them be involved in their children's learning.

LAP LINES

News & messages for parents
of children enrolled in the
LANGUAGE ACQUISITION PRESCHOOL

2101 Haworth
The University of Kansas
864-0649

Sept. 19, 1994   Editor: Annie Bowersox   Vol. 23, No. 4

 DISCOVERING WHAT BIG PEOPLE DO

MONDAY: The children will spend their day being construction workers. In dramatic play they'll build with cardboard, blocks, and tools; they will discover tools--hammers, saws, and screwdrivers. Art time will include building with Popsicle sticks. <u>A House Is a House</u> is the story and group will be about squares. "Johnny Works with One Hammer" will be our special music activity.

TUESDAY: This is the day to be a veterinarian. LAP will become very busy as the children care for animals of all kinds during dramatic play. The children will make puppets from paperbags at art time. They will read <u>Where the Wild Things Are</u>. Care of pets will be discussed in group. The special music song is "Herman the Worm."

WEDNESDAY: Today the Lappers discover all about being a big person working in an office. There will be typing, filing, telephone answering, stamping, and mailing during dramatic play. Easel painting will keep our children busy at art time. They will read <u>A Letter to Amy</u> at storytime. Group will be about the Letter "D." Lappers get even more alphabet practice in music when they sing the "ABC" song.

THURSDAY: Mechanics will be all over the place--they will be repairing cars, trucks, and buses. The wheels will go round and round, even in art! The children will use macaroni wheels to make necklaces. Our story for the day is <u>What's Under Your Hood, Orson?</u> Our group talk will center around seatbelt safety. "Going to Kentucky" will be the song of the day.

(continued)

An example of *LAPlines*, which is distributed to the parents and caregivers of the children enrolled in LAP at the beginning of each week. A newsletter such as *LAPlines* helps families stay informed and involved in their children's preschool program.

BIRTHDAY TIME!!!

Anthony turns three this week--
Tuesday, September 20th.   We
wish him a very happy day!!

Anthony, Happy Birthday!!!

ANNOUNCEMENT!!!

PARENTS' NIGHT WILL BE SEPT.
29TH!!!

THOSE NEEDING CHILD CARE PLEASE
LET US KNOW AS SOON AS
POSSIBLE.

WE'RE LOOKING FORWARD TO A
GREAT EVENING!!!

REMINDER!!

FIREFLY ORDERS DUE BY THURSDAY,
SEPTEMBER 22!!!

MORE LAP INFO-- MUSIC TIME

Music time is a favorite time
of the day for Lappers and for
parents watching from our
observation room.

The children act out many of
the songs with their hands or
bodies. For some songs a small
group of children will perform
for the others. The children
are all encouraged to
participate. None are
required. Some may not want
to sing. It can be scary to
stand up and act in front of
others. Also, sometimes at the
end of the day, the kids are
just tired.

The helper of the day has a
special job during music. He
or she helps the teacher lead
the "Goodbye Song"!

The children often learn words
to songs that relate to our
theme of the day. Monday is
construction worker day and our
song is about using a hammer--
"Johnny Works with One Hammer."
Singing fun songs with actions
helps children remember and
understand new vocabulary words
as well as enhancing learning
of body control.

Parents' Night - 7 PM
Thursday 9/29

`B`

Planning Guide Forms

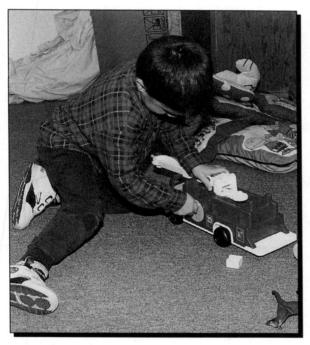

Blank planning forms are provided in this appendix (see Chapter 5 and Part III for examples of completed forms). These forms are provided for readers to use in developing additional activities. The first form, a monthly planning guide, is to be used for long-range curriculum planning. The second form is the weekly planning guide, which can be used to outline activities and list dramatic play props and other materials needed to complete the activity plans. The next form is a daily planning guide; its focus should be on ways to facilitate language, social, cognitive, and motor skills within daily activities. The next three forms are planning guides for specific dramatic play, art, and group activities. The final form is a sample therapy planning guide, which can be used for individual children (see Chapter 3 for an example of a completed therapy guide).

MONTH

Title

Theme	Activities	Monday	Tuesday	Wednesday	Thursday
	Dramatic Play				
	Art				
	Story				
	Group				
	Music				
	Dramatic Play				
	Art				
	Story				
	Group				
	Music				

Building a Language-Focused Curriculum for the Preschool Classroom, Volume II: A Planning Guide
by Betty H. Bunce   © 1995 Paul H. Brookes Publishing Co., Baltimore

CURRICULUM: WEEKLY PLANNING GUIDE

Semester Theme:

Weekly Theme: _____ **Week of:** _____

	Dramatic Play	Art	Story	Group	Music
Monday					
Tuesday					
Wednesday					
Thursday					

Suggested Props and Materials:

Monday	
Tuesday	
Wednesday	
Thursday	

Building a Language-Focused Curriculum for the Preschool Classroom, Volume II: A Planning Guide
by Betty H. Bunce   © 1995 Paul H. Brookes Publishing Co., Baltimore

CURRICULUM: DAILY PLANNING GUIDE

Theme: _____
Week of: _____

Monday	Tuesday	Wednesday	Thursday	

Dramatic Play	Art	Story	Group	Music

Language Skills Facilitated:

- **Vocabulary:**

- **Verb Phrase Structures:**

- **Adjective/Object Descriptions:**

- **Pronouns:**

- **Prepositions:**

- **Sounds:**

Social Skills Facilitated:

- **Initiating to peers and adults, responding to questions and requests from peers and adults**

- **Negotiating with peers for toys and materials**

- **Group cooperation:**

Cognitive Skills Facilitated:

- **Problem-Solving Skills:**

- **Classification Skills:**

- **Sequencing Skills:**

Motor Skills Facilitated:

- **Large Motor Skills:**

- **Small Motor Skills:**

Building a Language-Focused Curriculum for the Preschool Classroom, Volume II: A Planning Guide
by Betty H. Bunce   © 1995 Paul H. Brookes Publishing Co., Baltimore

DRAMATIC PLAY ACTIVITY PLAN

Dramatic Play: _____ **Date:** _____

Type of Activity: Central   Sequential   Related

Objectives: 1.
           2.
           3.
           4.
           5.
_____

General Description of Activity

Setting

Props

Roles

Verbal Productions

Adult Facilitory Role

Building a Language-Focused Curriculum for the Preschool Classroom, Volume II: A Planning Guide
by Betty H. Bunce   © 1995 Paul H. Brookes Publishing Co., Baltimore

ART ACTIVITY PLAN

Art: _____ **Date:** _____

Objectives: 1.
                2.
                3.
                4.
                5.

_____

General Plan

Supplies Needed

Building a Language-Focused Curriculum for the Preschool Classroom, Volume II: A Planning Guide
by Betty H. Bunce   © 1995 Paul H. Brookes Publishing Co., Baltimore

GROUP ACTIVITY PLAN

Group: _____   **Date:** _____

Objectives: 1.
           2.
           3.
           4.

_____

Introduction

Group Participation

Summary/Transition Activity

Materials Needed

Building a Language-Focused Curriculum for the Preschool Classroom, Volume II: A Planning Guide
by Betty H. Bunce   © 1995 Paul H. Brookes Publishing Co., Baltimore

THERAPY GUIDE

Child: _____

Clinician: _____

Date: _____

Theme: _____

Target Language Skill(s):

When to Emphasize Target Skills:

How to Emphasize Target Skills:

Special Props and/or Materials Needed:

Documentation of Progress (What Happened?):
[Describe on back of sheet success/failure of therapy procedures.]

Building a Language-Focused Curriculum for the Preschool Classroom, Volume II: A Planning Guide
by Betty H. Bunce   © 1995 Paul H. Brookes Publishing Co., Baltimore

Index

Page references followed by f indicate figures.